PLANNING TO MEET BASIC NEEDS

Also by Frances Stewart

TECHNOLOGY AND UNDERDEVELOPMENT
EMPLOYMENT, INCOME DISTRIBUTION AND
　DEVELOPMENT (*editor*)
THE ECONOMICS OF NEW TECHNOLOGY IN DEVELOPING
　COUNTRIES (*editor with Jeffrey James*)
INTERNATIONAL FINANCIAL COOPERATION (*with Arjun
　Sengupta*)
WORK, INCOME AND INEQUALITY (*editor*)

PLANNING TO MEET BASIC NEEDS

Frances Stewart

MACMILLAN

© Frances Stewart 1985

All rights reserved. No part of this publication may be reproduced or transmitted, in any form or by any means, without permission

First published 1985 by
THE MACMILLAN PRESS LTD
London and Basingstoke
Companies and representatives
throughout the world

Printed in Hong Kong

British Library Cataloguing in Publication Data
Stewart, Frances
Planning to meet basic needs.
1. Developing countries—Economic Policy
I. Title
339′.09172′4   HC59.7
ISBN 0–333–34018–3
ISBN 0–333–34019–1 Pbk

To Lucy

Contents

Preface		ix
1	A Basic Needs Approach to Development	1
2	A Macroeconomic Framework	14
3	Plans and Policies	36
4	Country Experience in Meeting Basic Needs	54
5	Economic and Social Variables and Basic Needs Performance	87
6	Basic Needs in Nigeria	106
7	A Macro Approach to Basic Needs in Nigeria	131
8	A Basic Needs Strategy for Nigeria	170
9	Basic Needs and the International Crisis: A Case Study of Tanzania	183
10	Conclusions	208
Appendix A: Table of Income, Life Expectancy and Adult Literacy		215
Appendix B: List of People who helped in Nigeria		219
Notes and References		220
Bibliography		232
Index		238

Preface

I started to work on the issues in this book during a year spent in Mahbub ul Haq's Department (Policy Planning Review) in the World Bank, 1978–9. I am grateful for many ideas on these issues, arising from discussion with Mahbub ul Haq, Paul Streeten, Jahved Burki, Norman Hicks and Paul Isenman, during that year. I also collaborated then with John Fei and Gustav Ranis, producing the macro-framework, which, in revised form, appears as Chapters 2 and 3 of this book. I am grateful for their stimulating collaboration and for their agreement to reproduce this work here. The case study of Nigeria, presented in Chapters 6 to 8, is based on work for a World Bank Mission to Nigeria in 1980, led by Irfan ul Haque. These chapters benefited greatly from discussions with Irfan ul Haque and with Selcuk Ozgediz. Chapter 9 was the outcome of work on an ILO/JASPA Mission to Tanzania in 1981, led by Shyam Nigam and Paul Streeten. They, and the other members of the Mission, made many helpful comments and suggestions. I am grateful to the World Bank and to JASPA for permission to use the work I did for them in this book. I would also like to record thanks to Harsha Singh who provided valuable research assistance.

FRANCES STEWART

1 A Basic Needs Approach to Development

A basic needs (BN) approach to development is one which gives priority to meeting the basic needs of *all* the people. The actual content of BN have been variously defined: they always include the fulfilment of certain standards of nutrition, (food and water), and the universal provision of health and education services. They sometimes also cover other material needs, such as shelter and clothing, and non-material needs such as employment, participation and political liberty.[1] The idea of making the meeting of certain fundamental human needs a development priority is not a recent idea nor a sophisticated one; it stems from the simple view that development should be concerned with removing absolute deprivation, as a first priority. This idea finds rhetorical echoes in the speeches of almost every statesman in developing countries, and every preamble to a development plan. But when it comes to translating the idea into action – into plans, policies and projects – the achievement of BN becomes more complex, both in terms of identifying the appropriate measures, and in terms of mobilising the required political will.

This book is concerned primarily with the first of these – translation of a simple human objective into plans and policies. This is a necessary first step to securing BN; but changes in the political system are generally also necessary. While BN planning is in part a technical matter, it is to a greater extent a political question, in which achievement depends on changes in the real world, rather than developments in the intellectual world. One aim of this book is to identify the types of political economy which tend to be successful in promoting BN. Such identification is helped by the planning framework (described in the next chapter) and by examination of actual country experience in meeting BN (Chapter 4). This first chapter is intended to set the scene for the analysis of planning and experience by examining the meaning of a BN-approach, and its place in development thinking.

Sometimes people write of a 'BN-strategy'[2], but this is an incorrect description. BN is an approach to development, not a strategy, in the sense that it consists of giving priority to a certain type of objective of development, but does not dictate the means by which this objective is achieved. In fact, as we shall see, very different types of strategies may be effective in meeting BN. Consequently, it is helpful to be clear, right from the start, that the BN-approach is concerned with the objectives rather than the mechanisms of development. But having settled that, it is not altogether clear what the objective is: the slogan 'meeting the basic needs of all the people' sounds clear enough, but in fact can be interpreted in various ways.

INTERPRETATION OF BASIC NEEDS

There is general agreement, in writings on BN, that a BN-approach involves focusing on the fulfilment of certain 'minimum human needs', but there is some confusion about the justification for selecting a particular bundle. This confusion is due to two different interpretations of the meaning of a BN-approach. Muddling the two leads to lack of clarity about the approach because they have rather different implications. It is important, therefore, to be clear about the view adopted, at the outset.

VIEW ONE The 'three acres and a cow' or the 'chicken in every pot' view.[3] This view asserts that there are certain goods and services which every human being ought to have in order to live a decent life. Basic needs defines these (minimally given LDCs' extreme poverty). A BN-approach to development is then one that involves giving extra (or even exclusive) weight to the achievement of the defined minimum. This view is attractive because it offers a well-defined set of targets for planning purposes: deficiencies can be measured; costs of meeting them estimated and so on; and it has strong political/ normative attraction – hence the long tradition among politicians of promising to secure specific goods for every person or household.

The problem about this approach is that of justifying any particular selection of items to be included in the bundle, and priorities between them. One way of selecting the bundle is on the basis that a particular bundle is what the society in question regards as the minimum decent bundle. This is indeed the justification (implicitly) of most political programmes of this kind. This makes the bundle to be selected society-specific. Moreover, most of the items are not wanted for themselves, but instrumentally as a means to improving the conditions of life: for example, it is not that the ultimate objective is x doctors per 1 000 people, but rather the conditions that will bring good health – which may or may not include x doctors per 1 000 people.

VIEW TWO defines the BN-objectives as being the improvement of conditions of life (or quality of life). The bundle of BN-goods are then selected according to whether or not they contribute to this ultimate objective – which for shorthand we describe as the 'full-life objective'. The full-life objective may be defined extensively or minimally. A minimal definition confines the objective to health and perhaps education. An extensive definition would include all sorts of other characteristics such as conditions necessary for the enjoyment of art, for entertainment generally, for full participation in the political process, and so on. The full-life approach to BN still leaves major problems of definition (as to which characteristics to include in the objective), but it ties the selection of BN-goods and services themselves firmly to a human welfare context, rather than being plucked out of the air in accordance with the whims of the observer.

According to this view the bundle of goods to be included as BN-goods[4] for planning purposes is selected according to the effects the various goods have on the full-life objective. This may lead to a different bundle from those chosen with respect to the first view. For example, a bundle of goods approach almost invariably selects access to clean water as one part of the bundle. But research has suggested that while access to a certain quantity of water is vital for health, quality (i.e. whether 'clean' or 'dirty') matters much less and indeed people can and do convert dirty water into clean, by boiling it (while similarly they can render clean water dirty).

This book adopts a 'full-life' interpretation of the BN-objective.

The characteristics of a truly full life of course include many elements – material, social, cultural and political. To include all these in the BN-objective would immensely complicate the process of planning for BN, since it would be necessary to ascertain the relationship between consumption of goods and services and achievement with respect to each of the characteristics of the full-life objective. Most of these relationships are not known; moreover, there is not even agreement about how to measure achievements (e.g. with respect to culture), and without that it would be difficult to investigate the relationships. To simplify and make the concepts operational, in most of this book a very minimal interpretation of the full-life objective is made: health and some degree of education are picked out as the major dimensions. This simplification makes the term 'full-life' rather pretentious, since so many of the conditions necessary for the achievement of a truly full-life are omitted. In defence three points may be made: first, while health and education do not tell the whole story, they are necessary conditions for enjoyment of other aspects of a full-life in poor societies; secondly, beyond the simple physiological needs, there is no objective way of ranking other wants or needs and hence of establishing priorities, and for planning priorities are necessary. Contrary to Maslow's theory of a hierarchy of wants (see, for example, Maslow, 1966, 1970), even people who are deprived of very basic physiological needs do consume non-basic goods and services. But the BN-objective is not (as will be discussed further below) exclusive, but leaves room for other objectives both at the level of the individual and of society. These may be viewed as taking care of the other aspects of a full-life. Alternatively, a richer interpretation of the full-life could be taken but at the cost of much complicating the planning procedure. Since a feature of human needs above a certain physiological minimum is that they are not readily and objectively to be ranked[5], but vary according to the individual and culture, there is a presumption that they are less amenable to planning than the basic minimum conditions for health and education.

The conceptual framework adopted would not be invalidated by a 'fuller' interpretation, but it would be complicated – first, it would considerably complicate the already difficult task of translating the objective into a bundle of goods; secondly, it would require some system of weighting (and measuring) the achievement of the various objectives. It is impossible to find an objective way of arriving at such a weighting[6] though this need not invalidate a multidimensional approach since achievements on the various aspects could be assessed individually and need not be added up.

Adoption of the 'full-life' view of BN means that it is necessary to identify the relationship between the consumption of certain goods and services (BN-goods) and achievement with respect to the full-life objective. This relationship, which is of fundamental importance to the procedure of planning for BN, is described in this book as the *meta-production function*. The relationship goes a step further than in most economic analysis and planning, since it is usually accepted that economic welfare is measured by income and therefore no attempt is made to identify how income gets translated into welfare. Without an independent criterion of welfare this would be a logically impossible step to take. But the BN-approach does take an independent definition – health and education – and consequently requires the extra step of identifying the meta-production function. As we shall see, identification of empirical properties of the meta-production function is very difficult, partly because this is not a normal part of economic planning, partly because of the complexity of the relationships, and partly because it seems likely that these will vary according to geography, culture, and class, among other dimensions.

Once the characteristics of the full-life objective have been determined, there remain further issues that have to be settled before it can be adopted as a planning objective. The three main ones concern distribution, time and exclusivity.

Distribution

In many poor countries a large proportion of the population may be far from having basic needs fulfilled; some are more deprived in this respect than others. Even the richest section of the population may have some needs which could be better met (e.g. more elaborate hospital care). The BN-approach may be taken to imply that the needs of the most deprived should be given priority. But it is difficult to go from there to defining precisely how much weight should be given to different groups, and at what point (if ever) zero weight should be given to further BN fulfilment. For most societies, some (rather arbitrary) cut-off point is adopted and the BN-objective is then targeted to people falling below this level. There are obvious difficulties about deciding the cut-off point, and there remains the problem that some may fall well below the level, others just below and it may be desired to give different weight to meeting the needs of these groups.[7]

Time

Like other objectives, different time-profiles of BN-achievement may be possible – e.g. there could be an alternative of meeting BN at one level today or devoting the resources to growth, meeting them at a lower level today, while generating greater BN-fulfilment at some date in the future.[8] In general, it seems to be part of the definition of the BN-objective to give strong preference to short-run fulfilment of BN, i.e. over a five or at most ten-year period. But if achievement over the immediate ten years were likely to endanger achievement over the subsequent twenty, then some thought would have to be given to the time-weighting of the objective. In practice, this may not prove to be a major problem because it seems that there need not be a conflict between BN-achievement and growth, as will be discussed more fully below.[9]

Exclusivity

Does a BN-approach to development mean that the BN-objective forms the *only* objective of development? If this exclusive view were taken then any income spent (by rich or poor) on non-BN items would have a zero weighting. The issue of exclusivity has distinct aspects. First, it concerns the issue of whether any weight should be given to those whose BN-achievement is above the cut-off point; secondly, whether a BN-approach would allow weight to be given to other objectives of society, such as independence, defence, cultural activities, apart from their instrumental role in helping to secure BN-achievement. Thirdly, there is the issue of whether any weight should be given to non-BN consumption, among poor people whose BN is below the minimum.

In general, no society ever gives *zero* weight to non-BN objectives, so that to suggest that this is part of the approach would be equivalent to getting it universally rejected. In any case, the rather minimal interpretation suggested here for the full-life objectives *requires that other conditions are also realised*, but it leaves them outside the mechanism of planning for BN. These other conditions include both other objectives of the state (including incomes of people whose basic needs are already met, cultural expenditures, etc.) and also expenditures among poor people (whose BN are not being met) on non-BN goods. Both have a valid role within a BN-approach. Expenditure on non-BN items among very poor people, whose own BN are patently not being met, may play an important role in making life tolerable: *drums* and *toddy* should not therefore be excluded.[10] But detailed and specific planning for non-BN items is not part of BN-planning. What is required is to recognise that some discretionary expenditure, for non-BN items, is necessary and desirable.

This does not answer the question of how much priority is to be given to BN, how much to other objectives, or other expenditures. The approach as such cannot answer this question, which is essentially political. In this respect the situation is similar to that where egalitarian income distribution is at issue; economists can show how different systems of weighting/poverty indices may be applied, but cannot select which is the correct index.[11]

The development objectives of any particular society are not settled by economists, but are the outcome of the political process. The BN-approach to development gives explicit priority to meeting BN. But, as discussed above, this is rather vague: for planning the objective has to be more tightly defined. The process of defining the objective more tightly, along the dimensions discussed previously, involves a set of political judgements and therefore, like the acceptance of the approach in the first place, is to be left to the political process of the country concerned. In practice, these judgements are likely to be made in a rather rough and ready way, sometimes by politicians, often by planners. Many of the judgements may be rather arbitrary, taken with little regard for logic, and in a way that does not resemble the smooth process of defining a 'social welfare function', implicit in much economic reasoning. A purist might consider these to be fatal flaws in the BN-approach, which appears to lose precision and consistency as an approach to development. But planning inevitably takes place in the real world, which is messy and inconsistent. So long as the major objective remains in sight – raising the welfare of the deprived – then the BN-approach to planning has something substantial to offer. In this book it may often seem that rather arbitrary judgements are made and short cuts taken, on shaky evidence: obviously it would be better if this were not so, and improvements made to minimise these elements. But the nature of the approach is such that arbitrariness can never be cut out altogether. If, nonetheless, we can identify why some societies succeed in securing a life expectancy for their people of over seventy in contrast to others where life expectancy is forty-five, then the approach will prove worthwhile.

This conclusion rests on the assumption that the BN-approach offers something additional to that of previous approaches to development planning. The remainder of this chapter will consider briefly how the BN-approach fits into the evolution of development thinking, in order to analyse the additional contribution it makes.

BN IN THE EVOLUTION OF DEVELOPMENT THINKING

The BN-approach to development evolved logically from earlier views on development.[12] In the early 1950s, growth maximisation and industrialisation were taken as the twin (and mutually supportive) objectives of development. These objectives met with considerable success, as indicated in Tables 1.1 and 1.2. But while there was a marked acceleration in growth rates, various aspects of the development process proved unsatisfactory.

Two strands of criticism of the 'growth-only' approach may be distinguished: on the one hand, there were those who emphasised the *dependent* nature of the development process, with the growing

TABLE 1.1 % *Annual growth in GDP per capita – selected countries, 1870 – 1975*

Country	1870–1913	1913–50	1950–7●
Egypt	n.a.	0.2	1.4
Ghana	n.a.	1.2	0.7
India	0.7	0.2	1.5
Taiwan	n.a.	0.7	5.3
Malaysia	n.a.	2.2	2.6
Philippines	n.a.	0.1	2.8
Argentina	1.5	0.7	1.9
Brazil	n.a.	2.4	3.7
Colombia	n.a.	1.4	2.0
Mexico	1.2	1.2	2.7
Peru	n.a.	1.5	2.5

Source: D. Morawetz, *Twenty-five years of Economic Development* (World Bank, Johns Hopkins, 1977) table 2.

TABLE 1.2 *Industrialisation, 1960–81 annual % growth, constant prices*

Country group	GDP		Industry	
	1960–70	1970–81	1960–70	1970–81
Low–income	4.6	4.5	6.6	3.6
Mid-income	6.0	5.6	7.4	6.8
Industrialised	5.1	3.0	5.7	2.9
	Industry as % GDP			
	1960	1981		
Low-income	25	34		
Mid-income	30	38		
Industrialised	40	36		

Source: *World Development Report, 1983* (World Bank)

economies increasingly (rather than decreasingly as had been hoped) dependent on the developed economies for goods, capital, technology and markets. This type of criticism has been widely adopted in Latin America, focusing on the centre/periphery relationships as the major problem facing developing economies.[13] On the whole, this view has little direct bearing on BN although at a political level there is often believed to be some conflict between concern with *dependency* and concern with BN. On the other hand, the growth-only approach was criticised because of the problems of unemployment, under-employment, income distribution and poverty that growth seemed to have left in its wake. The thinking arising from this second type of criticism forms the direct precursor of the BN-approach.

While economic growth accelerated in most countries, levels of unemployment remained consistently high;[14] moreover, it was soon noted that open unemployment formed only a small part of the 'employment' problem in poor countries. Under-employment, variously defined, was thought to constitute a much more substantial problem in many countries.[15] The first major move away from growth maximisation took the form of emphasis on *employment* as a development objective.[16] But the complexity of employment problems in poor countries soon revealed this to be unsatisfactory: while open unemployment and people working short hours constituted one aspect of the employment problem, to which additional employment was an appropriate response, people working long hours with very low productivity and incomes constituted another significant element in the problem. For the latter, it was not additional employment as such that was required, but improved productivity and incomes. The focus on employment tended to draw attention away from these productivity/incomes aspects. In this light employment was seen primarily as a vehicle for raising incomes, rather than an objective in its own right. While employment is one such vehicle, there are others: once raising incomes of the poor is taken to be the prime objective, then a direct focus on such incomes is more effective than an indirect one, filtered through employment.

Such direct focus was also suggested by the apparent failure of the growth process to 'trickle down' its benefits in the form of incomes of the poor. While average per capita incomes grew quite fast, generally the incomes of the lowest income groups appeared to grow less fast, and in some cases not at all. This was as expected if the negative association between income level and equality of income distribution, first noted by Kuznets,[17] remained valid. Adelman and Morris have claimed, on the basis of cross-section data, that 'development is accompanied by an absolute as well as a relative decline in the average income of the poor'.[18] The evidence of what has happened in individual economies over time is often scanty, but it seems that there have been different tendencies in different countries.[19]

Nonetheless, the balance of the evidence suggested that growth alone was not sufficient, except in quite unusual[20] cases, to eliminate poverty or even to reduce the numbers in poverty.[21] The Redistribution with Growth approach,[22] briefly espoused by some at the ILO and the World Bank, suggested that development efforts should be focused directly on raising the incomes of the poor. The approach contains both a suggested objective and a strategy for realising it. Although presented together, the two are distinct. As an objective, it was suggested that simple GNP maximisation should be replaced by some weighted average of incomes, in which the incomes of different groups should be weighted inversely to their income level.[23] The actual system of weighting was left for others to decide; in principle, a system could be adopted which placed exclusive weight on the incomes of the lowest income groups, or some less egalitarian position might be taken. The strategy associated with this objective was to continue with a high growth strategy but redistribute the fruits of growth in the form of investment resources to be conferred on the poor, who would then be able to raise their own incomes in a sustained way. The proposed strategy was subject to a number of criticisms, both as to its economic and its political realism.[24] It seemed unlikely that the growth strategy could be maintained while additional incomes were redistributed and investments relocated; in addition, it was argued that in most societies political opposition would prevent redistribution of the type advocated. However, the suggested objectives of maximising a weighted average of income is quite independent of the process advocated for its achievement. It is the objective, rather than the strategy, which forms a further step along the road to basic needs.

Making the incomes of the poor a major focus of development, seems to reach to the core of a good deal of concern about under-development – that is, the desire to eliminate poverty and deprivation. But that being so, it is not incomes as such which are important but the ability of the poor to acquire certain essential goods. In most societies this ability depends to a large extent on household incomes. But it also depends on the availability of essential goods at prices the poor can afford. In some societies, with considerable government interventions, incomes may be rather unimportant in ensuring adequate access. The BN-approach, then, sees access to the basic goods and services as the objective; incomes remain important but as a means of acquiring these goods, not an end in themselves.

The BN-approach to development is consistent with Sen's entitlement approach.[25] In Sen's initial formulation, the entitlement approach was developed to deal with the question of famine. Entitlements were defined as claims over food, which were made up of direct (subsistence) production of food, money incomes arising from the sale of goods, wage-labour and other sources, and transfers including transfers from the government; the value of these entitlements depends on the availability and price of food. A 'non-famine' set of entitlements can then be identified. In a similar way if the set of goods were extended to include all the BN-bundle, the set fulfilling some minimum BN standards could be identified. In contrast to the famine set, however, a simple cut-off point would not be objectively identifiable; in addition, it would be necessary to place more emphasis on government provision of various BN-goods than is typical in the case for food. Finally, it would be necessary to have a meta-production function to convert the BN-entitlements into full-life achievements.

The value of the entitlement approach is that it provides a comprehensive description of the factors determining people's consumption of particular items (be it food or, more extensively, all

BN-goods). Such a comprehensive account may be achieved in other ways – indeed, the intention of the planning framework described in the next chapter is to do just that. While it could be translated into the language of entitlements, it is not clear that much would be added by so doing, other than a change in presentation.

While a BN-approach can be readily fitted into the entitlement approach, it is more difficult to fit it neatly into the main conventional schools of economic analysis; the apparatus of neoclassical economics is designed to treat incomes as the indicator of welfare, and not to discriminate between different types of goods, as the BN-approach does. The BN-approach represents a quite explicit departure from the normal assumption about consumers' sovereignty, revealed preference and welfare optimality. That is not to say that a BN-approach necessarily involves dictating consumption patterns to individuals or households; but it does involve selecting certain types of goods for special attention, regarding these as non-substitutable in certain respects with other goods. When it comes to policy prescriptions, there need be no conflict, as we shall see: after all, the neoclassical approach permits exceptional treatment for public goods, which form a large part of BN-goods, and is consistent with redistribution of income, in accordance with preferences in social welfare function. But while policies towards BN, especially those which use incomes as the major vehicle, are consistent with the neoclassical approach, deriving a target income distribution, in order to generate a particular level of consumption of a particular set of goods, is not. In contrast this is precisely what the entitlement approach *is* designed to achieve.

The Marxist concept of 'use-value' is very much in the spirit of a BN-approach: production is to be oriented towards meeting the BN of the people (that is, production for use-value) as against production to maximise aggregate incomes (production for exchange-value). Marxism is also relevant in so far as it provides analysis and predictions of developments in the economy. Perhaps most of all, the Marxist understanding of political economy has bearing on the realism of the political requirements of a BN-approach. But simply interpreted, a Marxist view of development and political economy leaves little room for manoeuvre on BN. Marx and Engels were inspired in their prognostications of capitalist development by the evident deprivations caused by the industrial revolution in Britain in the nineteenth century, and found these to be an unavoidable consequence of such capitalist development. Essentially determinist, Marxist analysis leaves little hope for BN-improvements in the context of capitalist development. This is at sharp variance with the intent of a BN-approach which is to bring about such improvements. One critical issue then is to ascertain whether there exist possibilities of improving BN-performance in practice, in the light of theoretical analysis and political realities.

PLAN OF BOOK

The next chapter develops a planning framework for BN, while Chapter 3 considers alternative policies in the light of that framework. Chapters 4 and 5 examine BN-achievements in recent years in different countries, looking for shared features in 'successful' and 'unsuccessful' BN-performers. Chapter 4 concentrates on identifying 'good' and 'poor' performance and looks at types of political economy associated with each. Chapter 5 considers performance on particular economic and social variables related to good and poor BN-performance. Chapters 6 to 8 report on a detailed case study in Nigeria, applying the macro-framework developed in Chapter 2. Chapter 9 treats the theme of 'Basic Needs in Danger', looking at whether adjustment programmes made necessary by the crisis in the world economy need be at the expense of BN-achievements. While the chapter looks at the specific experience of Tanzania, the problem has become a very general one. Finally, Chapter 10 deals with some apparent conflicts and comes to some conclusions.

2 A Macroeconomic Framework*

If BN is to form a part of planning and policy formulation in LDCs, it is important to place it within the overall economic system. Below we develop a preliminary macroeconomic framework for this purpose. The framework has three aspects: first, a production aspect – which is institution neutral; secondly, an organisational aspect, which describes the productive activities according to their organisational setting; thirdly, an income framework which develops the income side of a BN-approach. This general economic system serves a number of purposes. It describes the set of important phenomena encountered in the BN-approach in a systematic fashion. The framework resembles a traditional national income accounting flow system which helps us to identify the behaviour of variables relevant for any rational analysis of BN. It also enables us to identify possible areas of intervention for planning and policy.

THE PRODUCTION FRAMEWORK

For a better understanding of the potential of a BN-approach it is essential to place the concept explicitly in the context of the broader

*This chapter and Chapter 3 were written in collaboration with John Fei and Gustav Ranis.

A Macroeconomic Framework

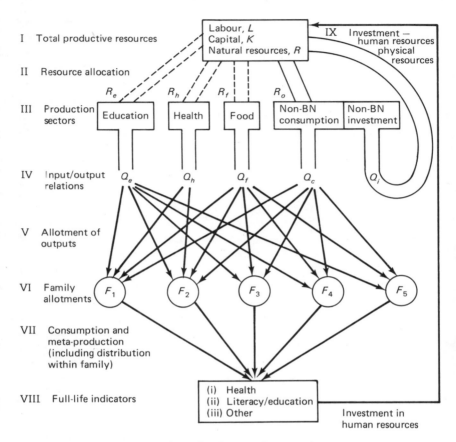

FIGURE 2.1 *Production framework*

economic system of which it is inevitably a part. A preliminary view of such a general framework incorporating the essential *production phenomena* involved in the BN-approach is provided in Figure 2.1. The production framework shows how resources are converted into basic needs achievements. The framework starts with resource endowment (labour, capital and land) and shows the processes of resource allocation, production and consumption, by which these primary resources are converted into BN-achievements.

At any moment of time, the economy is endowed with a stock of total productive resources consisting of the labour force (L) and the capital stock (K) and natural resources (R) indicated at Level I of the figure. During any given year these productive services are allocated to alternative production sectors (R_e, R_h, R_f, R_o) as inputs, as indicated at Level II. These sectors may be divided into 'Basic Needs' sectors, and 'other' or non-basic needs sectors. Basic Needs sectors consist in those sectors which produce goods and services which directly affect the 'full-life' objectives. They thus include education (R_e), health (R_h), food (R_f), and so on. The precise list of sectors will depend on the definition of the full-life objectives. With respect to the 'other' or non-BN sector, the injection of inputs R_o gives rise to two types of output, namely non-BN consumer goods (C) and investment goods (I).

There are some difficulties about the idea of 'Basic Needs sectors' because within any broad sector – e.g. health – many of the services may not be basic (i.e. may not affect the full-life objectives as defined – e.g. chiropody), whilst some of the basic services may go to consumers who already have more than the defined minimum level of services. The BN-sectors should, as far as possible, only include 'basic' goods and services (e.g. basic health care, not luxury; primary education, not higher). The BN-elements of these sectors should be included in the 'other' sectors. But the question of the distribution of such basic services as between higher and lower income consumers may be better dealt with in analysing the allocation process than in the definition of the sector itself, because to define a sector in such a way as to include the distribution of the product in the definition would make the concept difficult to handle from an operational point of view.

For each production sector the injection of inputs (R_e, R_h, R_f, R_o) leads to the output of goods and/or services: BN-goods and services in the BN-sectors, namely Q_e (the output of education services), Q_h (the output of health services), Q_f (the output of food) and non-BN consumption, Q_c, and investment goods, Q_i, as indicated at Level III of the figure. An important aspect of planning for BN concerns conditions of production in the BN-sectors – that is the technological conditions or production functions for each of the production sectors involved.

There is some interdependence between the various sectors, in an input – output sense. The output of some sectors – notably that of the education sector – forms an intermediate input into other sectors. When the various production sectors are viewed as a system it is necessary to investigate these interdependencies. But we shall ignore interdependencies in the discussion that follows.

Household or family structure and the allotment of output

Households or families represent the basic unit of social organisation. In Figure 2.1 they are represented as F_1, F_2 ... F_5 at Level VI. The composition of these families is assumed to be independently given. The labour force (L) postulated in the total productive resources box (Level I) comes from families; family members also of course include the dependent population (young and old, inactive and incapacitated).

Family members are the basic beneficiaries of any outputs (Q_e, Q_h, Q_f, Q_o) that emerge from the production sectors. For example, the total output of food Q_f is allocated in some fashion to the individual families (Q_{f1}, Q_{f2}, Q_{f3}, Q_{f4}, Q_{f5}) forming a pattern of food allotments (see Level V). The BN-approach is concerned not only with the volume of total output or per capita output but also with the pattern of allotment, i.e. the equality or inequality of the distribution of particular outputs or services among the individual families, taking into consideration the family requirements in the light of the composition of the families as well as the allocation within families.

Basic needs are met (or not met) at the level of *individuals*, not families. How far individual needs are met depends not only on family levels of income and consumption of BN-goods and services, but on distribution within the family. In addition, the effectiveness with which individual BN are met – for any given production and allotment of BN-goods and services – depends on how efficiently the BN-goods and services are converted into BN-achievements. Going from the level of family allotment (Level VI) to individual BN-satisfaction then involves two steps; an allotment among individual members of the family and a conversion. We describe these two steps as the *meta-production function*.

It is important for planning for BN that a 'regular' functional relationship, as described by the meta-production function, exists in the real world and can be approximately estimated empirically. Some of the relationships are supported by relatively hard evidence, some are still in the realm of (reasonable) beliefs. For example, it is likely to be true that a higher value and/or more equally distributed pattern of health services will increase a population's overall life expectancy. (Such a statement describes an implied characteristic of the meta-production function which may be expressed as a property of the partial derivative.) The BN-approach is based on a number of such assertions, some formally stated but most not so, concerning the properties of the meta-production function.

This meta-production function should be clearly distinguished from the ordinary production relations postulated earlier at Level IV of Figure 2.1. The ordinary production relations are an engineering and technological construct much investigated by economists. The meta-production function, on the other hand, has been studied much less, especially by economists. Economic demographers pay some attention to it in the context of the demographic transition, as do education specialists in relation to the achievement of functional literacy. But in spite of the difficulties limiting full understanding of these relationships, progress in these directions is virtually indispensable for any viable BN-approach. It is obvious that we cannot speak of a rational plan for meeting BN-requirements at a national level without some notion of the terms of the full-life indicators flowing from the allocation of resources to BN-sectors and the allotment of BN-outputs.

Problems involved in estimating the meta-production function are an important reason for adopting a rather restrictive definition of the characteristics of the 'full-life'.[1] Adding to the list of indicators to give the 'full-life' additional richer dimension, e.g. including human rights, love of art, will, of course, only add to the difficulties of estimating the meta-production relationships. While some of the relationships involved in the meta-production function may be universal, others may well be country-specific because of a critical dependence on stage of development, historic circumstances and cultural factors. The country-specific element poses a major problem for planning in countries where there is a dearth of evidence on empirical relationships.

Resources devoted to investment make no immediate contribution to BN but add to productive resources in the next period, as shown by the feedback in the diagram. Similarly, improvement in full-life indicators represent investment in human resources, which also add to productive capacity. Empirical values for the returns to such investment in human resources are difficult to estimate. The meta-production function and the better known 'returns to investment in human resources' represent crucial relationships while being the most difficult to estimate empirically, and thus the weakest links, in the entire BN chain of reasoning.

From the point of view of economic planning, the production framework incorporates the essential variables for planning for BN:

these include the quantity of resources available, the allocation of resources to BN sectors, the production relations within the BN sectors, the allotment of BN output to families (to be discussed more in the Incomes Framework below), and the meta-production function, or the conversion of these BN-outputs into achievements with respect to the ultimate objectives. In the longer run, investment (both physical and in human capital) is also relevant in determining the availability of resources in the future. The framework represented in Figure 2.1 essentially describes a closed economy. In principle, of course, exports/imports could be added in order to make it an open economy. In so far as the BN-goods and services are traded (either exported or imported) this would make a substantial difference since the availability of BN-goods and services would then not depend solely on internal resource allocation (as shown in the figure) but also on international trade. In fact, for BN-goods other than food, trade does not offer, even potentially, a way of adding to (or subtracting from) the availability of BN-goods, to any substantial extent, because these goods (for example, health services, education services, water, shelter) are not fully tradable. While food is a tradable commodity – and is in fact widely traded in some economies – food imports or exports normally form only a marginal addition/subtraction to available food resources. But where trade is important, then this should be incorporated into the framework for planning production for BN.

II ORGANISATION AND EFFICIENCY OF PRODUCTION

The resources flow framework of Figure 2.1 is institution – or organisation – neutral in the sense that the same set of functions (allocation, production, allotment, consumption, meta-production, capital and human resource investment) must be performed regardless of the broad institutional arrangement (for example, capitalism or socialism) and/or the specific organisational devices (i.e. local government or farmer associations). The lack of an organisation element to the production framework is a common feature of many exercises in economic planning and resource allocation. But organisation elements are particularly relevant to a BN-approach. This is because, for rather different reasons, household, public and 'hybrid' (i.e. co-operatives, farmers' organisations, and so on) organisational forms play an important role in basic needs activities.

Households and 'full' income

The household sector is of major significance as *producer* and as *consumer* of BN-goods and services. In subsistence and near subsistence economies, households are responsible for providing their own means of subsistence – for food, and shelter, health and education services. As monetisation and the market economy spreads, these functions are gradually taken over by the market system. But for many poor economies, households remain significant if not sole producers of these goods and services, which constitute the major BN-sectors. In addition, the households form the consumption unit, while the efficiency of consumption, as formally depicted in the meta-production function, is a vital element in the BN production framework. In defining and measuring national income with a BN-approach then it is essential to measure *full income* (i.e. including imputed household activity) as well as the usual monetary GNP. According to some estimates, inclusion of household activities may add as much as 40 per cent to GNP in some countries.

The public sector

The basic needs sectors are peculiarly subject to organisational variations because so many of the goods and services involved have elements of 'public good' characteristics, but are not 'pure' public goods. This aspect of the BN-sectors explains why public intervention (in the form of outright public production or subsidies, for example) is often justified from the point of view of welfare efficiency to a greater extent than in many other sectors; the partial public good characteristics explain the variety of organisational forms relevant and the need for institutional innovation. Indeed, apart from using a BN-approach as a means of redistributing income to the poor, the main justification for special support for BN sectors arises from these public good characteristics. It is therefore worth exploring these characteristics in a little more depth.

Goods may be produced in the public sector for reasons of history/accident/politics. Economic reasons for public sector production or intervention[2] may arise from production or consumption characteristics of goods.

With respect to production (a) there may be large production externalities, but this is rare. There may be (b) indivisibilities and economies of scale; in theory this is consistent with private production (although in relation to marginal conditions of optimality, underproduction will occur where marginal cost is less than average cost). But in practice it may mean – particularly in LDCs – that no suitable large scale entrepreneur is available. (c) There may be high risks, which the community may be prepared to undertake, but not private firms. Finally, there may be (d) need for a long time horizon, which, similarly, the community may perceive but not private firms. These last two conditions together explain, for example, why nuclear power is normally a public sector activity.

With respect to consumption (a) there may be non-appropriability of benefits – as with environmental improvements and defence; this does not mean that the benefits are not, in principle, allocable but that individuals cannot choose whether to consume or not. Second there may be (b) high externalities among divisible goods; this is a matter of partial inappropriability and applies, for example, to vaccination, to other health practices, to some parts of education. This consumption characteristic of public goods is intimately tied up with the nature of the meta-production function.

It is important to note that these public good characteristics are not absolute but relative to the size of the decision-making unit. For example, indivisibilities in production and consumption (as with a school) might justify the relevant area (say two or three villages) co-operating in building and running a school, but does not require central government participation. Similarly, the inappropriability of benefits, or a high ratio of inappropriable to appropriable benefits (for example, types of health) may often apply to a level higher than the normal consuming unit (the individual family) but a level much lower than the whole economy. Hence the most appropriate organisational form – from the point of view of optimal motivation and efficiency – varies according to the level at which public-goods type characteristics apply. One reason why BN-sectors may have been relatively neglected in some areas is the absence of suitable organisational forms, which in many cases fall somewhere between the family and the central government.

Apart from 'public-good' characteristics, other reasons for public support for production or consumption include using such support as a vehicle for income redistribution, and changing consumption patterns. As the matrix below indicates, many of the sectors commonly defined as BN-sectors have some public-good characteristics.

Reasons For Intervention:	I. PRODUCTION			II. CONSUMPTION			III. OTHER	
BN Goods	Externalities	Indivis.	Risks	Time Preference	Non Appropriability	Externalities	Income Distribution	Tastes
Food							*	*
Health		*		*		* *	?	*
Education		*		*		*	?	
Water: Sanitation		*			*	*	?	
Shelter							?	

Full income and the organisation of production

Figure 2.2 describes the productive activities of Figure 2.1 according to the organisation in which production takes place. Labour resources are specified (Level I) in terms of age, sex, marital status, etc. in conformity with the full income approach. Except for the very young (i.e. infants and those in early years of primary school), it is virtually certain that all age groups produce certain net BN-services, for example, via child rearing or improvements of personal hygiene levels, etc. In this way the labour force (plus the capital stock) produces the full income F at Level II (of Figure 2.2) which consists of a monetised component (Y_m) and a non-monetized component (Y_u). While the latter is not explicitly valued in the market place, a monetary value can be imputed to it through a scheme of shadow pricing.

At the aggregate level, there are two subdivisions representing different organisational choices. The monetised component, Y_m, is made up of the output of two types of production organisation, private firms in the market, and public sector production units. For the non-monetised components (Y_u), the services may be supplied by at least two types of organisation, families or communities (i.e. farmer associations, co-operatives, tribal groupings, neighbourhood associations); see Level III of Figure 2.2. Some organisational units – such as some co-operatives – are hybrids, with part of their activities in the monetised sector and part in the non-monetised.

These possible variations in production organisation may occur in each of the production sectors as illustrated in Level IV. For

A Macroeconomic Framework

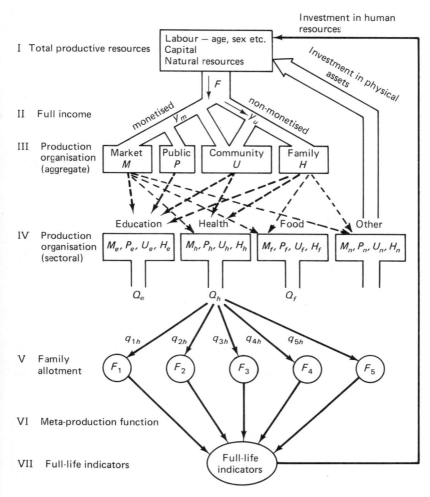

FIGURE 2.2 *Full income and organisational choices*

example, for the health sector, the total output of health services, Q_h, is the sum of the outputs of these four types of production organisations, i.e. the firms, M_h (representing private hospitals and clinics), public enterprises, P_h (public health, sanitation departments), H_h family and U_h (communal fly eradication groups). The same fourfold organisational choice may appear for the other BN-production sectors. In the food sector in many LDCs, the whole output may be produced by small peasant families so that there is a coincidence of the family as the production and consumption units.

One special organisational characteristic of all the BN-sectors (health, education and nutrition) is the importance of the family as a production unit. With minor exceptions this is not so for the 'other' or non-basic needs sectors for which there exists a sharper distinction (i.e. a sharper functional specialisation) between families (as consumption units) and firms (as production units). It is not solely accidental, especially in poor communities, that the household is often a significant producer in BN-sectors but not in non-BN-sectors. In a purely subsistence economy the family produces its own consumption items, which largely consist of BN-goods and services. Elements of such subsistence production remain in the BN-production of many poor economies.

The existence of a multiplicity of possible production organisations in any given basic needs sector, for example, health, arises because there exist many types of health services which in different circumstances can be produced with different organisational structures. For example, caring for the dependent population (old, young and sick) is normally handled by families in most LDCs. In different societies these same services may be produced by other organisations such as nurseries (in socialist countries) and old age homes (in the industrially advanced countries). For an output characterised by efficiency of large-scale production or natural monopoly (e.g. an immunisation programme) the government may be the best organisational form. An agreement to clean the local environment may be best handled by village associations, etc. Many central BN policy issues focus on the design of measures to promote efficient organisational devices.

It is helpful to distinguish between two types of institutional issues. On the one hand, there is the question of organisational capacity or efficiency within units: whether or not a sanitation department is collecting rubbish efficiently; whether a farm is producing food efficiently; whether a household is spending the family budget wisely; whether or not co-operatives are diffusing technological information effectively. On the other hand, there is the problem of the efficiency of the co-ordination of activities among the production sectors: co-ordination through the market mechanism under capitalism; or through central planning in controlled economies; or through some combination of the two in a mixed economy.

III INCOMES, ALLOTMENT AND BASIC NEEDS

The first part of the discussion presented a framework in which the production conditions for a BN-approach might be analysed; the second an organisational framework. In both approaches, the BN-goods produced by the system are allotted to families who use them to achieve full-life indicators (Level VI in Figure 2.1 and V in Figure 2.2), but so far we have not considered the system of allotment. The level and distribution of achievement in relation to full-life indicators depends largely on how these goods are allotted. This section considers the determinants of this distribution or allotment.

Figure 2.3 presents an accounting framework. The value of full income F is shown, as before, at the top of Figure 2.3 (Level II). Full income is divided into wages W, property income π (i.e. interest and profits), government revenue G, and imputed household (and community) income H (Level II).[3]

Each of these categories of income is divided among society's families F_1, F_2, F_3, F_4 as shown in Level III. In principle any family may receive five kinds of income: income from employment which depends on the composition of the family and employment opportunities; income from property, allocated according to ownership of capital assets; monetary transfers from the government or from other families; goods provided free (or at subsidised rates) from the government (or local community); and household income.

Conceptually, a family pattern (level and distribution) of full income is then determined, as in Level III of Figure 2.3. Full income consists in the sum of the family wage pattern (W_1, W_2, W_3, W_4), family property income (π_1, π_2, π_3, π_4), family receipts from transfers (T_1, T_2, T_3, T_4), public goods (P_1, P_2, P_3, P_4) and household income (H_1, H_2, H_3, H_4). We describe the full income distribution which consists of the sum of these elements as $V = (V_1, V_2, V_3, V_4)$.

The first two items (wages and property income) together constitute primary family income distribution. We describe this as $Y = (Y_1, Y_2, Y_3, Y_4)$. Disposable money-income includes wages, property income and transfer payments. The distribution of money-income among families (normally before and sometimes after including transfer payments) forms the focus of much of the literature on family income distribution on which both causal analysis and measurement has been concentrated. However, it is the distribution of full income

26   *Planning to Meet Basic Needs*

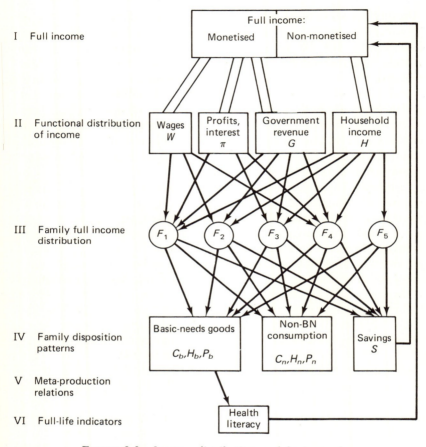

FIGURE 2.3 *Income distribution and basic needs*

(V), including household income and public goods as well as money-income, which is the relevant concept in analysing family consumption of basic needs.

The critical element in a BN-approach is family consumption of BN-goods which forms the input into the meta-production function and determines achievements on full-life indicators. For any given distribution of full income, family consumption patterns of BN-goods depend on how family full income is disposed of as between BN-goods, non-BN consumption goods and savings (see Level IV).

Different types of decision determine disposal patterns for the goods produced by the three sectors – private firms, household sector and the public sector. For goods produced by the private sector, families allocate their disposable income between the various categories. In the case of both household and public-sector goods, for both of which family income is imputed, decisions on consumption patterns are normally made in the process of making decisions about production patterns. In the case of the household sector, the family controls the decisions; in the case of public goods, disposal into BN and non-BN goods is largely determined within the public sector, and outside family control.

We may formally summarise these disposition patterns as follows: suppose there are two production sectors (i.e. a Basic Needs and a non-Basic Needs production sector) such that each sector contains three productive organisations, firms, families and governments.[4] Since the private firms involved in non-BN production can either produce consumption goods or investment goods, each family can spend its total income in seven ways leading to seven family income disposition patterns. In notation these are:

$C_b = (C_{1b}, C_{2b}, C_{3b}, C_{4b})$ family consumption of BN-goods produced by private firms

$C_n = (C_{1n}, C_{2n}, C_{3n}, C_{4n})$ family consumption of non BN-goods produced by private firms

$H_b = (H_{1b}, H_{2b}, H_{3b}, H_{4b})$ family consumption of BN-goods produced by families

$H_n = (H_{1n}, H_{2n}, H_{3n}, H_{4n})$ family consumption of non-BN goods produced by families

$P_b = (P_{1b}, P_{2b}, P_{3b}, P_{4b})$ imputed benefits to families of government expenditures on BN-goods

$P_n = P_{1n}, P_{2n}, P_{3n}, P_{4n})$ imputed benefits to families of government expenditures on non-BN goods

$S = (S_{1n}, S_{2n}, S_{3n}, S_{4n})$ family savings pattern

The subscripts 1,2,3,4 refer to different families.

A prime concern of a BN-approach is these allotment patterns.

The consumption pattern arising from the generation and distribution of full income and from the disposal of this income into the various types of goods must be consistent – as with any system of national accounting – with the patterns arising from the production framework (Figure 2.1).[5] In accounting terms, this is shown by the identity of family consumption patterns (Level IV Figure 2.3) with the production patterns generated in the production framework (Level VI Figure 2.1); both then lead, through the meta-production function, to achievement in terms of full-life indicators. This is not just an accounting identity but has important implications for any BN-approach to macro planning: any BN-approach must ensure that allotment conditions (i.e. distribution of full income and its disposition as between different goods) are realised as well as production conditions.

Analysis of allotments

The accounting framework enables us to identify some of the critical elements determining the allotment pattern. For convenience we consider the three sectors – market, public and household – separately. Analysis of allotments is a two stage process: the first stage consists in the question of how income is distributed among families; the second, how it is disposed of as between the various categories of goods. This forms a clear distinction for the market sector but for the other two sectors – where income is imputed – income distribution and disposal are largely determined simultaneously.

Economic analysis has very largely concentrated on the market model and in what follows we have much the most to say about this sector. However, for BN the other two sectors may prove at least as important. The market analysis can thus tell only part of the story.

The market model

The focal point of analysis of traditional functional income distribution is the investigation of the forces which determine the wage and property share. Much current analysis of family income distribution (FID) is concerned with the distribution of monetary income (Y_m above). This is being actively investigated in a number of ways.[6] One possible approach – still in a formative stage – is to attempt to link FID theory to classical income distribution theory. Such a link would lie at the foundation of a positive BN-theory as well.

The determination of FID is clearly critical to the determination of the market aspects of BN. But since it has been much studied elsewhere, here we do not discusss it further, but take the pattern of income distribution as given. Below we explore the relationship between a given pattern of family income, both as to level and distribution (characterised by the mean income $\bar{Y}$, and its distribution as indicated by the Gini co-efficient, G_y) and the disposal of this income on BN-goods, non-BN-goods and savings.

Neglecting the government and family production sectors of Figure 2.3, we have a private market model. Let us assume there are n-families $(F_1, F_2, \ldots, F_n)$, and two production sectors (of which the first is BN-production) as well as a saving sector. In addition to the total family income pattern $Y = (Y_1, Y_2, Y_3, \ldots, Y_n)$ there are thus a set of three patterns (C_b, C_n, S) representing the family consumption patterns of BN-goods (C_b), non BN-goods (C_n) and family savings (S). Then $Y = C_b + C_n + S$. A model of this type is a minimum analytically useful model incorporating FID and BN, in view of the fact that both Y (the total family income pattern) and C_b (the consumption pattern of a BN-good) must appear if FID and BN are to be analysed together.[7]

'Regression' assumption Let us assume that the primary data of our model (Y, C_b, C_n, S) is available as shown by the points in the three (vertically lined up) scatter diagrams of Figure 2.4. We have assumed that there are four families, while total family income patterns (Y_1, Y_2, Y_3, Y_4) are indicated by the points on the horizontal axes. The patterns for C_b, C_n and S are similarly indicated on the vertical axes. In presenting these primary data, we have made the simplifying assumption that a 'simple' functional relationship exists between Y and each of its C_b, C_n and S components. Some such regular pattern of functional relations must be postulated if any analytical approach to the problem is to be feasible. To simplify the technical difficulties further, we have assumed that linear relations exist between Y and C_b, C_n, S.

We may fit four linear regression lines (shown in Figure 2.4 with the estimated parameters as the intercepts b_b, b_n, b_s and slopes a_b, a_n, a_s). These constitute familiar consumption and savings functions in the Keynesian and Engels curve traditions. In view of the basic accounting equation $Y = C_b + C_n + S$ it is obvious that $a_b + a_n + a_s = 1$ and $b_b + b_n + b_s = 0$ (when the parameters are estimated by the method of least squares).

In order to analyse levels and distribution of BN-consumption both the mean value of BN, for *all* families, $\bar{C}_b$, and the inequality in the consumption of the good as measured by the Gini co-efficient $G(C_b)$, are relevant. Diagramatically $(\bar{Y}, \bar{C}_b)$ is represented by the mean point on the regression line $C_b = b_b + a_b Y$. In addition, it is sometimes useful to define a critical minimum value, for the consumption of BN goods C_{bm} – as indicated on the vertical axis in the lowest deck of Figure 2.4 which stands, for example, for the caloric

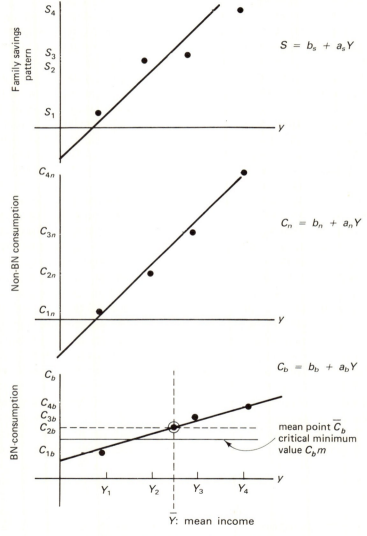

FIGURE 2.4 *Regression Analysis*

minimum food requirement where the BN-good in question is food. An understanding of the relationship between these indices is necessary for greater clarity concerning the relation between growth, distribution and basic needs.

In the linear model, a useful linking equation is given by $G(C_b) = e_b G_y$ where $e_b = a_b \bar{Y}/\bar{C}_b > 0$ when $(a_b > 0)$. e_b is the elasticity of the regression line at the mean point. If $e_b = 0.8$, for example, then $G(C_b)$ is 80 per cent of G_y and the inequality of the BN consumption pattern is less than total income inequality. e_b is positive if and only if the slope of the regression line is positive (i.e. $a_b > 0$), or the consumption of the particular BN-goods increases with income. Empirical information on the values of the parameters is needed to strengthen the analytical foundations of a BN-approach; many of the assertions made depend on the magnitude of the regression slope a_b.

Whether a BN-good is more or less equally distributed than total monetary income depends on whether the value of e_b exceeds or is less than one – i.e. whether the consumption function for BN-good is elastic or inelastic at the mean point. Intuitively, it seems likely that as incomes rise families will increase their consumption of BN-goods less than proportionately with income, while non-BN consumption and savings will increase more than proportionately. Thus our *a priori* hypothesis is that: $0 < a_b < 1$ or $G(C_b) < G_y$, i.e. the basic needs good is distributed more equally than total family income. It is also reasonable to assume that for BN-goods, the slope of the regression line a_b, as well as the vertical intercept b_b, are both positive. The BN-commodity, in other words, is likely to be of the type of which every one must consume some and of which everyone will consume more – but not proportionately more – as incomes rise. A second and related question concerns the impacts of an increase of $\bar{Y}$ (i.e. an increase of per capita income) on the consumption pattern of BN-goods. The equation which is essential for answering this question is provided by substitution $C_b = b_b + a_b \bar{Y}$ in the linking equation above

$$G(C_b) = e_b G_y \text{ where } e_b = a_b\bar{Y}/(b_b + a_b\bar{Y}) = a_b\bar{Y}/\bar{C}_b$$

$$= \frac{1}{1 + b_b/a_b\bar{Y}} < 1$$

This equation is useful for analysing the relationship between BN and the family income distribution in the context of growth.

The attempt to solve the BN issue through growth alone is often rejected as being too slow, and indirect. The linking equation shows that through time, the change in $\bar{C}_b$ and $G(C_b)$, (the per capita consumption of BN goods and the equity of its distribution) are determined by the changes of $\bar{Y}$ and G_y through time. Suppose the increase in per capita income is unaccompanied by any change in G_y, then the equation suggests that the effect on $G(C_b)$ is exercised entirely through e_b. In the linear case (where the marginal propensity to consume is constant) e_b increases as $\bar{Y}$ increases, so that BN-goods tend to be more unequally distributed as per capita income increases, even when the overall distribution of income is not getting worse. However, in the more realistic non-linear case, where the marginal propensity to consume the BN-good declines as incomes rise, the distribution of BN-goods may get more equal as incomes rise.

An increase in the relative inequality of BN-consumption may, of course, be accompanied by a reduction in the number of families falling below the critical minimum or absolute deprivation line, since any increase in income going to the most deprived is likely to increase their consumption of BN-goods.

In a BN sense, immiserising growth can be defined as occurring if, as growth proceeds, the number of families falling below the critical minimum consumption of BN-goods rises. This would only occur if a sharp deterioration in income distribution accompanied growth.

It is necessary, therefore, to estimate the empirical values of the four main variables in order to assess the policy options for a particular country. Fast growth of a particular kind – without a severe worsening of FID – may solve the BN-problem over time. BN-failure may be due either to inadequate growth or to a growth path which is accompanied by a severe worsening in income distribution. The recent experience of Taiwan seems to indicate that rapid (and equitable) growth can solve the BN problem. Experience in other more typical LDCs indicates that the absolute deprivation of BN-goods may at least be alleviated even if family income distribution worsens somewhat under growth. In some countries, however, the worsening of income distribution has been such that little progress in BN has been recorded. (For example nutrition levels of the poorest in Indonesia and Brazil have shown little improvement in recent years.) Country experience is analysed in more depth in Chapters 4 and 5.

The public sector

Both theoretical and factual investigations are much less advanced with respect to the other two sectors (public and household). This is particularly unhelpful for a BN approach since, as shown earlier, both play a critical role in BN-production; both must complement and may substitute for market sector production. It is generally assumed that the public sector would play a very significant part in a BN-strategy; but this cannot simply be assumed. It is necessary to analyse patterns of government behaviour with respect to fiscal transfers and public goods.

Research is needed in analysing the determinants of the pattern of transfers ($T = T_1, T_2, T_3, ...$). The rather piecemeal evidence suggests that for most LDCs (T) tends to be distributed in much the same way as (Y);[8] however, there clearly are exceptions, as in Sri Lanka before 1977, where government transfers had a major egalitarian effect.

The more direct role of the public sector in BN is through the distribution of public goods. Income from public goods may be imputed to families. This imputation process may be rather uncertain and indirect for some types of goods (for example, defence, police, general environmental measures), or fairly direct and clearcut, as for example, with education and health and specific environmental measures.

Public sector goods may be divided into BN-goods and non-BN goods (P_b, P_n); such that $P_b = \Theta P$. Each category is associated with particular distribution among families, such that $P_b = (P_{1b}, P_{2b}, P_{3b}, P_{4b})$ and $P_n = (P_{1n}, P_{2n}, P_{3n}, P_{4n})$.

A BN-approach requires knowledge of the determinants of P_b. For this it is necessary to investigate the determinants of total expenditure on public goods, and its distribution. There is an obvious analogy here with investigation of the determination of the distribution of BN-market goods, discussed above. But in the market sector, because of the long history of research in this area, we are confident about the main elements involved in both distribution and disposition. In the public sector we have little knowledge about either.

Political, sociological and economic factors are involved. One approach would be to assume that political factors are responsible for determining the share of the public sector in national income P/Y, its disposition ΘP and distribution (G_n, G_b), then for any given set of political factors, P_n and P_b would be uniquely determined by the level of per capita income. But very preliminary and tentative findings suggest that there is some (loose) association between the distribution of money-income and the distribution and disposition of public goods, such that in countries with more egalitarian monetary income distribution, there is some tendency for a more egalitarian distribution of public goods, and an associated tendency for a higher proportion of public goods to be BN-goods. The positive relationship between public good distribution and money-income distribution might be explained by connections between political power over the administrative machine and economic power. There are also more straightforward economic explanations.

The consumption of public goods often involves heavy opportunity costs in terms of foregone earnings, for example resulting from school attendance, and other complementary costs, as for clothes, transport and so on, such that public good consumption is positively related to money income. If this finding were firmly established then P_b would appear to be a function of the level and distribution of money-income, in a similar way (though with looser connections) to that in which the consumption of marketed goods is related to the level and distribution of money income. 'Regression lines' could then be drawn relating the consumption of public goods to levels of money-income. Whereas, for market goods, differences in the observed relationships are attributed to relative prices, tastes, culture, etc. for public goods such differences would be related to political factors, although these political factors might in turn be explained by economic factors.

Policy options *vis-a-vis* public BN-goods are again analogous to those for market goods: indeed one could use the same equation as for market goods showing the relationship between BN-consumption, income levels and distribution. Again growth of income and improved distribution would tend to increase the consumption of public BN-goods, but at this stage of our knowledge we are much less certain about how much. The major difference lies in the determination of the factors underlying these relationships. For market goods, we take given tastes as the determining factor. For public goods, we have to assume, 'political factors' are the underlying determinants. But we know little about the stability of these factors and therefore of the underlying relationships. For market goods, one policy option is to change tastes, changing the propensity to consume any given good; for public goods, the analogous change is a change in the underlying political decisions. But whereas for market goods we know about the kind of changes necessary to achieve this (relative prices, information, etc.) for political factors we are more ignorant.

Potentially it seems that public goods could substitute largely for private goods in a BN-approach. Investigation of the determinants of public good disposition is therefore essential to illuminate the possibilities.

Families as producers of BN-goods

Finally, we need to consider the family as a producer of BN and non-BN goods – indicated by the family production sectors in Figure 2.3 leading to the allotment patterns $H_b = (H_{1b}, H_{2b}, H_{3b}, H_{4b})$ for BN-goods and $H_n = (H_{1n}, H_{2n}, H_{3n}, H_{4n})$ for the non-BN goods. This sector is important since household production may account for as much as 40 per cent of full income and a greater proportion of BN-production.

Recent research and analysis on the distribution of household income has produced the not unexpected result that non-monetised household income is more equally distributed than the monetised components of income. This means that full income is more equally distributed than monetised income, although in normative terms this may not mean much since standards of equity have to be adjusted to allow for the inclusion of full income.

The distinguishing characteristic of household production and allotment is the directness of the allotment process. This is due to the very fact of the coincidence of the families as both beneficiaries and producers. There exists a large incentive to produce more efficiently whenever such a coincidence exists.

CONCLUSIONS

The accounting framework presented here illuminates some of the issues which are widely discussed in relation to BN. Apart from providing an orientation for research and data collection, it enables us to comment on the role and usefulness of a resource-planning approach; it also identifies the potential points of intervention and thus provides a framework in which to consider planning for policy change. The next chapter is devoted to issues of planning and policies.

3 Plans and Policies

The last chapter presented a macro framework for basic needs. The framework permits a more organised analysis of some of the issues that arise in planning for BN. This chapter looks at two of these, in the light of the discussion of the framework: first, a 'target-planning' approach to BN; secondly, identification of policies for BN.

TARGET-PLANNING FOR BN

There is a strong current of thought within the BN-approach which emphasises resource-oriented targeting[1] – both for national planning in developing countries and at the international aid-giving level. The approach has much in common within the 'planning school' of development (associated, for example, with Tinbergen and Chenery), which formed an important part of development thought in the 1950s and 1960s. This approach deployed planning models emphasising the need for technical and financial consistency in the use of resources in achieving development targets.

A typical simple planning model is provided with the Harrod–Domar framework which generates the familiar growth equation, where the rate of growth of capital and of output are expressed in terms of the saving rates 's' and the capital–output ratio 'v'. When the parameters are estimated econometrically, the equation becomes a planning equation in which the target growth rates of GNP and of the capital stock are determined by the instruments, 's' and 'v'. The model emphasises a consistent pattern of resource allocation between consumption and investment to ensure intertemporal resource allocation, in order to reach a targeted GNP growth rate, and a particular level of GNP by a certain date.

Similar ideas are inherent in much thinking underlying the BN-approach: it is felt that (a) the BN-approach should focus on the number of persons below the poverty line (or some similar target group) and that a time-phased target should be set for the reversal or elimination of that condition; (b) that eliminating poverty or meeting specified basic needs requirements over a specified period of time entails a demand for productive resources which may possibly run into conflict with growth; and (c) that this threatened conflict may be dominated (or at least softened) because the BN-expenditures may in turn promote the growth of GNP since they also constitute investments in human resources, etc.

It should be apparent that issues of this type can be analysed in terms of a framework similar to a dynamic version of a planning model directly descendant from those of the earlier vintage. The general economic system presented in Figure 2.1 in the last chapter may help in thinking about the construction of a resource-oriented planning model in support of the BN-approach.

Referring to that figure we can see, for example, that total resources may be allocated either to the BN-sectors (R_e, R_h or R_f) or to the non-BN sectors (R_o) that produce ordinary consumption (C) or investment goods (I). Hence a clear case of possible conflict may arise necessitating consistent resource planning. As suggested by the figure, the first step would be to estimate the production functions: $Q_i = f(K_i, L_i)$ (i = education, health, food and other) relating the outputs to inputs, from an engineering standpoint. In the BN literature these production functions are usually interpreted as the specification of certain costs associated with the provision of certain BN-services.

The next step in the planning process is the allotment of every component of the BN (and non-BN) output to all the families (Q_{1i}, $Q_{2i},...Q_{ni}$). These patterns are in turn linked to the 'full-life' indicator values through the relations postulated for the meta-production function, $J = F(Q_{1i}, Q_{2i},...Q_{ni})$. If maximisation of indicator J is taken as the ultimate objective of the society then the optimisation process should determine how a consistent resource allocation and basic needs allotment plan can be constructed. If J is, moreover, specified for a future target date (for example, life expectancy and/or literacy should reach stated target levels in twenty years), the solution to the dynamic resources allocation model yields the appropriate decisions. If J is also regarded as contributing to the human capital stock we have an additional feedback, a complication, but still a planning model involving target setting and consistent resource allocation.

Feasibility of target-planning for BN

Although the BN planning approach just outlined is simple enough in theory, there exist well-recognised difficulties when one tries to implement it statistically. Many of the difficulties arise from measurement of the meta-production function.

The input–output relations inherent in the production function are neither static nor instantaneous. In order to produce a literate population or a long life it may take the cumulative effect of consumption (of BN-goods) over a considerable stretch of time before a significant relationship can be detected. Statistically, a full-life indicator value in one year may be affected by the lagged values of consumption of many years in the past.

In order to produce a long life or a longer life the input of additional education, health, and food may exhibit certain relations which are complementary or substitutable. Without education services the health sector may not, for example, be effective in producing long life, i.e. education and health services may be complementary in production. On the other hand, food may constitute a substitute for health services in producing a long life, i.e. they are substitutable. There are also dynamic lead and lag factors. Thus it may be the case that education expenditures must precede health expenditures in time, to secure dynamic resource allocation efficiency. While it is easy to specify these possibilities, it is very difficult to establish the relationships empirically.

In the normal resource planning case a single key target variable (for example, the rate of growth of per capita GNP) is usually identified and maximised. But in BN, the multi-dimensional characteristics of the full-life indicators $J = (J_1, J_2, ..., J_n)$ render simple maximisation more difficult. Moreover, the full-life indicators describe the quality of life for the entire population. Implicit in the BN-objective is not only a high average life expectancy or low infant mortality but also that the variance should be low, although how low is rarely specified.

When the various quantities of outputs (Q_e, Q_h, Q_f, Q_o) are fixed, the full-life indicators values may vary with variation in the patterns of allotment among families, and the distribution within families. For example, a given volume of total food output may be allotted more or less equally among families, leading to different results in the state of longevity. In the case of health an unequal allotment of public health services (e.g. smallpox inoculations) or environmental sanitation (for different districts in a city) may hurt the health of all families.

A whole new set of problems arise once the qualities described by the full-life indicators are also regarded as human resources investments that augment the system's future productive capacities. We need to take into account the substitutability of the various human skills and capacities as productive inputs in the ordinary production function sense. Aptitude tests, administered by the employment offices of certain industries, may provide some clues to these issues. Others can be gathered from research results in the relevant labour market/human capital literature. From an investment point of view, the allotment of BN-goods will influence the effects on productivity. The relationships are likely to vary according to sector and even product. For example, in health, it is probable that with adequate average health a more equally distributed increase in health services for the entire population is more productive than an unequally distributed one. On the other hand, in the case of education this may be inaccurate to the extent that a modernising economy is likely to require a skill hierarchy of workers, differentiated in education. Such societies may require a small fraction of very highly educated workers (doctors, engineers, etc.), and a larger group of professionals, resting on a still larger base of unskilled labour.

Planning models focused on the demographic transition have investigated one key dimension of full-life indicators – the relationship between the reproduction rate and the age structure of the population – and in so doing have illustrated some of the difficulties of a resource planning approach. The demographic simulation models show that even among expert demographers the question of the determinants of change in the reproduction rate is far from settled. Usually, instead of employing a meta-production function to determine life expectancy through changes in birth and death rates, the reproduction rates are postulated exogenously, i.e. the planning exercise is conducted for alternative fertility assumptions. This inability to analyse one relatively simple dimension of meta-production relations underlines the difficulties facing a resource-oriented planning approach to BN.

Thus while there is something very appealing about a target-setting approach, it does not appear, at this stage, that there is sufficient knowledge about the underlying relationships to justify it in most cases. Target setting may fulfil a political function, but if the targets are unrealistic in terms of resources or of achieving the postulated objectives, they may prove counterproductive in the long run, politically as well as economically.

This conclusion does not mean that planning for BN is impossible. As discussed in detail in the case of Nigeria (Chapters 6–8), a macro economic approach, involving all three aspects of the framework, is of considerable relevance to a BN-approach to development. It enables one to make an assessment of government's actual priorities; it reveals the major sources of deficiencies with respect to each of the aspects – reasource allocation and production, organisation and incomes – and indicates where corrective action is needed; it also reveals the need for consistency with respect to the various aspects, and demonstrates the choices (and conflicts) facing governments. What it cannot do is provide a watertight prescription for planning for BN, either from the point of view of resource allocation or incomes. This deficiency arises primarily because of lack of knowledge about some of the underlying relationships, which are critical to BN-achievement. But in addition it arises because aspects of political economy enter in such a way that not only does government often not have the power and/or the will to make certain choices, but also the relationships themselves have political as well as technical content.

POLICY OPTIONS FOR MEETING BN

The foundation of planning for policy must be the presumption of a reasonable amount of knowledge of how the economic system behaves independent of changes in government action, for such policy and policy change is in large part devised to modify individual behaviour. Hence understanding underlying behaviour is an essential prerequisite for devising policy with respect to BN.

It is assumed that policies related to a BN-oriented strategy will have as their main aim the achievement of a higher level of full-life indicators. The framework presented earlier enables us to identify, in principle, the potential points of intervention from a BN-oriented point of view. While, as already stated, more work is needed for a fuller specification of many of the relationships, and therefore before we can be confident of the magnitude (and sometimes even the direction) of the effects of these policies, it may be useful to provide a brief categorisation of the points of intervention which seem indicated.

Before going into some details, three (intuitively obvious) points emerge from the earlier analysis, which deserve some emphasis:

1. That it is necessary to operate consistently with respect to the conditions represented by the three aspects of the framework: i.e. that changes in production may only be effective if accompanied by corresponding changes in organisation and distribution. Failure to recognise this is another weakness of the resource–planning approach.

2. That there is not a single road to Rome, but many roads. For example, a particular level of full-life indicators may be achieved through a high rate of per capita income growth, with a low share of public goods in output and unequal income distribution, or by a low growth in per capita income accompanied by a high share of public consumption and an equal income distribution. These are the grand macro choices. There are other route choices at almost every step of the way: for example, there is a choice between changing the pattern of consumption among families at a given income level by education, by changing relative prices, by supply management or by changing intra-family allotment patterns. At every stage the appropriate choices will depend on the consequences of different choices in terms of efficiency with respect to both normal production functions and the meta-production function, upon initial conditions, upon what is politically and economically possible, and upon political preferences. The function of this type of analysis is to illuminate these choices and their implications, *not to make them.*

3. That different paths will be relevant according to the objectives of the country: it is assumed that a country pursuing a BN-approach is giving *special* weight to full-life indicators, and that this weight is greater than would be justified with reference to human resource aspects alone. But this assumption by no means provides a full or sufficiently well-specified objective for decisions about policies, as was noted in Chapter 1. The following remain undetermined and require elucidation:

(i) How much special weight is given to full-life indicators? Some appear to wish simply to correct market imperfections which lead to underinvestment in BN-sectors. Others wish to go much further than this. Few would go as far as giving 100 per cent weight to the achievement of full-life indicators and no weight to, for example, other consumption, or defence expenditures.
(ii) The aim, according to most BN-analysis, is not to be defined solely in terms of *average* full-life indicators but also in terms of their distribution; but the weight given to improvements at different levels is not specified.
(iii) The content of the full-life indicators to be considered varies. Moreover, there is the question of how much weight to give to the individual elements (e.g. how much to health, how much to education).
(iv) The objective needs to be specified with respect to *time*.

Policies and resources allocation

The most obvious policy area here is increasing the share of resources devoted to BN-sectors: such an increase may be at the expense of non-BN consumption (both public as well as private) or at the expense of investment, or some combination. Decisions on how many resources to devote to BN-sectors and at the expense of which other sectors are the most critical ones with respect to resource allocation. Decisions on both these questions will depend in part on the total availability of resources, and the compressibility of resources in each sector. Other areas in relation to production concern increasing the productivity of the BN-sectors and increasing the productivity of the meta-production function.

Policies and BN-allotment

The resource allocation side of a BN-approach appears most critical, according to the resource-planning approach. But from a policy point of view the generation of appropriate allotments may be of greater significance.

There are a number of alternative routes to the achievement of any

Plans and Policies

specified level of consumption and distribution of the output of BN-sectors. Significant alternatives include:

1. Generating a sufficient growth in primary incomes among the poor, through economic growth, so that their expenditure on BN-goods rises to adequate levels.
2. Generating a sufficient level of primary incomes among the poor through redistribution of assets (e.g. land reform).
3. Generating a sufficient level of *secondary* incomes among the poor through government transfers (including cash payments and the provision of free or subsidised goods).
4. Changing the pattern of consumption for any given income distribution by changing relative prices, availability of different goods and influencing tastes, so that the poor spend a greater proportion of any income on BN-goods.

Which of these options is feasible is closely related to the political economy of each country, as will be illustrated in the next chapter which looks at how different countries have performed. It also depends partly on economic realities: i.e. in countries with very low incomes the redistribution option may not produce adequate levels of BN. Moreover, the 'growth' option (option 1 above) may not be possible for countries with very poor growth prospects, nor for countries where growth tends to be accompanied by worsening income distribution. While the options have been classified into four, in fact countries can and do opt for combinations of the four (e.g. some growth, some redistribution of primary incomes and some secondary redistribution.)

The figure below illustrates different ways of achieving a target level of BN-consumption. Assume initially the typical 'target group' consumer has income shown by $i^o i^o$ budget line, relative prices of BN and non-BN items are represented by the slope of that line, and consumer preferences are shown by indifference curves $p^o p^o$, $p'p'$. Initial consumption of the BN-good is OC^o. Assume the minimum desired level of consumption is OC_m which is above OC^o. In order to secure this desired level the following options are possible.

(a) Raise incomes (either through improved economic opportunities or through transfers) to $i'i'$, so that the consumer's desired position shifts from a^o to a'.
(b) Alter relative prices (e.g. by subsidies or by subsidies on the BN-good and taxes on the non-BN goods) so that the relative prices shift to ii and consumption shifts to a''.

(c) Alter preferences, by advertising/propaganda, or by altering intra-family income distribution and/or power, such that with a new indifference curve, pp, preferences are more heavily weighted towards BN-goods so that the desired level of expenditure on BN is achieved at a'''.

In the figure any one of these options is feasible and the choice between them is then a matter of political decision in the light of the implications for economic efficiency, administrative burden and political objectives. But in some cases some of the options may not be feasible, and in extreme cases none may be feasible. For example, if the minimum income, Ym, to achieve minimum consumption, Cm, is above the mean income of that society, then even complete equality will not produce a sufficient transfer of income to realise the minimum desired consumption level. In that case, the transfer of income would have to be accompanied by policies to increase the proportion of income spent on the BN-good. There could be a situation in which that combination also was insufficient to realise the desired minimum. This would be the case if the mean income budget line fell below the desired minimum consumption of the BN-good, as in Figure 3.2 below, if we assume that ii represents the mean income.

Figure 3.2 shows that options (b) and (c) will not be feasible to achieve the desired objective without improvements in incomes, when the actual income (as shown by the budget line ii) falls below the line representing minimum BN-consumption.

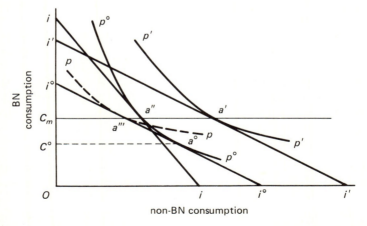

FIGURE 3.1 *Different ways of achieving a target level of BN-consumption*

In very poor societies then (or where the minimum desired consumption of BN-goods is set rather high), no policy combination may be sufficient to achieve the objective, and economic growth becomes a necessary precondition for its achievement. In richer economies, with unequal income distribution and very poor consumers, influencing tastes through advertising, etc. and changes in relative prices may also be insufficient to achieve the desired objective and income redistribution then becomes essential as part of the solution. Subsidies on BN-outputs can themselves form an important source of income transfer to the target groups.

Identification of which policies are feasible is important. It is sometimes suggested that many poor economies fall into the category just identified, where no amount of redistribution will be sufficient to secure minimum BN-consumption, and consequently growth and 'trickle down' represents the only workable policy. In so far as this argument is taken as a justification for not pursuing (and even sometimes dismantling) egalitarian policies, the better to promote growth, it involves an immediate sacrifice of BN – i.e. the BN-element in consumption is actually further reduced below the critical minimum level because non-BN resource use (in the form of investment goods, and incentive consumptions goods) is believed to be necessary to achieve growth and hence eventually a minimum desired level of BN-consumption. Whether or not this argument is correct depends on:

1. Whether it is true that redistribution could not achieve adequate levels of BN. The case of Sri Lanka – described in Chapter 4 – shows

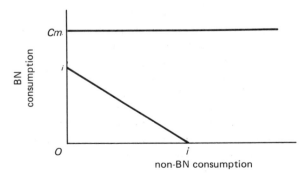

FIGURE 3.2 *Mean income budget line below minimum consumption of the BN-good*

how great BN-achievements may be *even in very poor economies*, if radical policies of subsidies and income transfers are adopted. Since Sri Lanka's average per capita income in 1980 was 18th in the whole world, i.e. only seventeen countries had lower income and seventy-two developing countries had incomes per capita above her, the applicability of this argument should be limited at most to the minority of countries, (the seventeen), with lower incomes than Sri Lanka. But since Sri Lanka's policies, though fairly egalitarian were by no means completely egalitarian, BN through redistribution is probably a real possibility for many of the seventeen. As a very rough suggestion, it might be argued that at most eleven countries (those with incomes per head in 1978 of below $150) fall into the category of countries for whom growth is the only solution to the BN problem.

2. Whether the pursuit of growth need be at the expense of current fulfilment of BN. This depends on whether sufficient investment resources can be obtained from non-BN sources, how far 'luxury' (i.e. non-BN) consumption is necessary as an incentive, and how far any sacrifice of BN-expenditures itself threatens growth by reducing human potential. With the current evidence on the significance of human resources for development and growth,[2] and the absence of evidence on links between inequality, incentives and growth, it would seem that arguments for sacrificing BN now in order to promote it later through growth have very shaky foundations.

Income transfers

The 'disincentive' effects of income transfers are often cited as an argument against them, in the normal case where a sufficient transfer could achieve the desired level of BN-consumption. The effects on incentives depend on the *form* the transfers take. As is well known lump sum taxes and transfers need not affect incentives, but they are difficult to devise and administer. Nonetheless some approximation to this form of taxation is possible. At the lower end of the income scale any disincentive effects of receiving benefits may easily be offset by improved productivity resulting from improved health and nutrition. The magnitude of the effects (negative and positive) will be related to the magnitude of the transfer.

In some instances, political economy factors may limit the use of monetary transfers to achieve BN-objectives. Most of the empirical evidence suggests that governments rarely succeed in having a major effect on inequality through fiscal transfers alone, particularly when primary income inequality is great. But, as argued in the last chapter, this is an area which requires more research.

Public goods

Another form of transfer is via greater provision of public goods for BN-raising (P_{1b}, P_{2b}, P_{3b}, P_{4b} – see p. 27). Potentially this could apply to any BN-goods although in practice it is liable to be concentrated among goods normally produced in the public sector, which account for a large proportion of BN-output. Any disincentive effects of such a policy would be less than with fiscal transfer because families would need more money-income in order to provide the complementary resources required for the effective consumption.

A major problem with a public good BN-approach is that of 'hijacking' such that the public goods are not received by the groups in need. An associated problem is that of targeting to reduce the cost of the policies.

It should be noted – with respect both to fiscal transfers and public goods – that where income inequality is very great a quite small additional expenditure can make a major difference to income levels among the poorest groups. For example, if the income share of the bottom 20 per cent is 2 per cent, as in Brazil, increasing public consumption by one-fifth and directing the increase to that group would double the income level of the group.

Relative prices and consumption patterns

Government may attempt to change families' consumption patterns, altering the proportion of income spent on BN-goods. This may be achieved by controlling the price of a particular BN-good (e.g. lowering food prices) and/or by education/information policies (options (b) and (c) above). Income levels need not be affected, although in practice where the good forms a large proportion of total consumption of the poor, they often are.

When governments change relative prices (e.g. by lowering food prices, through price control), this may require other measures of direct control such as rationing, food coupons, etc. to effect a smooth

48   *Planning to Meet Basic Needs*

delivery of the BN-goods, especially in the short run.[3] In the absence of such rationing devices, the government may impose a tax on the wealthy families, the revenues of which are used to subsidise food prices for the benefit of the poor. Analytically, the price intervention policy would then be combined with an income transfer policy so that incomes become more equal.

Nominally, a relative price policy represents a partial equilibrium solution affecting BN-goods. But the policy, when effective, also has general equilibrium implications. In the model, outlined in the last chapter, these take the form of the other (non-BN) regression lines, which must consequently move downward and become steeper in a compensatory fashion. As the per capita consumption of BN-goods increases, the per capita consumption of non-BN goods and/or savings must drop.

When there are n-families and m-goods, the allotment patterns form a matrix which may be listed in Table 3.1 as follows:

TABLE 3.1

Families Goods	F_1	F_2	$F_3 ... F_n$	Total (all families)
BN – items				
1) Food	C_{11}	C_{21}	$C_{31} ... C_{n1}$	C_1
2) Health	C_{12}	C_{22}	$C_{32} ... C_{n2}$	C_2
3) Education	C_{13}	C_{23}	$C_{33} ... C_{n3}$	C_3
Non – BN				
4) Clothing	C_{14}	C_{24}	$C_{34} ... C_{n4}$	C_4
5) Entertainment	C_{15}	C_{25}	$C_{35} ... C_{n5}$	C_5
m) Savings	C_{1m}	C_{2m}	$C_{3m} ... C_{nm}$	C_m
Total	$Y_1\ <$	$Y_2\ <$	$Y_3 ... <Y_n$	Y

Note: The block marks off those BN-items among those families whose consumption falls below some defined minimum requirement.

The family income distribution pattern is indicated as the row sum in the bottom row while various consumption patterns ($C_1, C_2, ..., C_m$) are indicated by the column sum at the right-hand margin. Traditional theory of production and consumer preference explains the determination of the column sum through resource allocation. FID analysis is concerned with the equity of the row sum. The BN-approach marks off a block (shown by the block in this matrix) corresponding to BN-goods for the low incomes families. The specification of critical minimum values (indicated roughly by the right-hand margin of the box) can then be used as exogenously postulated land mark values to assess performance.

Of the range of policies listed above, doubts are often voiced about the legitimacy of intervening in family consumption patterns. It is important to be clear about the sort of grounds on which such intervention is justified: first, the policy may simply be a form of income transfer through subsidised consumption. The use of a subsidy may be justified for reasons of administrative economy, because it makes it easier to prevent hijacking and because it is politically more acceptable than other forms of income transfer. Secondly, intervention may be justified to provide families with improved information and to offset the distorted information they receive in the form of some advertising. Thirdly, interventions may be justified as a means of correcting intra-family misallocations: school meal subsidies are an example. Fourthly, there are the usual public goods reasons for intervention – externalities, etc. These reasons – which all fit into a consumer sovereignty liberal approach to economic welfare – are themselves sufficient to justify the sort of interventions proposed in most BN policy–making.

It should be recognised, however, that non-individualistic systems of consumer choice are in being in many parts of the world. In many political systems, generally those which adopt a more holistic and etatist approach to political economy, ranking of human needs is not regarded as something which must be left to the individual family, but as a co-operative and essentially political decision. All economies share an element of this more dirigiste philosophy in their requirements for compulsory education, minimal standards of child care, consumption priorities in times of crisis, etc. These are sometimes described as 'merit' wants by neoclassical economists. But this is really only a way of saying that the usual consumer–sovereignty type arguments do not apply. In some economies collective ranking occurs more systematically – as in the way, for example, that centrally planned economies determine consumption priorities, or Communes or Kibbutzim. Such systems do not necessarily mean that the individual has less choice *in toto* – since by affecting collective consumption he may have more influence over total decisions than if he only affected his own. Recent developments in consumer theory, recognising the interdependence of much consumption, suggest that this form of choice might even be preferred if individual utility remained the sole criterion. Selection of *systems* of consumer choice must essentially be a political decision. The justification for intervention in family consumption patterns will differ according to the system of choice in being. It should also be added that a strong BN-orientation might itself cause a country to select a particular system of choice.

POLICIES AND ORGANISATION

Policies related to organisation are of greater relevance to a BN approach than to more conventional development strategies for three reasons:

1. Because as argued in Chapter 2 it is a distinguishing characteristic of most BN-sectors that output may be produced in a variety of organisational forms; because of the semi-public good characteristics of the goods it is by no means always obvious which form of organisation is more efficient. In many cases these characteristics are such that the most appropriate form might fall somewhere between the pure public sector and the purely private sector, and somewhere between the central government and the family in terms of coverage of the producing/consuming unit. Institutional gaps – in some countries – may prove to be a significant source of deficiency with respect to BN. Identifying and filling these gaps then may be one area of BN-oriented strategy.

2. The efficiency of the organisation, as ordinarily defined, is not the only criterion for organisational choice, in a BN-approach. In addition to the normal efficiency criteria, participation (both moral and financial), may be a significant criterion for choice of organisational form. Such participation – which includes some voice in decision-making and a commitment to the success of the institution – is required on a number of grounds: first, to the extent that a BN-approach involves ascertaining people's 'felt needs', participation enables the producer and consumer to exercise some genuine control and choice (in a sense it is a counter to the loss in consumer's sovereignty discussed above). Secondly, such commitment may be necessary to ensure the long-run sustainability of the producing units – to deal, for example, with the problem of recurring costs of schools and health clinics; thirdly, participation and commitment may be critical to the effectiveness of BN-outputs in relation to full-life indicators – i.e. the efficiency of the meta-production function may

depend, apart from other things, on the extent of popular participation. It has also been argued that the full life requires not only health and education but also some degree of control over one's life. For this reason participation itself is sometimes included as one of the full-life indicators.[4] We do not include it here because it would put too much burden on the meta-production function; here we regard participation (formally) as a means rather than an end.

3. As argued above, the family is the prime input (as well as being the recipient of the output) of the meta-production function. Hence the efficiency of the family, in this respect, becomes critical to the approach.

GOVERNMENT AND ORGANISATION

All governments allocate part of their budget to the production of BN-commodities, e.g. education and health. The amounts allocated depend on social and political forces in the country. It must be assumed that if governments decide to adopt a BN-approach, then along with this decision goes some commitment to increasing the provision of BN-commodities. But governments which have adopted such an approach are still subject to constraints which may limit their freedom of manoeuvre in terms of size and allocation of the budget. There are certain measures likely to reduce these constraints: these include providing information on the benefits of BN-outputs, in terms of full-life indicators, which may increase popular pressure for the provision of such outputs.

The allocation of expenditures *within* a given budget can be as critical as the total size of the budget. As stated earlier, too little is known about how to achieve effective redistribution of public expenditure at all levels, central, regional and local.

In general it seems that a socialist society, in which the method of production appeals to the co-operative rather than the competitive instincts, is more likely, *ceteris paribus*, to have a large budget and a more egalitarian allotment within it. This is one of the reasons why socialist societies are likely to achieve higher BN-standards at any particular level of development.

Organisational deficiencies can affect achievement on BN in two ways: first, there may be an inappropriate organisational structure (for example, a centralised structure for the public sector, making it difficult for appropriate local units to develop); secondly, there may be deficiencies within any organisational structure which reduces its efficiency. Policies then can be designed to respond to both these (somewhat interconnected) phenomena.

As far as the first category is concerned, the appropriateness of any set of institutions tends to be unique to each society, depending on historical evolution, cultural factors and political preferences. In many cases, there are alternative ways (institutionally) of meeting any given BN. For example, food may be produced collectively, co-operatively, through capitalist farming or household/family farms. The choice depends on many historical/political factors: but the choice is relevant to the meeting of BN and therefore the implications for BN could form a major consideration in determining the organisational choice. The relevance to BN comes in three ways: first, the organisational choice affects the distribution of income and hence the ability to meet BN from the point of view of incomes.[5] Capitalist farming tends to be inegalitarian compared with collective or family farms. Secondly, the choice of organisation affects what is produced – that is, food for self-consumption, food for the market, or other cash crops – which may in turn affect a society's ability to meet its BN through production. In general, collective/co-operative farms and households tend to give greater priority to producing food for self-consumption than capitalist farms. Thirdly, the mode of production affects the efficiency of the unit – i.e. production for any given inputs and therefore the ability of a society to meet its BN from the point of view of production.

Within any given organisational structure, BN-achievements are much affected by the efficiency of each of the major units. In some societies inefficiencies within the organisations appear to be one of the major obstacles to achievements. For example, the rural health services in some LDCs often lack vital drugs, while schools are poorly staffed and have minimal equipment. To some extent these deficiencies may be due to low expenditure, but efficiency of delivery systems and of use when delivered is also a major factor.

THE HOUSEHOLD

The household is a major focus for BN because of its dominant role both as producer and as consumer of BN-goods. It is in the latter role that the household determines the relation between BN-outputs and

BN-achievements, or what we have described as the meta-production function. It is the activities of the household which determine, for example, how far health clinics are used; the extent to which children go to school; what food is consumed ... and so on. The efficiency of the household then may be the critical factor in determining the success or failure of a BN-strategy. If the household fails to make use of BN goods and services, then ensuring their availability will not be sufficient. Moreover, an efficient household can counter many deficiencies of supplies – e.g. in making good use of what there is, following hygienic practices and so on. Thus a major area for policy *vis-à-vis* organisations concerns the efficiency of the household. In practice, this often means the women of the household who tend to be the people primarily responsible for BN-type consumption, choosing the food, doing the cooking, responsible for family hygiene, for teaching the children, taking them to health clinics, to school and so on. Policies towards household efficiency then largely come down to policies towards women: such policies concern female education (as adults and as children), female work and productivity and allocation of time to BN-activities; female access to money-income and their disposition of that income; and more generally, the role of women in the family and in society.

Recently developments in household economics,[6] have begun to focus on allocation of time within the household. Attention has, however, been directed towards measuring the contribution towards production, as normally defined, rather than the BN-type full-life indicators with which we are concerned.

CONCLUSION

The last two chapters have attempted to provide a framework for planning for BN, both with respect to resource allocation and policies. The discussion has been rather general and speculative. In contrast, the remainder of this book is specific and empirical. The next two chapters look at how different LDCs have performed on BN, in an aggregate way, during the past twenty years or so. The subsequent section takes the experience of one country – Nigeria – and relates its performance to the framework presented above. It is intended that these chapters will serve to put flesh on the framework developed in Chapter 2.

4 Country Experience in Meeting Basic Needs

There is a very great variety of experience in meeting BN among developing countries[1]. This variety encompasses differences in political framework, ideals and objectives, in strategy of development and in the way in which each strategy is carried out in practice. Alongside these major differences in how countries go about meeting BN, there are also very big differences in achievements with respect to BN. Taking life expectancy as a measure, performance varies from forty (Ethiopia, 1979) to seventy-two (Cuba, 1979). This chapter is devoted to exploring these differences to see how far it is possible to arrive at general conclusions about country strategy towards meeting BN, in order to identify the type of political and economic strategies that tend to be successful in achieving it and the type that tend to be unsuccessful.

To analyse this question, it is necessary to have some criterion for success and failure in BN-performance. This requires two things: first, a measure or indicator of BN-performance; second, a norm against which country performance can be assessed.

As far as identifying *indicators* is concerned, it is helpful to go back to the discussion of the meaning of a BN-approach to development, in Chapter 1. There it was argued that it is essential to distinguish carefully between the immediate means necessary for BN-achievements (the basket of goods and services) and the ends to which these inputs contribute. The ends of a BN-approach were defined there, in a rather minimalist way, as a healthy life for all, with each person being educated up to a minimum standard. Of course, the quality of life depends on more than this. But, as argued in Chapter 1, considerable complexities and arbitrariness enter once one leaves the minimalist position. Moreover, the minimalist interpretation focuses very clearly on critically important needs for very poor people. Taking this approach, life expectancy becomes the simplest measure of achievement with respect to health, while literacy is the relevant measure for education. These measures have the additional advantage that they are among the most widely available statistics, other than income. There are problems, however, about using these measures.

Firstly, there is the question of the accuracy of the measures. International statistics about life expectancy provide a single figure for each country. Yet anyone working in a particular country almost always finds that the figure is uncertain, based on guesses rather than facts, and could more legitimately be described by a range rather than a point estimate. It sometimes appears that the best guess range lies outside the internationally published statistics.[2] Similar problems apply to literacy; standards required for 'literacy' may differ between countries. Changes over time or differences between countries can be due to methods of measurement as much as any actual differences.

Secondly, there is the problem that neither measure fully reflects the objectives of a BN-approach. For example, people may have long life expectancy while suffering debilitating diseases. With respect to education, numeracy may be as important as literacy. Life expectancy, however, does seem to be highly correlated with other relevant statistics (for example, child mortality and incidence of diseases). The same is probably true of literacy and other measures of the spread of education. Moreover, these are the only widely available statistics and they also avoid the weighting problems which would arise were we to devise a composite measure.

Thirdly, there is the problem of *distribution*. A fundamental aspect of a BN-approach is that everyone should have access to health and education. But the measure of life expectancy is an average for each country and might therefore conceal maldistribution. The problem is much smaller than for many other average figures, such as income per head, since physiological factors put an upper limit on life expectancy even for the very rich and thus limit the range within which life expectancy varies between different income groups. Consequently, while upper income groups do generally enjoy higher life expectancy than lower income groups, differences in distribution of life expectancy among different groups are unlikely to be a major factor in explaining differences in the *average* achievement between societies. In other words, if one country shows a markedly higher life expectancy than another, this is likely to reflect higher standards for the majority of people in that society and not simply very high life expectancy among upper income groups accompanied by low standards for the mass of the people. The literacy figure is not subject to the same problem of distribution since it is not an average but a measure of the proportion of the (adult) population who are literate. The adult literacy rate shows how far education has reached the currently adult population. It does not therefore tell us much about the extent of education among children and therefore future adult literacy rates.

The Table in Appendix A shows life expectancy (in 1979) and literacy rates (for 1976) for 122 countries. The countries are shown in (ascending) order of income per capita. As can be seen, there are considerable variations in BN-performance as shown by these two indicators. It is clear from a glance at this table that there is a positive association between average income per capita and life expectancy and literacy rates. Low income countries generally have a life expectancy of below fifty years and a literacy rate of below 50 per cent, while middle income countries have a life expectancy of between fifty and seventy and a literacy rate over 50 per cent. The richest countries have life expectancy of over seventy years and a literacy rate of nearly 100 per cent. One would expect BN-performance to improve as income per capita rises. This is indicated by the framework (see Chapter 2) where incomes provide the resources from which BN are met and the purchasing power over BN-goods and services. With higher incomes, private expenditure on BN-goods is likely to rise. In addition, for any given proportion of national income spent on social services, absolute expenditure per head would rise with rising per capita incomes.

Taking the low, middle income and industrial economies as a group, there is a clear positive relationship between BN-goods and services and levels of income, as Table 4.1 illustrates.

Statistical analysis of the relationship between per capita incomes and life expectancy, and per capita incomes and literacy across countries supports the view that average per capita income is a

TABLE 4.1

	BN-goods and services					BN-achievements	
	Population per Doctor 1977	Nurse 1977	% of population with access to safe water 1975	Per capita calory supply 1977	No. enrolled in primary school as % age group 1978	No. enrolled in secondary school as % age group 1978	Life expectancy at birth 1979	Adult literacy 1976
Low income countries	6150	6200	29	2231	83	36	57	51
Middle income	4380	1820	58	2581	95	41	61	72
Industrial market economies	620	220	100*	3377	100	89	74	99

Source: *World Development Report 1981*, (World Bank) Annex, table 22 and 23.
* not given, estimated.

TABLE 4.2 Statistical relationships between life expectancy and income per capita, and income per capita and literacy

Relationship	No. observations	a	b	c	Adjusted r^2	F-Statistic	D–W Statistics
1. Life expectancy and income per capita							
a. All countries, linear LIEX = a + by	112	53.99 (0.986)	0.20 (0.002)		0.43	1,110 : 84.22	0.68
b. All countries, quadratic LIEX = a + by + c²	112	50.62 (0.992)	0.0057 (.0006)	−.0000003 (.0000006)	0.58	2,109 : 78.4	1.16
c. All countries, semi-log LIEX = a + blogy	112	11.36 (2.941)	6.9 (0.416)		0.71	1,110 : 275.1	1.35
d. All countries, inverse LIEX = $a + \frac{b}{y}$	112	66.2 (1.002)	−3391 (321.4)		0.50	1,110 : 111.3	0.83
e. All countries, ex oil surplus linear	108	53.65 (0.958)	.002 (.0002)		0.49	1,106 : 103.4	0.75
f. All countries, ex oil surplus quadratic	108	49.1 (0.92)	.008 (.0007)	−0.000005 (.00000006)	0.69	2,105 : 120.3	1.26

g.	All countries, ex oil surplus: semi-log	108	8.03 (2.736)	7.46 (0.39)		0.77	1,106 : 366.0	1.66
h.	All countries, ex oil surplus inverse	108	66.6 (1.03)	−3472.5 (323.4)		0.52	1,106 : 115.3	0.79
i	Excluding oil surplus and industrialised linear	90	48.7 (0.967)	.0078 (0.00069)		0.59	1,88 : 126.8	1.37
j.	Ex. oil surplus and industrialised quadratic	90	43.8 (1.145)	.0186 (.00187)	−.000002 (.00000047)	0.71	2,87 : 107.8	1.95
k.	Ex. oil surplus and industrialised semi-log	90	0.52 (3.99)	8.69 (0.615)		0.69	1,88 : 199.3	1.81
l.	Ex. oil surplus and industrialised inverse	90	63.4 (1,172)	−2827 (336.9)		0.44	1,88 : 70.4	1.01
2.	*Literacy and Income Per Capita*							
a.	All countries, for which data available, linear	81	51.63 (3.67)	0.00571 (0.00127)		0.28	1,79 : 31.84	1.06
b.	All countries for which data available, semi-log	81	−48.6 (11.30)	16.72 (1.65)		0.57	1,79 : 103.16	1.75
c.	All countries for which data available, inverse	81	84.53	−7991.03		0.50	1,79 : 79.88	1.58

significant factor in explaining BN-performance. The results of this analysis are summarised in Table 4.2. A substantial proportion of the vaiation in life expectancy and literacy between countries can be 'explained', at least in a statistical sense, by variations in per capita income. The adjusted r^2 varies, as shown in Table 4.2, depending on the countries included, the form of relationship adopted and the variable in question.

The two indicators of performance, life expectancy and literacy, are required to indicate performance with respect to the two main features of the BN-approach, health and education. However, as suggested by a casual glance at the country figures in the appendix and shown in the scatter diagram (Figure 4.1) there is a very high correlation between country performance with respect to life expectancy and country performance with respect to literacy.[3] This high correlation between literacy and life expectancy probably indicates an important causal relationship, running from education/literacy to life expectancy. Apart from this, it permits the use of a single indicator, life expectancy, as an indicator for achievement with respect to both the major aspects. The statistical analysis of 'good' and 'poor' performers (see discussion below) also shows a close relationship between exceptional performance on life expectancy and

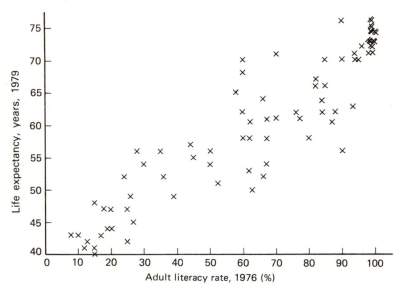

FIGURE 4.1 *Correlation between literacy rate in 1976 and life expectancy in 1979*

literacy. Hence in much of the rest of the discussion, unless explicitly stated, life expectancy alone will be used as an indicator of country achievement with respect to basic needs.

The precise statistical relationship between life expectancy and per capita incomes depends on the countries included in the sample. There are strong grounds for excluding four major capital exporters/ oil surplus countries (Iraq, Saudi Arabia, Libya and Kuwait) since their incomes rose sharply in a short period of time, due to the rise in the price of oil, and are in a sense artificially high, exceeding their stage of development. These countries are sometimes called 'rich–poor countries'. Apart from Kuwait, their BN-performance is well below what might be normal at their apparent income level. Excluding these countries from the sample relating per capita income to life expectancy considerably improves the relationship (see Table 4.2). There may also be a case for excluding the industrialised countries – partly because we are not primarily concerned with these countries in this analysis; and partly because beyond a certain income level, diseases of the rich predominate and hence the relationship between incomes and life expectancy might be expected to change. The

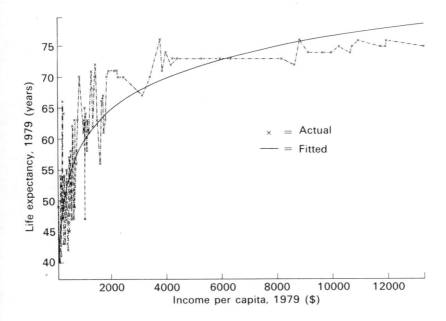

FIGURE 4.2 *Relationship between life expectancy and per capita income, 1979*

analysis relating income per capita to life expectancy tests the relationships including and excluding the industrialised countries.

As far as the *form* of the relationship is concerned, it seems likely that the relationship will exhibit some diminishing marginal returns, in the sense that a given increase in income is likely to result in a smaller increase in life expectancy as incomes (and life expectancy) rise. Thus at very low levels (e.g. life expectancy of around forty), an increase of income of, for example, $500 per capita might lead to a substantial increase in life expectancy (and income), say of ten years, but at much higher levels of life expectancy (and income), say around seventy, such an increase would be negligible in relation to existing income levels and would be unlikely to affect life expectancy. At high income levels, a much higher absolute (and also proportionate) increase in income would be necessary to secure an increase in life expectancy of any particular amount. These 'diminishing marginal returns' may be captured, in a rough and ready way, by a linear relationship with a large constant, a semi-log relationship, a quadratic relationship or an inverse relationship. The linear and inverse relationships gave poorer fits (see Table 4.2). The quadratic relationship was deficient when the industrialised countries were included because at these levels of income the regression showed life expectancy *declining* with income. But for developing countries alone, the quadratic relationship provided a good fit and gave an adjusted r^2 of 0.71. The semi-log relationship was just about as good statistically; in this case the relationship was similiar both including and excluding the industrialised countries. But when the industrialised countries were included they all showed negative deviations, suggesting that the relationship shown is not very good at high income levels.

The finding that about 70 per cent of variation in BN-performance among LDCs can be explained by differences in average per capita incomes is of major significance. It suggests that the growth maximising strategy does appear to produce considerable 'trickle down' in terms of BN-achievement. From this point of view there would not appear to be any necessary conflict between a BN-approach and a growth maximising approach. In terms of particular country performance, countries which have generated high average income per capita through rapid growth rates, like Taiwan and Hong Kong, have raised their average life expectancy to developed country levels (70 or above). But other countries, with above average growth rates, have done much less well on life expectancy. For example, S. Korea with a growth in GNP per capita of 7.1 per cent p.a. (1960–79) had life expectancy of 63 in 1979, well below that of Jamaica (70) and Taiwan (72), countries with similar levels of per capita income. Brazil is another example, with high growth in per capita income (4.8 per cent p.a. 1960–79) and quite a high level of per capita income, and yet a life expectancy of only 63. While the correlation between levels of per capita income and life expectancy shows that life expectancy is likely to increase with incomes, these cases show that the connection is not invariable, but depends on other factors as well as average incomes. This is shown also by the few very low income countries which have succeeded in achieving very high levels of life expectancy. Most notable, is the case of Sri Lanka with a life expectancy of sixty-six and one of the lowest per capita incomes (at $230 in 1979). While income is significant, we need to explain why some countries are able to perform much better and others do worse than might be expected on the basis of per capita income alone. The regression relationships between life expectancy and per capita incomes provide a sort of bench mark, against which actual performance may be judged. Countries whose actual BN-performance (as measured by life expectancy) is markedly better than would be predicted by per capita incomes alone are especially good BN-performers, while countries whose actual achievements are significantly below that which would be expected on the basis of per capita incomes are poor performers.

This approach to measuring 'good' or 'poor' performance on BN is subject to a number of potential defects. First, it is highly dependent on the accuracy of the estimates of both life expectancy and income per head. This is clearly indicated in the case of China, whose performance is very good using this approach, with life expectancy nearly 30 per cent above predicted level. But this assessment hangs entirely on the figure of sixty-four for life expectancy. If this is wrong,[4] then the assessment falls to the ground. As far as incomes are concerned, apart from the many statistical and administrative problems which prevent accurate measurement, there are also special problems raised by the use of official exchange rates to convert the various local currencies into dollars. Official exchange rates give misleading results; exchange rates in LDCs are often overvalued. Moreover, the price of non-tradables tends to be lower, the lower per capita incomes, so that using official exchange rates, which broadly reflect relative prices of tradables, would tend to overstate the incomes of the higher income countries relative to the lower. Purchasing power parity (*PPP*) estimates of real income are designed to correct for this.[5] It might be expected, therefore, that the use of PPP estimates in relating income per capita to BN performance would change the results. However, the case for using PPP estimates, especially in this context, is not proven.

Apart from correcting the obvious biases in the exchange rates due to heavy protection, the PPP estimates also correct for divergencies in the price of non-tradables. These divergencies arise mainly from differences in labour costs, which form a large component of non-tradables. In general the effect is to raise the real income of poor countries, where the opportunity cost of labour is low and hence the labour cost component of non-tradables tends to be lower; and reduce real incomes of rich countries, where the opposite is true. The lower cost of non-tradables in poor countries in one sense does raise their (relative) real income, since it means that for any given money-income more non-tradables can be purchased, but against this some allowance should be made for lower standards of quality. But viewed as an indication of productive potential – as against consumer welfare – the low price reflects genuinely lower productive potential, due to the poorer alternative productive possibilities for labour in poor countries. For the production aspects of a BN-plan (the first two aspects of the framework discussed in Chapter 2) the unadjusted figures are probably more appropriate. As far as the incomes aspect is concerned, to the extent that the adjustments affect the prices of BN-goods and services then they are relevant to measuring the ability of a society to meet its basic needs.

Lack of up-to-date data actually rules out the use of purchasing power parity estimates for most of the investigations. But it is possible to use them for 1970, for which detailed estimates are available for ninety countries. The results can be compared, for the same year, with estimates using ordinary incomes, thus indicating how far the results are changed by using purchasing power parity estimates.

For 1970, for 107 countries (including industrialised countries but excluding capital exporters), the relationship between life expectancy and incomes per head is:

$$LIEX = 0.471 \quad + 9.21 \; log \; y$$
$$(3.088) \quad\quad (0.514)$$

Adjusted $r^2 = 0.754$

Using PPP estimates, for the ninety countries for which evidence is available gives:

Table 4.3 *'Good' and 'poor' performers in 1970*

	'Good'			'Poor'	
Country	% deviation 'ordinary' incomes	% deviation PPP	Country	% deviation 'ordinary' incomes	% deviation PPP
Lagos	19.6	n.a.	Portuguese Timor	−12.2	n.a.
Burma	18.8	21.2	Mauritania	−11.7	−11.6
Sri Lanka	39.8	37.5	Sierra Leone	−12.6	−21.3
Thailand	16.8	15.6	Cameroon	−15.4	−16.2
Liberia	10.7	11.5	Senegal	−16.9	−18.1
Philippines	10.4	(6.5)	Swaziland	−17.9	−16.2
Paraguay	17.5	15.0	Guinea Bissau	−26.4	n.a.
S. Korea	26.3	22.5	Mozambique	−18.8	n.a.
Taiwan	25.2	n.a.	Ghana	−14.6	−16.9
Brazil	10.2	(7.1)	Equatorial Guinea	−20.2	n.a.
Portugal	12.7	11.1	Angola	−36.1	n.a.
Cyprus	15.9	14.3	Congo	−21.8	−23.4
Malta	15.4	12.6	Ivory Coast	−23.8	−24.8
Hong Kong	16.1	15.7	Zambia	−18.4	−21.6
Uruguay	10.6	(6.2)	Nicaragua	−11.2	−13.1
Spain	12.0	10.0	Gabon	−57.1	−31.5
Greece	11.4	10.0	S. Africa	−25.8	−19.3
Rwanda	(5.6)	12.9	Papua New Guinea	(−9.1)	−10.5
Lesotho	(7.5)	12.5			
Sudan	(9.0)	10.3			

$$LIEX = -24.4 + 12.05 \log yp$$
$$(4.43) (0.662)$$

Adjusted $r^2 = 0.788$

Analysis of the countries which perform particularly well/badly in relation to 'expected' performance according to the regression shows very substantial similarity. Table 4.3 shows the countries which performed particularly well (with life expectancy of 10 per cent or more than the predicted level) and particularly poorly (10 per cent or less than predicted levels.) Of the seventeen good performers using 'ordinary' incomes, with PPP estimates twelve of the countries fell into the 'good' category, while for two of the countries PPP estimates were not available. The performance of the remaining three was each fairly good, using PPP estimates (i.e. over 5 per cent but below 10 per cent of predicted levels). Similarly, the three countries which PPP picked out as particularly good, which were not picked out by the 'ordinary' estimates, were all in the 5–10 per cent above predicted category in the 'ordinary' estimates. Among the seventeen particularly poor performers, as indicated by ordinary income estimates, for three no PPP estimates were available, but all the remainder were also picked out by PPP estimates. Only one country showed up as particularly poor according to PPP but not ordinary income estimates, and this narrowly missed classification in the ordinary estimates (being 9.1 per cent below predicted levels). Analysis of the countries in the groups 5–10 per cent above and below predicted levels shows a similar degree of overlap between the two methods.

While the precise relationships differ, both PPP and ordinary income estimates show a similar relationship for 1970, explaining a very similar proportion of the total variance and giving an almost identical list of good and poor performers using the criterion of 10 per cent above or below predicted levels. It therefore seems likely that the use of PPP estimates for later years would be unlikely to make a substantial difference to the results and to the list of good and poor performers.

'GOOD' AND 'POOR' PERFORMERS, 1979

Table 4.4 lists the countries whose performance, as measured by life expectancy at birth, was significantly better/worse than predicted,

Country Experience in Meeting Basic Needs

TABLE 4.4 *'Exceptional' performers in basic needs (life expectancy) 1979*

Country	'Good' Av. % deviation on 3 methods† 7.5% or more above predicted		Country	'Poor' Av. % deviation on 3 methods, 7.5% or more below predicted level
1. Sri Lanka*	37.2		1. Ivory Coast*	− 22.0
2. China*	30.9		2. Angola*	− 20.3
3. Albania*	20.3		3. Yemen Arab Rep*	− 19.8
4. Burma*	18.2		4. Senegal*	− 18.0
5. [Bangladesh*	16.4]		5. Yemen PDR*	− 15.8
6. Jamaica*	14.2		6. Mauritania*	− 14.7
7. Cuba*	13.7		7. Cameroon*	− 14.0
8. Thailand*	12.5		8. Algeria*	− 13.2
9. Philippines*	12.3		9. Niger*	− 12.6
10. El Salvador*	12.1		10. Congo People's Rep*	− 12.4
11. India*	11.1		11. Central Africa Rep*	− 11.4
12. Panama*	10.7		12. Afghanistan*	− 11.1
13. Mongolia*	9.5		13. Guinea*	− 11.0
14. Syrian Arab Rep††	8.1		14. Ethiopia††	− 10.0
15. Malaysia††	8.0		15. Burundi*	− 9.7
16. Kenya†††	6.7		16. Nigeria*	− 9.5
17. [Bhutan††	6.5]		17. Papua N.G.††	− 8.9
18. Hong Kong†††	6.4		18. Zambia††	− 8.8
19. Costa Rica†††	6.2		19. Sudan††	− 8.6
20. Uruguay††	5.4		20. Bolivia††	− 8.3
			21. Togo††	− 7.9
			22. Upper Volta††	− 7.5
			23. S. Africa†††	− 6.6
			24. Chad†††	− 5.4
			25. Venezuela†††	− 5.2
Taiwan ⊕	12.8		Iran ⊕⊕	− 21.2
Vietnam ⊕	35.6		Saudi Arabia ⊕⊕	− 27.0
			Iraq ⊕⊕	− 21.5
			Libya ⊕⊕	− 21.8

†   The three methods involve comparing actual achievements on life expectancy with that predicted by 3 of the equations in Table 4.2 (that is, g, j and k).
*   Achieve 7.5% or more above/below predicted on each of 3 methods.
††   Achieve 7.5% or more above/below on 2 of 3 methods.
††† Achieve 7.5% or more above/below on 1 of 3 methods.
      [ ]: countries with lowest incomes per capita in sample.
⊕   Using estimates for 1979 income per capita.
⊕⊕ Oil exporters, not included in regressions.

using 1979 data. The percentage deviation from predicted levels shown is the average deviation using three methods. This list of countries then provides some indication of the sort of countries that perform particularly well and those that perform particularly badly on BN, in relation to what might normally be expected at their level of per capita income.

The list is not complete, since very small countries (population below ½ million) have not been included. Data was estimated for certain countries, including some which appear in the list in Table 4.4 as exceptional performers – for example, Vietnam, with life expectancy of sixty-three and income per capita (probably) around $170–180. As far as exceptionally good performers are concerned, the list tends to understate the achievement of countries which have done exceptionally well in raising incomes and therefore may appear as 'normal' achievers because of their high incomes. An obvious case is Hong Kong, with life expectancy of seventy-six – as high as any country – but whose high income makes this performance only 'exceptional', as defined here, according to one of the three equations. There are also some problems at the very low end of the scale of incomes: under certain measures both Bhutan and Bangladesh, the two poorest countries, appear as good performers, but this is largely due to the shape of the fitted curve at the low extreme. Given these, and other problems, the precise content of the list of good and poor performers should not be taken too seriously. But the method does enable us to take a look at the *type* of countries that do well and do poorly, while in most cases the exceptionally good/poor performers would appear exceptional on almost any test.

Table 4.4 shows the 'exceptional' performers, using life expectancy as the BN-indicator. Table 4.5 shows which countries appear exceptional if literacy is taken as the indicator. The country coverage is smaller and the estimates for literacy probably less reliable than life expectancy estimates. Nonetheless, a comparison between the results using life expectancy and those using literacy is instructive. As far as the 'good' performers are concerned, of the twenty countries shown in Table 4.4 (excluding Taiwan and Vietnam), eight also appear on the list of good performers on literacy; for seven literacy data is not available. Of the remaining five, two did very well on literacy too (El Salvador's literacy exceeded that predicted – using the semi-log relationship method – by 18.2 per cent and Hong Kong by 13.4 per cent). India did slightly better than predicted (2.4 per cent), while two countries, Malaysia and the Syrian Arab Republic, had literacy

Country Experience in Meeting Basic Needs

TABLE 4.5 *Exceptional performers on basic needs (literacy), 1976*

Country	'Good' % deviation from predicted level,[1] more than 20% above		Country	'Poor' % deviation more than 20% below	
1. Burma*	113.3		1. Senegal*	− 80.4	
2. Sri Lanka*	112.6		2. Yemen Arab Rep.*	− 70.2	
3. Somalia	100.1		3. Niger*	− 69.7	
4. Tanzania	72.7		4. Ivory Coast	− 65.9	
5. Philippines*	69.3		5. Mauritania*	− 65.1	
6. Thailand*	65.7		6. Mali	− 64.8	
7. S.Korea	54.5		7. Togo*	− 63.9	
8. Cuba*	49.2		8. Sudan*	− 56.7	
9. Nicaragua	45.0		9. Zaire	− 55.8	
10. Indonesia	44.2		10. Chad*	− 52.2	
11. Paraguay	41.4		11. Morocco	− 50.5	
12. Lesotho	39.6		12. Algeria*	− 47.5	
13. Romania*	34.1		13. Ethiopia*	− 47.2	
14. Costa Rica*	33.3		14. Liberia*	− 44.0	
15. Uruguay*	29.9		15. Guinea*	− 43.1	
16. Ecuador	29.6		16. Yemen PDR*	− 40.8	
17. Peru	26.7		17. Nepal	− 39.5	
18. Argentina	25.4		18. Afghanistan*	− 39.3	
19. Madagascar	25.1		19. Kuwait	− 37.9	
20. Bolivia	23.7		20. Iran*	− 35.8	
21. Mexico	20.0		21. Pakistan	− 35.7	
			22. Libya*	− 28.3	
			23. Zambia*	− 26.5	
			24. Malawi	− 26.5	
			25. Burundi**	− 20.5	

[1] Semi-log relationship, covering all countries (81) for which data is available.

* Also appear as 'good', 'poor' performers on life expectancy on Table 4.4.

performance below that predicted, by 6.8 per cent and 7.5 per cent respectively. Ten countries did well on literacy but not on life expectancy. Of these ten, five had life expectancy a bit above that predicted, for one there was no data, and for five countries performance on life expectancy was *below* that predicted.[6] These five countries were Argentina (−1.3 per cent), Mexico (−0.8 per cent), S.

Korea (−3.1 per cent), Madagascar (−4.0 per cent) and Bolivia (−5.9 per cent).

As far as the 'poor' performers are concerned of the twenty-five performers on life expectancy (excluding the oil countries), fourteen also did poorly on literacy, for eight literacy data was not available. Of the remaining two, Bolivia did well on literacy (+23.7 per cent), while Venezuela did roughly as predicted. Five (non-oil) countries appear as poor performers on the literacy test, but not the life expectancy. Of these, two did well below predicted on life expectancy (Nepal, −4.7 per cent, Mali, −7.2 per cent), two did about as predicted (Malawi and Morocco), while one, Pakistan, did substantially above predicted on life expectancy (+7.3 per cent).

For both 'good' and 'poor' performers, then for those countries where data is available, the great majority perform the same way on both literacy *and* life expectancy. Only two countries did well on life expectancy and *not* at all well on literacy, while only one country did well on literacy and poorly on life expectancy. This close correspondence provides further justification for using life expectancy of good and poor performers as the sole BN-indicator. For the rest of the analysis, therefore, we use the list of countries shown in Table 4.4.

In considering country experience in relation to BN, the list of exceptional performance is useful in two respects: first, as giving some indication, at a broad level, of the types of political and economic strategies that tend to be successful and those that tend to be unsuccessful; secondly, in permitting rather detailed analysis of particular variables (e.g. public expenditure) that tend to be associated with good and poor performance. The rest of this chapter considers the broad strategies. The next chapter analyses performance on particular economic and social variables.

POLITICAL ECONOMY

'Good' performers

A glance at the countries in Table 4.4 listed as 'good' performers shows that they are a very disparate lot, from any point of view. All three continents are represented; large countries (India and China) and small; countries of every political persuasion are on the list; and countries which have pursued very different economic strategies, for example, the export orientation of Taiwan and Hong Kong, the import substitution of India and the Philippines among others. The breadth of experience, in nearly every dimension, shows that *any* country should be able to improve its BN-performance, by at least around 10 per cent in relation to typical or average experience of 1979.

Among the disparate experience indicated in Table 4.4, it is possible to pick out three major types:

1. Socialist countries – this category includes China, Cuba, Albania and Mongolia. These countries have succeeded, in relation to BN, by planning production to meet BN, by egalitarian income distribution and by rationing/allocating BN-goods to reach all the people, irrespective of income. Education tends to receive high priority in such countries partly for political reasons.

2. Market-oriented (mainly capitalist) countries, with rapid and labour-absorbing economic growth. This category includes Hong Kong and Taiwan. These countries have succeeded in BN primarily through raising incomes of the poor, as a result of the labour-absorbing growth. Whereas, the prime emphasis among the socialist countries tends to be on planning production (and consumption), among these countries, production has been broadly left to the market to adapt to the demands generated by the economic growth process. In terms of the earlier classification of planning frameworks, among these countries, then, incomes have been the 'moving' sector, with production adapting.

3. The third category are the mixed economies, which have succeeded in BN by welfare state-type government interventions. Sri Lanka provides the prime example where government provision of health and education services, plus extensive rice subsidies have ensured a very high achievement on BN, despite very low levels of income. In this case, secondary transfers and government expenditure provided the main impetus, not the income levels generated by the economic process (the primary income distribution), nor production planning. While Sri Lanka is the most notable example, other countries – such as Jamaica and Costa Rica – fit broadly into this category.

In terms of the three frameworks presented in Chapter 2, the lead framework differs among the different categories of success. Nonetheless, for success *ex post facto, all* of the three frameworks must be realised. Thus in the socialist case, where planning production was arguably the lead aspect with considerable emphasis on public sector organisation, an egalitarian distribution of income (plus some rationing) was necessary to ensure a satisfactory allocation of BN goods and services. In the capitalist 'success' economies, public sector provision of education and health services played an essential role, alongside the growth of private incomes, while the success of the food-producing sector ensured that rises in food prices did not eliminate the rise in real incomes of the poor. In the case of the welfare state successes, government interventions operated both with respect to production (especially the provision of public services), and incomes (through subsidies). It was also essential that changes in production and incomes following economic developments were not such as to negate government interventions towards BN. This model – the mixed economy, welfare state category – apparently offers the most feasible model for economies which do not have a socialist system and where it seems unlikely that the dramatic successes of Taiwan and Hong Kong, in labour-absorbing economic growth, can be duplicated. Yet, the most severe question marks fall over this category for two reasons: first, the successful countries in this group have managed to use government intervention in a progressive way. But there are many apparently similar mixed economies, where government interventions (e.g. public expenditure and food subsidies) have been widespread, but have tended to help the middle classes, rather than the poor. The government machine has been 'hijacked' by the élite. Hence the political and economic conditions for successful use of government intervention in the context of a mixed economy needs further exploration. Secondly, there is the question of the sustainability of this model. Sri Lanka changed its policies towards the end of the 1970s, dismantling many of its services, as a result of rather poor economic performance and consequent internal and external pressures. Similarly, and dramatically, Jamaica did a complete U-turn, following her foreign exchange problems, confrontation with the International Monetary Fund and internal political changes. More recently, Costa Rica's programmes have come under fire from the IMF.

The economic performance of countries in this success category has not been particularly unsuccessful, against the background of general performance of all LDCs, but like all countries which are not outstandingly successful, they have met difficulties – especially in recent years. Their programmes are particularly vulnerable to such difficulties, presenting an obvious target (both internally and externally), in times of difficulty. Hence the problem of sustainability is as much a political as an economic problem. The other two categories do not meet the same problems: among socialist countries both beliefs and systems are tougher when they come up against adverse developments, than those of the mixed economy welfare states. But even here they are (to some extent) vulnerable, as indicated by the recent changes in China. The success of the capitalist countries is firmly based in the economic process, and does not depend much on government interventions. Hence the achievements are only threatened if the economic system falters. '

The discussion above has emphasised the need for production and incomes to be consistent with good achievement in BN, irrespective of the actual lead aspect. The third aspect of the framework – organisation – must also be adequate: this involves performance with respect to each of the three sectors – public, private and household. In general, among the 'success' stories a high level of household performance can be observed. This is a vital feature, for example, of the Sri Lanka case, where high levels of household hygiene have been noted as an important contribution to her high standards of health. Organisation tends to be a necessary condition for success, rather than a 'lead' aspect in any obvious sense (inadequate organisation is, as we shall see below, a prevalent feature of 'poor' performance). The adequacy of organisation in the success stories is probably related to high levels of education (as indicated by the earlier discussion of literacy) and particularly by high levels of female education.

The three-fold categorisation of success becomes more meaningful when the cases of particular countries are considered in more depth. Below three cases are briefly described – Cuba, Taiwan and Sri Lanka – as examples of the three categories identified.

Examples of success in BN

Cuba[7]

Cuba is a small country (population nearly 10m) with a socialist system of government, which was initiated in the years following the revolution in 1958.

In 1979, Cuba's life expectancy at birth was seventy-two (just one year below that of the UK) and her adult literacy rate was estimated at 96 per cent, while her per capita income, at $1 410, was below such countries as S. Korea, and Brazil whose life expectancy was much lower at sixty-three years.

Cuba has devoted a high proportion of her national income to health and to education services, spending about 12 per cent of GNP or about twice the proportion typical in developing countries with similar income levels.

In 1980 there were 1.59 doctors per 1 000 people and 2.74 nurses, compared with 0.93 and 0.74 in 1958. (For middle income LDCs as a whole there were 0.23 doctors and 0.53 nurses per 1 000 people in 1977). Educational enrolment ratios were also very high in Cuba, with universal primary education. Average calory supply in 1977 was 118 per cent of requirements compared with 108 per cent on average for middle-income countries. Equitable food allocation was ensured by a fairly strict system of rationing. Food rationing was accompanied by price controls and food subsidies.[8]

The socialist revolution in Cuba was accompanied by a radical redistribution of income. The data is not good. However, one estimate suggests that the share of income of the lowest 40 per cent of income earners increased from 6.5 per cent before the revolution to 17 per cent in 1972. The Gini co-efficient of family income distribution was estimated to be around 0.47 in 1959, around 0.35 in 1962 with some further reductions in the 1970s.[9]

Cuba's success in BN can then be attributed to action with respect to each of the three aspects of the planning framework, but especially production and incomes. Allocation of resources was such as to secure adequate provision of health, education and food. Rationing, food subsidies and the radical redistribution of income ensured that each family had sufficient command over resources to meet their needs. Were these achievements at the expense of economic growth as is sometimes claimed? Because of statistical problems, it is difficult to be confident about what has happened to Cuba's growth rate since the revolution. There was a period of stagnation (possibly negative growth) from 1958 to 1965, followed by sustained growth in per capita income, with a particularly rapid spurt between 1971–5.[10] World Bank statistics show a growth of 4.4 per cent p.a. in GNP per capita between 1960–79. While this is well below the very high growers among middle-income countries, it is above the average for middle-income countries as a whole. Statistical deficiencies make it difficult to establish precise figures, but the evidence does not suggest that in Cuba growth was sacrificed to meet basic needs.

While Cuba provides one example of success in BN, its experience is special and may not be widely duplicable. It had a radical socialist political system, strong economic support from the USSR and started the period with considerable social infrastructure.

Taiwan[11]

Taiwan, like Cuba is a smallish (population 17 million) island economy, with a political regime that was radically changed as a result of decolonisation and political revolution. But in the case of Taiwan the main revolution was elsewhere (in mainland China); the Taiwanese system was the result of the retreat to Taiwan of the mainland anti-communists led by Chiang-Kai-Shak and their takeover of the Taiwan government from the Japanese colonial administrators. Since then the Taiwan government has supported a mixed system, with strong capitalist leanings and though there have been active government economic policies, these policies have operated largely through the market system.

Taiwan is a success judged by our two BN-indicators. With per capita income of $1400[12] (1978), life expectancy is the same as Cuba (seventy-two years) and literacy rate in 1975 was estimated to be 82 per cent. These represent substantial improvements; in 1952 life expectancy was fifty-nine years, while in 1946 55 per cent of people over six were illiterate.

The achievements were the result of a high and egalitarian rate of economic growth, which led to increases in incomes among the poor sufficient to permit them to buy the marketed BN-goods. At the same time, government provision of BN-goods and services – education, health services and sanitation – also expanded rapidly. Between 1960 and 1978 growth in per capita income was 6.6 per cent p.a. However, it was the egalitarian nature of this growth which was significant from a BN point of view. The Gini co-efficient for family income distribution declined from 0.56 in 1953 to 0.44 (1959), 0.32 (1964), 0.29 in 1972.[13] It remained at around 0.29 during the 1970s. By 1972 Taiwan's income distribution was more egalitarian than that estimated in Cuba, and the change had also been more substantial. There are a great many factors which go to determine family income distribution, but two stand out in the case of Taiwan.[14] First, a very radical land reform in the early period. Owner-cultivation of land rose from 56 per cent (1948) to 86 per cent (1960) and the Gini of land concentration fell from 0.62 (1952) to 0.46 (1960). Secondly, economic growth in Taiwan has throughout the period, but especially during the phase of rapid growth in manufactured exports in the 1960s and 1970s, been very labour-using. Employment outside agriculture grew rapidly and labour surplus was eliminated by the end of the 1960s. Rates of absorption of non-agricultural labour were around 3 per cent p.a. in the 1950s and 6 per cent p.a. in 1960s. The rapid growth in employment was egalitarian because it enabled most families to participate in the growth in incomes, through wage-employment.

In Taiwan then a major factor responsible for success in BN, was the *incomes* aspect, with egalitarian economic growth leading to the spread in incomes sufficient for BN. Production of BN-goods kept pace with expansion in demand. Average per capita calorie consumption rose from 2078 (1952) to 2845 (1978) while protein consumption rose by over 60 per cent in the same period. Living space per head increased nearly four-fold. While rising incomes permitted expanded consumption of these marketed goods, public provision of vital BN-goods and services also rose rapidly. The educational system expanded dramatically: the enrolment ratio in primary schools rose from 79 per cent (1952) to 100 per cent (1978); the secondary ratio from 48 per cent to 90 per cent. The proportion of households served by piped water rose from 14 per cent in 1949 to 64 per cent (1979).[15] The number of doctors per person was substantially above the average for middle-income countries in 1977.

Like Cuba, Taiwan's experience may be unique and not readily replicable elsewhere. The particular political situation that accompanied liberation from Japan permitted a very radical land reform, [16] which was carried out by newcomers from the mainland, and *not* by local Taiwanese. The economic success was supported in the initial period by substantial financial support from the US. It was also due to cultural factors and historic heritage. But policies played a part[17] – in particular liberal price/exchange rate policies which permitted Taiwanese labour-intensive goods to compete on world markets.

It is noteworthy that these two countries, Cuba and Taiwan, at two extremes of the political spectrum, and opposites in terms of historic heritage, one subject to the influences of Spain and then the US, the other to Japan and China, should be so similar in BN-achievements. In both countries it was the combination of growth and equality (a combination achieved in different ways in the two countries) which permitted the sustained achievement of BN.

Sri Lanka[18]

Sri Lanka is also a small (population 14.5 million) island economy, which was a British colony until 1948. Since independence Sri Lanka has been a rather typical mixed economy. Until recently, there was a fairly strong socialist element to political and economic policy. There was a change in government in 1977 and since then there has been a markedly greater capitalist/market orientation.

Sri Lanka is a very poor country, with a per capita income in 1979 of $230. Its life expectancy was sixty-six and its literacy rate 85 per cent. These BN-indicators are remarkably high for such a poor country: for example, Benin, with similar level of per capita income, has a life expectancy of forty-seven. The achievements are all the more remarkable because Sri Lanka is not, in contrast to Taiwan and Cuba, particularly unusual politically or economically. It has followed rather ordinary, undistinguished economic policies, trying to diversify away from dependence on tea, and promoting industrialisation through import substitution policies.

Sri Lanka's achievements seem to be mainly due to government policies which gave priority to BN-expenditures. Some of these policies have a long history: compulsory primary education was introduced, on paper at least, in 1901. Food rationing was introduced in 1942. Government policies in the 1960s and 1970s aimed at universal primary education and basic health care for the whole population. In addition, there were rice rations and substantial rice subsidies. In 1973, food subsidies amounted to 14 per cent of the incomes of low-income earners (incomes below 400 rupees a month.) In 1969–70 the ration provided about 20 per cent of calorific intake for such low-income families. Only 5 per cent of the population had calorific intakes below 1900 calories a day. In contrast in Bangladesh, 25 per cent of the population consumed less than 1700 calories a day. The significance of the rice ration for nutrition and mortality was indicated by the effects of cuts in 1974 when the death rate increased from 7.7 to 8.9 per 1 000.[19]

Social programmes and food subsidies amounted to about 40 per cent of current government expenditure. Primary income distribution in Sri Lanka (before allowing for taxes and subsidies) was not especially equal in 1963, with a Gini of 0.49, but over the next ten years although economic growth was slow (2.0 per cent p.a.) it was egalitarian so that the incomes of the bottom 60 per cent rose by 4.6 per cent p.a. and the Gini co-efficient fell to 0.40.[20] Because of the importance of food subsidies, which although they extended to rich as well as poor, had the greatest proportionate significance for the poor, the post-tax and post-subsidy distribution must have been significantly more equal than the primary distribution. The egalitarian nature of Sri Lanka's economic growth between 1963 and 1973 was such that while Sri Lanka ranks bottom in GDP growth among a group of thirteen countries, it comes fifth in growth of incomes of the bottom 60 per cent with a growth of twice as much or more than Peru, Brazil, the Philippines and India, each of whose overall growth rate was above that of Sri Lanka.[21] As far as meeting BN is concerned, it is of course growth in incomes among the bottom 60 per cent rather than aggregate growth which is most relevant.

In terms of the three aspects of macroeconomic planning, Sri Lanka's success was due to achievements with respect to all three aspects of the framework described above. On production, government expenditure on health and education ensured adequate facilities, while for some years rice production kept pace with the high demands generated by the rice rations/subsidies. Primary income growth among the poor was relatively rapid, which, together with the food subsidies, ensured that the poor generally had sufficient incomes to meet their minimum needs. The long history of near universal primary education also meant that Sri Lanka was efficient on organisation aspects. For example, standards of health and hygiene within the family were high, as evidenced by the tendency for people to boil water before consumption and by the high levels of health despite the rather poor provision of safe water (only 20 per cent of the population was estimated to have access to safe water in 1975).

The Sri Lankan story is particularly interesting because it illustrates how a low-income country with a mixed economy can succeed in a BN-approach. But in recent years, with difficult economic circumstances and a change in government, there has been a quite marked turning away from the BN-programmes. Food subsidies have been drastically cut. While in 1977, food subsidies amounted to nearly 22 per cent of government recurrent expenditure, in 1980 the proportion was 2.3 per cent and the provisional estimates for 1981 showed them to be almost negligible.[22] In addition, expenditure on social programmes (health, education, housing) has been curtailed. Current expenditure on these programmes fell from 21 per cent of total government current expenditure in 1977 to 16 per cent in 1980. Total expenditure on BN-programmes (current and capital on social services plus food subsidies) fell from 8.6 per cent of GDP in 1977 to 4.2 per cent in 1980.[23]

The reduction in subsidies resulted in part from pressure from the international community, with reports from the World Bank, the ILO and the IMF each criticising the subsidies which went to everyone, rich and poor. From 1970 domestic rice production lagged behind consumption and the import bill for rice became very large. In the face of the acute balance of payments difficulties following the oil price rises, the international community acquired more power than before, while the new rather conservative government was antipathetic to the heavy emphasis on BN expenditure: 'a 180° turn was executed ... changing attitudes away from the welfare orientation of the past which has stressed equality and the State's responsibility for providing basic needs, towards a society willing to tolerate, even encourage accumulation of wealth, greater income disparity and a preference for goods over state services'.[24]

There are already some slight indications that the shift away from a BN-emphasis is affecting BN-achievements. The estimated life expectancy fell between 1977 and 1980[25] while in other low-income countries there were large improvements during these years; rates of child mortality rose slightly. The number of doctors per person has fallen, as has the number of central dispensaries. Meanwhile, the greater emphasis on private consumption led to a rise in the imports of motor cycles from 700 in 1979 to 18 000 in 1979 and of cars from 2 500 in 1977 to 10 000 in 1979.

The changes in economic policies which occurred in 1977 – representing greater emphasis on the market, and less on controls – appear to have been successful in boosting Sri Lanka's growth rate, improving the balance of payments, and reducing unemployment. If this progress continues, the economy will be in a much better position to sustain BN-programmes. The economic policy changes could, however, have been introduced without major changes in social programmes, while despite the stronger economy the present government seems unlikely to use the strengthening of the economy as a basis for giving priority to BN.

The Sri Lanka case illustrates the vulnerability of a BN-approach which is heavily reliant on government intervention, as compared with BN-achievements which are a more intrinsic aspect of the economic system, as in Cuba and Taiwan. The problem is not that governments cannot finance such programmes. In fact Sri Lanka's public expenditure was quite modest – 13 per cent of GDP went on public consumption in 1960 and by 1977 this had dropped to 10 per cent, the former ratio being a bit higher and the latter a bit lower than among low-income countries on average. Nor is it the case that this approach to BN need be at the expense of economic growth. With a fairly low proportion of GDP going to public consumption, investment need not be adversely affected. Moreover, the investment in human capital that the BN programmes represent may increase the growth rate. Sri Lanka's investment ratio during this period was generally above rather than below that of other low-income countries. Consumer subsidies need not discourage production: they can be designed to encourage, discourage or be neutral *vis-à-vis* production. Richards and Gooneratine find no evidence that the net effect of government subsidies to consumption and production was to discourage production. Growth in agricultural production in Sri Lanka was 3.0 per cent p.a. from 1960–70 (compared with 2.5 per cent p.a. for low-income countries as a whole), while Sri Lankan growth in GNP per head, at 2.0 per cent p.a. during 1960–78, was above the average for low-income countries.

The problem of sustainability that arises stems from political factors rather than economic. When governments are under pressure because of adverse economic circumstances, social programmes represent an easy target. It is *political* vulnerability, rather than intrinsic defects in the programmes, that cause long-run problems for this approach to BN. However, as the Sri Lankan approach probably represents the most feasible of the three paths for many LDCs, since they cannot expect to become as radically socialist as Cuba or as economically successful as Taiwan, the programmes should not simply be dismissed as non-sustainable, but rather political threats stemming both from the international and the national community need to be tackled directly.

Because of these political problems, any approach which can base BN achievements firmly on the economic system, rather than on the political system, may prove to be more sustainable: that is to say economic policies which produce sustained growth in primary incomes among the poor are likely to provide a firmer political base for sustained BN-achievements.

'Poor' performers

The list of 'poor' performers in Table 4.4 also contains a wide variety of countries in terms of economic development and political system. But one feature may immediately be noted: a very large number of the countries are in sub-Saharan Africa (twenty of the twenty-five excluding the oil-surplus countries). This may be due to some special geographic/climatic characteristics of sub-Saharan Africa, although one should note that Kenya appears on the 'success' list. It may also be due to common colonial experience in Africa. If the regression is carried out excluding sub-Saharan Africa, Bhutan and Bangladesh are added to the list of 'poor' performers, although as these two countries come at one extreme, being the poorest countries, the method is not really appropriate for them.

The poor performers include countries which have recently become socialist (Angola and Ethiopia), semi-socialist countries (Algeria) and many examples of mixed economies, primarily of a capitalist nature (Ivory Coast, Nigeria, Bolivia, S. Africa). It includes countries that have had a fairly rapid rate of economic growth (e.g. Ivory Coast, Nigeria) and countries whose per capita income has grown hardly at all (e.g. Zambia, Central African Republic).

Low-income countries typically have rather weak BN-fulfilment. Our method picks out, as particularly poor performers, countries whose BN is weak in relation to their income level. A general reason why this occurs is because income is concentrated, so that poverty is high in relation to average income levels. Different types of economic development tend to have this consequence. First, the capital–surplus oil countries, such as Iran, Iraq, Libya and Saudi Arabia, where incomes of those in the bottom half of the income distribution and social services lag behind the high average incomes which were created by the large oil price rises of the 1970s. Another group are mineral rich countries. These include copper producers, like Bolivia, Zambia, Congo People's Republic, and oil producers, like Venezuela, Nigeria and Algeria. Among these countries, the incomes conferred by minerals tend to be rather concentrated, while public expenditure is also primarily directed at upper income groups. Nigeria, described in detail in Chapters 6 to 8, provides an example. Growth based on industrialisation may also produce an inegalitarian income distribution and fail to meet the BN of the poor. Even agricultural growth may not extend its benefits to the most deprived, especially if public expenditure on BN is inadequate. The Ivory Coast provides an example of economic growth – based on both agriculture and industry – which has not made a significant contribution to improving BN.

In addition to failure of the economic system to allocate sufficient resources and incomes to BN, a general feature of the poor performers on BN is organisational deficiencies. The weakness extends to all three sectors: the household sector is weak, mainly because of lack of education, so that full use is not made of those BN-goods that are available; the organisation of the public sector is inadequate to meet basic needs, especially in the rural sector; and a weak private sector means heavy dependence on imported managers and technology, large-scale productive units and little spread of employment and income-earning opportunities. The story of organisational weakness extends in one way or another to nearly all the sub-Saharan countries in the sample.

Below, sketches of developments in Zambia, the Ivory Coast and Ethiopia provide examples of types of countries which have had especially weak BN-performance.

Zambia[26]

Zambia (population 5.6m), heavily dependent on copper for exports (in 1978, 94 per cent of exports were accounted for by minerals and metals), appears as a poor performer on BN in both 1970 and 1979. In 1979, her life expectancy was about 9 per cent below that which might have been expected at that level of income. At forty-nine years it was below the East African countries (with lower levels of income) and only just above that of much poorer countries such as Malawi, Bangladesh and Sierra Leone. The number of people per doctor in Zambia was over twice that of middle-income countries as a whole (among which Zambia with per capita income of $500 in 1979 is classified) and also above that of the average for low-income countries. Zambia also shows poorly on other indicators – calory supply being on average 87 per cent of requirements in 1977, access to clean water extending to 42 per cent of the population, and adult literacy estimated at 39 per cent in 1976. Enrolment in primary education has increased rapidly from a very low base, especially among females, where primary enrolment was only 34 per cent in 1960 and had risen to 89 per cent by 1978. Secondary enrolment remains very low.

Zambia's weak performance on BN has occurred despite explicit government commitment to meeting basic needs: in a speech in 1968,[27] President Kaunda gave a moving description of his aims for 1980 – aims which encompass all the major facets of a BN-approach to development: by 1980 the rural inhabitant should have opportunities to earn adequate incomes, equal access to health and education services, clean water and 'suitable balanced diets to meet the challenge of rural development'.

Zambia's poor BN-performance seems to be largely due to two aspects of her development: first, a lop-sided development, which has tended to benefit the few rather than the deprived masses; secondly, organisational weaknesses, especially within the public sector. Both aspects are clearly brought out in the recent ILO report on BN in Zambia.

Economic development in Zambia has tended to be concentrated on the production of copper and on import-substituting industrialisation financed through the proceeds of copper: 'the urban sector and large-scale modern industry have increasingly pre-empted the lion's share of resources pledged in plans of rural revival, employment creation and basic needs for all.'[28] From 1969 to 1979 there was a fall in output per head in agriculture. Rural-urban terms of trade have deteriorated substantially – by 65 per cent since 1965 and by 29 per cent since 1973. It was estimated that in 1980, 80 per cent of rural households had incomes below a BN-defined minimum (compared with 25 per cent of urban households).[29] There were high degrees of malnutrition in the rural areas in 1970–2, with only 24 per cent of children under five suffering from *no* malnutrition; 'the balance of expert opinion in the country is that the position since 1972 had deteriorated not improved.'[30] In recent years, all sectors of the Zambian economy were badly hit by international events, especially sharply deteriorating terms of trade. Nonetheless, the problems of poverty and poor BN-performance, especially in the rural areas, predate and are of deeper origin than the recent international crisis.

While the process of economic development has hardly extended to many in the rural areas, leading to inadequate income-earning opportunities for BN, the situation has been compounded by severe organisational deficiencies in the BN-sectors. These, according to the ILO Report, are to be seen in all sectors and at all levels: rural clinics operate without minimal supplies of basic medicines and equipment; schools lack books; government field staff have been depleted through transport problems. Some of these deficiencies are due to financial problems associated with the economic crisis, but they also stem from administrative weaknesses, compounded by political and personal factors which contribute to an urban bias. According to the ILO Report, it is:

> Our strong conviction that the process of implementation goes

wrong not by a single deliberate decision to subvert the Country's – and the Plan's – basic needs objectives, but by a succession of smaller decisions in which the original objectives are lost. It is in the process of translating Plan into budget and budget into the Ministry programme, and Ministry programme into day-to-day actions that the biases *against* rural development priorities and basic needs concerns assert themselves.[31]

The Ivory Coast

In 1957, the President to be, Felix Houphouet-Boigny challenged Ghana's President Nkrumah: 'We will meet again in ten years. Then we will see which of our systems has done more to raise the living standards of the people.' For Ghana, a dismal story of economic failure followed, with a negative growth in per capita income from 1960–79. The Ivory Coast became one of Africa's rare success stories, judged by conventional criteria; growth in per capita income was 2.4 per cent p.a. over the same period. As one commentator noted in 1980: 'There can be no doubt today about who won that bet.'[32] Yet, taking BN-achievement as the indicator, there seem to be no winners. In 1979, the Ivory Coast's life expectancy was forty-seven years, below that of the acknowleged failure, Ghana (at forty-nine years) and substantially below the East Africa countries with much lower incomes. Other social indicators show similar deficiencies – the adult literacy rate in 1976 was estimated to be just 20 per cent. In the mid-sixties[33] it was estimated that 57 per cent of the population had calory deficits compared with health requirements. Since 1969–71 food production, although it has grown fast, has not kept pace with population, so that per capita food production (1971 – 1977–79) is estimated to have declined by 0.9 per cent p.a.[34] It therefore seems unlikely that nutritional standards have improved since the 1960s. Thus while the Ivory Coast has had an impressive performance in terms of economic growth, this has not been reflected in BN-performance.

The Ivory Coast has firmly followed a capitalist development path with a continued dominating French influence; its industrialisation strategy seems to have been very similar to many other countries at an early stage of development – a strategy of import substitution, with high levels of protection making heavy use of foreign technology and European managers, with the consequence that the pattern of industry has tended to be rather large scale and capital-intensive. In the African context, the Ivory Coast has been unusual in also successfully promoting agriculture. Among middle-income oil importing African countries, it ranks third in growth of agricultural output and first in food output.[35] Moreover, despite some big projects, the major focus has been on small-holder agriculture. In contrast to many other countries (e.g. Zambia) the terms of trade during the past decade did not turn against agriculture.

The Ivory Coast's failures with respect to BN are a reflection of a number of deficiencies: on the incomes side, the Ivory Coast exhibits severe inequalities. The bottom 40 per cent of the population, in 1975, were estimated to account for 10.4 per cent of income, below the average for that income level, and the Gini co-efficient was over 0.5.[36] For 1975, it was estimated that 25 per cent of the population were below the poverty line.[37] With some decline in per capita production in the agricultural sector, where most of the poor are, it seems likely that this proportion has increased. Secondly, public provision of BN-goods and services has been very low. In 1977, there were over 15 000 people per doctor, nearly three and a half times as many as for middle-income countries as a group, and two and a half times as many as the average for low-income countries. Clean water extended to only 19 per cent of the population. Educational enrolment rates were substantially below those for middle-income countries, and also below the average for low-income countries. Female enrolment ratios were particularly low – only 54 per cent of girls were in primary school in 1978. This ratio had been much lower – at 24 per cent in 1960. Thus there must be a very low level of education among the adult female population, which is likely to be felt in terms of BN-inefficiencies within the household.

The Ivory Coast is an example of a country which has succeeded in achieving sustained economic growth, but failed to get this growth transformed into basic needs achievement. A major responsibility for this failure appears to stem from deficiencies in public supplies of BN-goods and services.

Ethiopia[38]

Ethiopia's present performance is rooted in the political and economic system which preceded the 1974 revolution. A feudal state, which made little attempt to promote economic growth or fulfil social needs, Ethiopia then had the shortest life expectancy in the world (37.5 years for men), a very high rate of infant mortality, the lowest ratio of doctors to population, and the lowest per capita calory consumption of any country in the world. Illiteracy was over 90 per cent in the rural areas and over 50 per cent in the cities.

At this time, the failure to meet BN was due to major deficiencies on each aspect of the framework: extremely low and unequally distributed income; deficiencies on production with low levels of food production per head and low and maldistributed expenditure on health and education; and very poor organisation resulting from the lack of education.

The 1974 revolution dramatically changed the political and economic structure; the feudal system was destroyed; redistribution of land brought about a substantial increase in the incomes of the peasantry (by perhaps as much as 50 per cent). A mass literacy campaign was initiated in 1979. By October 1981, about 11.5 million people had participated in literacy classes and 5.4 million had completed the course. The estimated national literacy rate in 1981 was 45 per cent, with very little illiteracy in the urban areas.

There has been a marked improvement in measures of BN-achievement since the revolution – life expectancy was estimated to be forty-four in 1980 – but the BN-indicators remain extremely poor, even in relation to the low levels of income. In large part, this poor performance is due to the historic heritage, which cannot be eliminated overnight. But in addition, there was little or no improvement in per capita incomes between 1973–4 and 1979–80, while agricultural production per head declined during this period. Health coverage increased – from an estimated 15 per cent (1974) to 40 per cent (1980) – but there was not a corresponding improvement in health, probably due to poor organisation and supplies in the health service, and low levels of education among the population.

Before 1974, Ethiopia's poor performance on BN was due to a combination of poor economic performance and inegalitarian policies, with a minimal commitment to meeting BN. Since 1974, the last two factors have changed radically – egalitarian policies have been initiated and there is a strong commitment to meeting BN. Continued poor performance is now due to the lagged effects of past deficiencies, which show up especially in all aspects of organisation, and to the continued poor economic performance, particularly with respect to food production.

5 Economic and Social Variables and Basic Needs Performance

The last chapter related performance on BN to the broad strategies countries have followed. Yet actual achievements in BN depend on specific performance with respect to specific variables – for example, how much food is actually consumed and by whom. Performance with respect to such specific variables depends largely on the general economic, social and political strategy adopted. But for planning for BN, it is important to identify the requisite achievements with respect to the specific variables, for while planning operates within a broad political economy context, it influences specific variables. This chapter, therefore, aims to explore the relationships between performance on specific variables and BN-achievements. The first part of the chapter investigates how successful and unsuccessful countries' performance on a number of economic and social variables has differed from the achievements of 'average' BN-performers. The second part summarises findings of other studies of this question. A comparison between these findings and our own permits some conclusions on the 'robustness' of the various findings.

There are some difficulties involved in identifying the relevant relationships – these are partly statistical but partly reflect the nature of the situation, i.e. that the relationships are inherently complex.

The question being investigated is how inputs relate to outputs, with respect to BN. This encompasses much of the three planning frameworks, identified in Chapter 2, and is particularly concerned with (though goes further than) the meta-production function, relating the consumption of BN-goods and services to output in terms of full-life indicators. We have already (Chapters 2 and 3) discussed some of the difficulties involved in identifying these relationships. These include:

First, the difficulty of identifying the full-life indicator to be used as a criterion of success. For reasons given already, we use life expectancy at birth as an indicator of BN-achievement. This approach is shared by some[1], but others[2] adopt multidimensional indicators, encompassing some non-material aspects, thus greatly complicating (but also enriching) the results. The use of a single indicator has the considerable advantage of simplicity. But it means that non-material aspects have to be considered separately, while at higher income levels the life-expectancy indicator may be too simple sufficiently to measure material aspects. However, where more complex and multidimensional indicators are used, the meaning of any results depend on the nature of the output indicator, so that for interpretation one has to get back to relationships with simple indicators.

Secondly, as noted earlier, there are complementarity and substitution relations between many of the variables, such that there is unlikely to be any simple relationship between variable X and BN-achievements. The relationships will depend then on the presence (or absence) of other variables, as well as the variable being investigated. This is true of most variables being considered. An instance is food supply. An increase in food supply *per se* could be totally ineffective if the poor had no money with which to buy the extra food, or if there were no way of transporting the food to where it was needed. In some situations, improved methods of food conservation would be far more effective than increased supply, but in other situations the opposite might apply. There may be no general relationships between particular variables across countries because of these complementarities/substitutions; and also because the same set of variables may have different effects according to social/political/economic milieu.

Thirdly, discontinuities are probable: for example, a certain amount of food is required for health, but beyond that more may actually reduce health. In other cases, there may be sharply diminishing returns to a particular variable, or a need for a change in the type of approach adopted. For example, the balance between preventive and curative medicine and the effects of each seem to change sharply as development proceeds.

Fourthly, the variables for which statistics are available are aggregates. These aggregates can conceal important aspects; one aspect that gets concealed with aggregation is the distribution of the goods and services. Clearly, for example, the impact of food on life expectancy will be heavily influenced by its distribution. Another element that is concealed is the precise nature of the good or service; for example 'health' expenditure includes doctors and nurses, hospitals and medicines, curative and preventive medicine. The same aggregate figure could involve different proportions of these elements, as well as a different distribution as between urban and rural areas, rich and poor. As research progresses, there is a tendency to break the aggregates down into more relevant items, (just as the BN-approach itself may be viewed as a breakdown of the aggregate 'income' into finer and more relevant categories), but we are still at a very early stage in this respect. And the non-availability of statistics limits greater breakdown.

Fifthly, many of the variables move together – in particular most of the social variables increase as incomes increase. Hence simple correlation analysis is unlikely to capture the true relationships. Multicollinearity among the variables reduces the value of multiple correlation analysis. Some sort of analysis of deviations (i.e. relating deviations from performance on the variables to deviations from predicted BN-performance) is therefore most likely to capture the presence of significant relationships. But such an analysis is heavily dependent on the 'normal' relationship adopted, since deviations are measured as the difference between actual performance and 'normal'.

These problems apply to all the attempts to relate variables to BN-performance across country – and may explain why many rather obvious variables do not appear to be significantly related to BN-achievements. Because of the difficulties we have adopted a very simple method below. The method is subject to the inherent problems/defects discussed as are the other more complex statistical investigations which have been carried out. It has the advantage that it is possible quickly to consider a very large number of variables.

We have taken the classification of 'good' and 'poor' countries identified in Table 4.4 in the last chapter, and compared the

TABLE 5.1 *Low income countries: BN-performance, 1979*

Variables		Strong assoc. +ve with good −ve with weak	Assoc. with good only	Assoc. with poor only	No sig. assoc.
Social					
Education					
Literacy rate	1976	★			
Enrolment in	1960	★			
primary school	1978	★			
Female enrolment as portion of total	1960			★	
	1970	★			
Enrolment in secondary school	1960	★			
	1978		★		
Female enrolment as proportion total in secondary schools	1960	★			
	1970	★			
Health Services					
Doctors p. person	1977		★		
Nurses p. person	1977	★			
Doctors p. person, rural areas	1975	★			
Nurses p. person, rural areas	1975		★		
Water % access to clean water	1975				★
Food Calory supply as % requirements	1977				★
Population, growth %	1960–70			★	
	1970–79		★		
Urban pop. as % total	1960		★		
	1980		★		
Economic variables					
Growth of GNP p. capita	1960–79			★	

TABLE 5.1 *Low income countries: BN-performance, 1979*

Variables		Strong assoc. +ve with good −ve with weak	Assoc. with good only	Assoc. with poor only	No sig. assoc.
Structure					
Gross domestic investment as % GDP	1960		★(neg)		
	1979			★	
Agriculture as %GDP	1979[b]		★(neg)		
Industry as % GDP	1960		★		
	1979		★		
Trade					
Change in ratio of exports to GDP	1960–79[c]			★(neg)	
Manufacturing exports as % total exports	1978			★	
Fuels, metals & minerals as % total exports	1960[d]			★(neg)	
	1978		★(neg)		
Public expenditure					
Public consumption as % GDP	1960[e]			★ (perverse)	
	1979[e]		★ (perverse)		
Central govt. expend. on health & educ. as % GDP	1978				★
Defence expenditure as % central govt.	1978[f]			★ (perverse)	
%GNP	1978[f]			★ (perverse)	
Income distribution					
Income share of bottom 40%				★ (perverse for poor performers)	
Income share of top 20%					
Gini co-efficient				★ (perverse)	
% of population in absolute poverty	1975		★		

92   *Planning to Meet Basic Needs*

TABLE 5.1 *cont'd.*

Sources: *1977 Compendium of Social Statistics* (UN, New York, 1980); *Demographic Year Book, special issue, Historical Supplement* (UN, New York, 1979); *Annual Abstract of Statistics, 1974* (CSO, HMSO, London, 1974); *Statistical Year Book of the Republic of China, 1981* (Directorate General of Budget, Accounting and Statistics, Republic of China, 1981): *Statistical Year Book, 1978* (UN, New York, 1979); *World Development Report, 1980* (World Bank, Washington DC); Jain, S., *Size Distribution of Income: A Compilation of Data* (World Bank, Washington, DC, 1975); Paukert, F. 'Income Distribution of Different Levels of Development: A Survey of Evidence', *International Labour Review*, 108, 2–3, 1973.

a. An association is defined as occurring where the proportion of 'good' countries whose performance equals or exceeds the average is 75% or more; and for poor performers the proportion of below average performance on the variable is 75% or more.
b. The association between agricultural as a proportion of GDP and good performance is a *negative* one.
c. 80% of poor performers had average or *above average* increase in ratio of exports to GDP.
d. 78% of poor performers had less than the average proportion of fuels, etc. as a proportion of total exports.
e. Public consumption exhibits a 'perverse' association with 75% of poor countries having *above average* ratios of public consumption in 1960; in 1979 all good performers had *below average* ratios.
f. Perverse relationship in that poor performers on BN spend *less* as a proportion on defence than average.

performance of the 'good' and 'poor' (divided into low and middle-income) countries on a number of variables, with the performance of 'average' BN-performers. Hence this is an analysis of deviations. For each variable we have calculated the proportion of countries in each category whose performance exceeds (or is the same as) the average; and the proportion whose performance falls below the average. Where three-quarters or more of good or poor performers' performance falls above or below that of the average, we have concluded that there is some significant relationship.

The variables selected consist of a set of social variables commonly associated with achievement on BN; and a set of economic variables

Economic and Social Variables

which have been hypothesised to have some (positive or negative) relationship with BN-performance. The social variables represent the BN-sectors (health, education, ...), while the economic variables represent elements in macroeconomic resource allocation.

Tables 5.1 (for low-income countries) and 5.2 (for middle-income) summarise the results of the exercise. The association between BN and particular variables has been divided into four types:

1. Strong association: this is found when the variable is positively associated with good performance and negatively associated with poor performance. Association has been defined to occur when 75 per cent or more of the 'good' countries do as well or better than average on that variable, and among 'poor' performers, 75 per cent or more do less well than average.
2. Association with good performers only. This occurs when there is a positive association with good performers, but no significant negative association with poor performers, who may do no worse than average.
3. Association with poor performers only. This occurs when there is a negative association with poor performance, but no positive association with good.
4. No association.

Before discussing the results, it must be emphasised that they are very tentative, especially since the sample of countries involved is often very small.

TABLE 5.2 *Middle-income countries: BN-performance, 1979*

Variables		Strong assoc.	Assoc. with good only	Assoc. with poor only	No signif. assoc.
Social					
Education					
Literacy rate	1976	★			
Enrolment in primary school	1960	★			
	1978				★
Female enrolment as proportion of total in primary school	1960	★			
	1970	★			
Enrolment in secondary school	1960			★	
	1978				★
Female enrolment as proportion of total in secondary schools	1960				★
	1970		★		
Health Services					
Doctors p. person	1977[a]			★ (perverse)	
Nurses p. person,	1977[a]			★ (perverse)	
Doctors p. person rural[b]		(perverse for good)			
Nurses p. person, rural[b]		(perverse for good)			
Water % access to clean water,	1975			★	
Food Calory supply as % requirements	1977			★	
Population growth %	1960–70[c]		★		
	1970–79[d]			★	
Urban pop. as % Total	1960			★	
	1980			★	
Economic variables					
Growth of GDP p. capita	1960–79			★	
Structure					
Gross domestic investment as % GDP	1960				★
	1979				★
Agriculture as % GDP	1960				★
	1979				★

Variables		Strong assoc.	Assoc. with good only	Assoc. with poor only	No signif. assoc.
Industry as % GDP	1960				★
	1979				★
Trade					
Change in % exports to GDP	1960–79				★
Manufacturing exports as % total	1978			★	
Fuels, metals & minerals as % exports	1960[e]	★			
	1978[f]	★			
Public expenditure					
Public consumption as % GDP	1960				★
	1979				★
Central govt. exp. on health & educ., as % GNP	1978				★
Defence expenditure as % central govt. exp.	1978				★
Income distribution					
Income share of bottom 40%				★	
Income share of top 40%				★	
Gini co-efficient				★	
% of pop. in absolute poverty	1975			★	

Sources: as Table 5.1.
a   Perverse association: i.e. 80% of poor performers had average or above average doctors p. inhabitant in 1977.
b   Perverse for good: weak performers have below average, good also below average.
c   1960–70 80% of good performers had average or *above* average pop. growth.
d   1970–9, 88% of poor performers had *above* average pop. growth.
e   90% of good performers, 1960, had average or *below* average ratio of minerals, etc. to exports, while 75% of poor performers had below average ratios.
f   In 1978, the good performers had *below* average share of minerals, etc. in total exports, while the poor performers had above average.

SOCIAL VARIABLES

For low-income countries almost all the education variables (literacy rates, and primary and secondary enrolment ratios) show a strong association. Although the results are a bit weaker for middle-income countries, there is some association for nearly all the educational variables. The results strongly support the view – also shown in the correlation analysis in the last chapter – that education is an important factor in determining BN at all income levels. It appears that female education is especially significant: the proportion of females in total education is related to BN-performance for both low and middle-income countries. This seems plausible, given the importance of women in determining BN household practices. However, it is also true that the proportion of women in schools tends to rise as total enrolment goes up, and we have not been able to disentangle these factors here.

The other social variables give more uneven results, with differences between low and middle-income countries. For low-income countries two variables – nurses per inhabitant and doctors per inhabitant in the rural areas – show a strong association. Doctors per inhabitant of the whole population and nurses in the rural areas shows a positive association with good performance, but not a negative with poor. The results therefore definitely suggest some association between the number of health personnel per person and BN as measured by life expectancy. For middle-income countries below average performance on doctors and nurses per inhabitant in the rural areas is associated with poor performance, but for doctors and nurses over the whole population (1977) there is a perverse result, with the weak performers having above average numbers of doctors and nurses.

For low-income countries there are no associations for calory supply on average as percentage of requirements or for percentage access to safe water. For middle-income countries, there are negative associations on these variables – that is, poor performers have significantly below average achievements on these variables.

On social variables, then, education comes out most strongly, especially female education; there is evidence for association with health personnel; and little evidence for association with calory supply or access to water. There is an interesting distinction, on this evidence, between low-income and middle-income countries; the associations for low-income countries are in general positive with good performance, rather than negative with weak – i.e. the good performers tend to do exceptionally well on various aspects, but the poor performers are not doing particularly poorly. In contrast, among middle-income countries, most of the relationships are negative – with poor performers doing below average, but good performers not doing especially well. This finding may be a reflection of the varying significance of growth and distribution at different income levels: 'at lower levels of income per capita it is growth that matters most in improving social indicators, while at higher levels of income, it is distribution' (Leipziger). For low-income countries, exceptional performance on BN would require exceptional supplies of BN-goods and services (education, health, water, etc.), while among middle-income countries, it is a question of the *distribution* of normal supplies to achieve good performance. Bad performance occurs among middle-income countries when supplies are exceptionally poor. The evidence on the varying significance of income distribution (see below) also lends the hypothesis some support.

Population growth shows a changing relationship, depending on period and group of countries, but nothing conclusive emerges. The proportion of population in the urban areas *is* associated with BN-performance for both groups of countries. For low-income countries it is positively associated with good performance. For middle-income it is negatively associated with poor performance.

ECONOMIC VARIABLES

The method used here of identifying 'good' and 'poor' performers already allows for the very substantial influence of national income per head in determining performance. The variables in the table are concerned with explaining deviations from the BN-performance that would be expected for a particular level of per capita income.

There is no particular association with economic growth, although among middle-income countries, poor BN-performers had below average growth. There is no evidence here for any conflict with economic growth. This is supported by the evidence on the investment ratio, with no association between BN-performance and investment ratio among middle-income countries and a positive association for low-income countries, where in 1960 poor performers had below average investment ratio and in 1979 good performers had above average investment ratios.

The export variables were inserted to test how trade affects BN. The two results worth noting are for manufacturing exports and minerals. A low ratio of manufacturing exports to total exports (1978) was associated with poor performance (though a high ratio was not associated with good for either group of countries). As far as fuels, metals and minerals (including oil) is concerned, it was expected that a high proportion of fuels, etc. in total exports would tend to produce poor performance on BN because it raises incomes without spreading them widely.[3] In fact the opposite result was found for 1960 for both sets of countries; but for 1978, the results were in the expected direction; for low-income countries good performers had below average share of fuels, etc. ; for middle-income countries there was a strong association, with good BN-countries having a low ratio and poor performers having a high ratio.

Public consumption as a proportion of GDP shows no association for middle-income countries, and a perverse relationship for low-income, with poor performers having a higher public consumption ratio in 1960 and good performers a lower than average ratio in 1979. The figures for total central government expenditure on health and education show no association with BN-performance for either low or middle-income countries.

There is no tendency for defence expenditure to differ from the average (as a proportion of central government expenditure or GNP) for good performers among low-income countries and both good and poor performers among middle-income. But among low-income countries poor performers showed less than average expenditure on defence.

For low-income countries, the share of national income produced in the industrial sector is positively related to BN among good performers, while the share of agriculture is negatively related: this may explain (or be explained by) the positive association among good performers between the rate of urbanisation and BN-performance. For middle-income countries, the associations here are much weaker, although the poor performers have lower than average rates of urbanisation and lower than average shares of manufacturing exports in total exports. Taken together these relationships indicate a possible positive association between industrialisation and BN-achievement among low-income countries and rule out the opposite hypothesis – that BN and industrialisation are in conflict.

Income distribution; The data in this area is particularly sparse in quantity. The results obtained differed markedly between low-income and middle-income countries. For low-income poor performers the results were perverse (i.e. opposite to those expected) with the poor performers having better (i.e. more equal) income distributions on each of the measures than the average, although the good performers showed somewhat more equal distribution than the average. For middle-income countries, in contrast, while the good performers were not markedly different from average, the poor performers had distinctly worse income distributions than average on each measure. This finding supports the view, for example that of Selowsky (1981), that among middle-income countries redistribution of income would be sufficient to bring about good performance.[4]

The final line in the two tables shows the relationship between the proportion of the population in absolute poverty, as indicated by the proportion falling below an absolute poverty line[5] and our indicator of BN-achievement. Any international poverty standard is inevitably crude, not reflecting the particular needs and conditions of each country.[6] In addition, as Sen has forcibly pointed out, a poverty line says nothing about how far below the line various groups fall.

Among low-income countries, countries doing exceptionally well have a below average proportion of their population falling below the absolute poverty line, but poor performers do not differ significantly from the average. Among middle-income countries, poor performers have exceptionally large numbers below the poverty line. While there are many difficulties about defining a poverty line, especially across nations, the measure adopted *roughly* captures the money-income side of poverty. The BN-approach emphasises the supply elements also (especially among public goods), and hence perfect association would be unlikely. For middle-income countries, these results confirm those on income distribution – raising the incomes of the poor would be sufficient to avoid exceptionally poor performance. For low-income countries, too, the results are similar to those obtained from the income distribution measures: good performers do have better than average performance, but so (to a limited extent) do poor performers – hence redistribution of money-incomes may be necessary, but is not sufficient to bring about good BN-performance among this group of countries.[7]

COMPARISONS WITH OTHER FINDINGS

Systematic attempts to explore relationships of the variables associated with BN-performance across countries include those by Sheehan and Hopkins (1979), Hicks (1982) and Berg (1981). Although the methods differ quite substantially, for the most part the conclusions support the findings noted above.

Sheehan and Hopkins take a multidimensional approach to BN-performance, using calory consumption per head, protein consumption, access to water, life expectancy, infant mortality, deaths due to infectious disease, literacy, doctors per 100 000, nurses per 100 000 and inhabitants per room, in each country, as indicators of BN-achievement with respect to material aspects of BN, and protest demonstrations, death rates from political violence and electoral regularity, as indicators of non-material 'participation' aspects of BN. They thus include many of the variables that are regarded in our approach as *means* to BN as aspects of the *objectives* of a BN-approach. They use principal components analysis to reduce the large list of BN-indicators to four – calory consumption, life expectancy, infant mortality and literacy rate. Using discriminant analysis for 1970 BN-performance, they find that the major significant variables associated with BN are four: GNP per capita and number of years since independence, which are associated with good BN-performance; the significance of mineral exports in a country's economic activity, associated with poor performance; and major aid flows, associated with the two extremes – very good and very poor performance.

As far as changes in the BN-indicators between 1960 to 1970: 'We were unable to find any variables which significantly differentiated between slow and rapid basic needs progress', although a few variables (high per capita GNP, high per capita aid and rapid population growth) were common to the extremes, good and bad, as compared with average performers.

Sheehan and Hopkins also use an alternative methodology of regressing variables against each of their BN-indicators, while controlling for level GNP. The main positive findings were:

– health (as measured by life expectancy and infant mortality) is significantly related to the number of doctors per 100 000 of population;
– some evidence that education is a key input for life expectancy and infant mortality, but not for the other BN-indicators;
– income distribution was related to life expectancy, but not to most of the other BN-indicators;
– economic growth was not related to life expectancy, but was related to a few other indicators;

– heavy dependence on minerals was related to poor performance on most of the BN-indicators.
– dependence on international trade was not related to BN-performance;
– the most important variable 'explaining' BN-performance was GNP per capita;
– population growth was positively related to BN-performance, as indicated by life expectancy and negatively related to other BN-indicators;

TABLE 5.3 Ranking of variables

	Simple[a] correlation	Multiple[b] correlation	Analysis[c] of deviations-1	Analysis[d] of deviations-2	Total score
Literacy, % 1974	1	1	1	1	1
Pop. per doctors, 1974	3	4	3	2	3
Calory p. person, 1974	2	6	4	4	4
Ratio of females to total enrolment, 1975	6	7	2	3	5
% pop. with access to clean water, 1975	4	2	7	6	5
Income share of lowest 40% 1970–75	7	3	5	4	5
% pop. in urban areas, 1975	5	5	6	6	6
% public cons. in GDP, 1960–73	8	8	8	8	8

Source: Hicks (1982), table 6

[a] The correlation co-efficients for public consumption as % of GDP and income distribution were near zero.
[b] Only 4 variables – literacy, income distribution, water supply and doctors are significant at 95% level.
[c] This method relates deviations from an income p. capita related 'norm' of life expectancy to deviations of income related norms of achievements on each of the variables. The method is confined to good performers (i.e. above norm).
[d] This is similar to c, but whereas in c over-achievers on BN (life expectancy) are identified, and then their achievement on the variables is noted, here over-achievement on the variables is first identified and then related to achievement on BN (life expectancy).

– while they have some success, as just listed in finding relationships with their material indicators of BN, they did not find significant relationships with non-material aspects.

Hicks (1982) adopts the same unidimensional approach to BN-achievements, as used above, with life expectancy at birth as the measure of performance. Hicks's findings are summarised in Table 5.3. He uses four methods to sort out the relative significance of eight variables in 'explaining' BN-performance.

A third study using simple correlation analysis for the mid-1960s, for thirty-nine developing countries, showed that literacy, urbanisation and per capita calory deficit were the three variables explaining life expectancy.[8] Per capita calory deficits were calculated by combining data on income distribution with average per capita calory consumption in each country, to arrive at a hypothetical level of calory consumption for different income groups in the population.[9] The level of income of the poor affected performance through its effect on calory deficits, but once this was allowed for it did not have an independent influence. When the analysis was confined to thirteen countries in Latin America, child mortality rates were best explained by the share of the population having energy deficits, medical expenditure and urbanisation. In this case, literacy ceased to be a variable.

Table 5.4 summarises the various findings.

CONCLUSION

Despite the differences in methodology, there is considerable agreement on conclusions, as indicated in Table 5.4. Among social variables, most methods show that education variables are positively related to BN. In addition, the proportion of females in education appears a significant variable. There is agreement also that there is a positive association between doctors per person and life expectancy (with strong results according to two of the methods). There is also agreement that other social variables are not significantly associated with BN-achievement: these include percentage access to clean water, calory consumption per head and nurses per person. However, Berg finds a strong relationship between average calory deficits and life expectancy, where calory deficits have been calculated

TABLE 5.4 A summary of findings

Variables	Own results (around 1979) Low-income countries	Own results (around 1979) Middle income	Sheehan and Hopkins (around 1970)	Hicks* (around 1975)	Berg mid-sixties 39 countries	13 Latin American countries[+]
Social						
Education	positive – strong	positive – strong	positive – strong	positive – strong	positive – strong	no relation
Ratio of female to total in education	positive – strong	weak	n.a.	positive – medium	n.a.	n.a.
Doctors p. pop.	none	assoc. with poor perf.	positive – strong	positive – medium	n.a.	medical expenditure, positive
% access to water	none	assoc. with poor performance	weak	weak on most methods	n.a.	n.a.
Calory consumption			weak	weak on most methods	calory deficit affects life expect.	calory deficit positive
Urbanisation	some positive association		positively related to life expectancy; negatively to other indicators.	negligible	positive	n.a.
Population growth	nothing conclusive		n.a.	n.a.	n.a.	n.a.
Economic						
Growth of GNP	nothing conclusive	some	nothing conclusive some	positive some	n.a. incorporated in calory deficit	n.a. incorporated in calory deficit
Income distribution (degree of equality)	none		n.a.	none	n.a.	n.a.
Public consumption as % GDP						
Defence expenditure as % GDP/central govt. exp.	none		n.a.	n.a.	n.a.	n.a.
Dependence on trade	n.a.		none	n.a.	n.a.	n.a.
Dependence on mineral exports	some negative association		n.a.	n.a.	n.a.	n.a.
Manuf. exports as % total exports	association (negative) with poor performance		n.a.	n.a.	n.a.	n.a.
GNP per cap.	positive strong		positive strong	positive strong	n.a.	n.a.

* in Hicks (1979, 1980).
+ relates to rate of child mortality.

incorporating distribution of calories as well as average consumption.

As far as economic variables are concerned, the only item that comes out strongly positive on all methods is GNP per capita, while dependence on minerals is found to be negatively associated with performance. The equality of income distribution is not found to be strongly associated with BN-performance, but each approach finds some association. Our method finds more association for middle-income than low-income countries, as has been suggested elsewhere.[10] Public consumption as percentage of GDP is *not* associated with performance (positively or negatively), nor is defence expenditure. Public consumption might have been expected to show some (positive) relationship as an indicator of expenditure on social programmes. But since no positive relationship is found between any of the social variables and BN-achievement, it should not be surprising that none is found for public consumption.

Economic growth and BN-achievements are not negatively related, according to any of the methods, i.e. there is no evidence of any conflict. Hicks finds some evidence of a positive relationship between the two. Any such conflict – did it exist – would presumably have its basis in conflicts in resource allocation and income distribution, since it is often hypothesised that a high growth strategy requires high investment and a certain degree of inequality while BN-achievement is normally assumed to require high social expenditure and a high degree of equality. But empirically we have noted that the BN-achievers do not have lower investment ratios, nor higher ratios of public consumption, nor very markedly more equality, nor is the converse true of BN-failures. Moreover, high growers do not have significantly more inequality than low ones, according to Ahluwalia. Hence the basic elements of the hypothesised conflict are empirically false.

Another conflict that has been hypothesised is between industrialisation and BN-achievement. Our findings are that no such conflict obtains; indeed for some countries it appears there is a positive relationship, with good BN-performing low-income countries having above average rates of industrialisation. Further, poor performers among both low and middle-income countries have below average share of manufactures in total exports. Regression analysis across ninety-two countries showed that there was a positive relationship between the proportion of GDP which went to industrial output and life expectancy in 1979 (r-square 0.39). But this is to be expected since GNP per head and industrialisation are positively related.

The many negative findings confirm the view, advanced at the beginning of this chapter, that the relationships are complex and likely to vary according to the circumstances of each country.

The marked variations in our findings between low and middle-income countries suggest that it will be rare to find relationships which hold across *all* countries. The few positive findings then stand out as particularly robust, given that the relationships show up empirically according to a number of methods, despite the many reasons why they might not.

6 Basic Needs in Nigeria

INTRODUCTION[1]

The exploitation of oil resources in Nigeria in the 1970s brought about a rapid rate of economic growth, raising average per capita incomes to nearly $700, well in excess of most African countries.[2] Yet Nigeria's performance on basic needs has been very poor. Life expectancy is between forty and forty-five;[3] rates of infant mortality are very high (well over 100); most of the population suffers from chronic diseases; average levels of nutrition are below those set by the FAO; the rate of adult literacy is estimated to be around 20 per cent. The economic growth has had very little effect on basic needs. Standards of health and nutrition have changed very little over the past decade. Only in education has there been (quantitatively at least) any major progress.

The next three chapters contain a detailed case study of Nigerian performance on BN. This chapter records current status and recent progress on the main BN areas – health, food and nutrition, water and education. The next chapter attempts to apply the macroeconomic framework developed in Chapter 2 to BN-performance in Nigeria, since while each sector exhibits its own particular problems and deficiencies, it is the performance of the economy at the macro-level which is the major determinant of aggregate performance on BN.

Nigeria has been dominated in recent years by oil, which accounts for about one-fifth of national income, over 75 per cent of Federal Tax revenue and over 90 per cent of exports. It has influenced the productive structure of the economy, the distribution and location of employment opportunities and the distribution of income. It is impossible to understand recent developments or to analyse alternative macroeconomic strategies without an understanding of the role of oil. Chapter 8 considers the 'logic' of an oil economy in the Nigerian context, and analyses alternative BN-strategies in the light of that logic, as well as of the specific BN-performance revealed in this and the following chapter.

SOME BACKGROUND FEATURES OF THE NIGERIAN ECONOMY

Nigeria has much the largest population of any country in Africa: the 'best guess' of the present population is 70 million.[4] The country was carved out of a large and heterogeneous area, with marked differences in climate and soil, culture and religion in different parts of the country; while there are three main languages spoken in Nigeria by the largest ethnic groups as many as 400 distinct languages have been identified. Strong centrifugal tendencies culminated in the fierce civil war of 1967–70, some seven years after independence. Military rule, which began with a coup in 1966, continued until 1979, when civilian rule was reinstated.

Until very recently agriculture was dominant in the economy, accounting for half of output, three-quarters of employment and almost 100 per cent of exports. For the most part, agriculture is organised on a small-scale family basis. The few attempts to introduce State farms and plantations have mostly proved unsuccessful. The major cash crops – introduced by the British – are cocoa, cotton and oil seeds. In general there is no land shortage, nor landless labourers on a significant scale. The manufacturing sector, which including 'crafts' accounted for a consistent 7 per cent of GDP between 1965 and 1973, consists of the usual list of consumer import-substitution industries based on foreign technology and in many cases foreign ownership.[5] By the early 1970s Nigeria had reached the stage of exhausting the obvious first phase list of import-substitution industries and thus faced the dilemma, shared by many countries, of how to proceed. The discovery and exploitation of oil in the early 1970s, together with the escalation of its world price, had an enormous effect on the Nigerian economy.[6] Through exchange rate and other effects agricultural exports were eliminated; indeed agricultural products are now imported on a substantial scale. The oil revenues went largely to the government thus hugely increasing government revenues; the effect was to reduce the significance of other sources of revenue and to lead to an explosion in government expenditure: current federal expenditure rose from 5 per cent of GDP in 1965/6 to 22 per cent in 1977/8. The oil exports also temporarily removed any foreign exchange constraints, permitting a massive rise in imports – both capital and consumer goods. Much of the investment was devoted to economic infrastructure; some to large-scale manufacturing industry. Nigeria is beginning to move from first phase import-substitution to a second phase consisting of consumer durables/luxuries (e.g. the assembly of cars) and heavy industry (e.g. steel).

Nigeria's per capita income of $679[7] in 1979 put her among the middle-income countries: yet her social indicators – as we shall see in detail below – are among the worst in the world. But the 'high' per capita income is to some extent misleading, reflecting a high post-oil boom rate of growth of around 6 per cent p.a. and an overvalued exchange rate. At the beginning of the 1970s, Nigeria would have been classified among the low-income countries. Her economic and social infrastructure had been badly damaged by the civil war. While monetary GDP did grow in the 1970s, its growth was a peculiar and lopsided affair, as is often associated with a rapid rise in oil revenues. Thus despite the apparent riches conferred by oil, Nigeria remains a low-income country from most relevant points of view, and her performance in relation to BN should be judged accordingly.

Any analysis of the Nigerian economy is confronted by statistical deficiencies more acute than in many other countries. On the social side the statistics are even weaker than on the economic. While there are numerous micro-studies the aggregate statistics are often completely lacking, or known to be unreliable. Divergencies in estimates of the aggregate population, for example, amount to as much as 30 million; estimates for life expectancy vary from as little as thirty-eight to ten years more; literacy rates are unknown; estimates of nutritional status and infant mortality no more than informed guesses. The great regional and cultural differences within Nigeria compound the problem of statistical weakness, making any generalisation dangerous. Best guesses at a national level may be completely inaccurate at a local level. Differences in culture mean that solutions which would be applicable to some people may be totally irrelevant to others. For example, it has been observed that families in the *same village* have totally different diets because of differences in religion.[8] Statistical problems which are particularly marked in the BN-area, are worse than normal in a country at this level of development. They are not (solely) the accidental outcome of administrative deficiencies, but in addition a political solution to a host of problems – concerned with the distributional (between regions as well as classes) effects of development. Thus the statistical deficiencies, which affect most of the BN-questions should be seen as a symptom as well as a cause of failures in this area.

RECENT PROGRESS IN MEETING BASIC NEEDS IN NIGERIA

There is, as discussed in Chapter 1, considerable disagreement about the precise meaning of BN, which goods and services should be included, whether non-economic needs (e.g. 'participation') are essential aspects of BN as well as material needs, and so on. From the point of view of economic planning, it is the material needs that are most relevant (and also most easy to handle). This study of Nigeria, therefore, follows the approach adopted in the planning framework, regarding healthy and educated people as the major objective of a BN-approach, and health services, education services, water and food, as the major relevant sectors to achieve this objective. Housing has not been included below because it seems to have less direct impact on health, nutrition and education than the other sectors, although a strong case could be made for including it.

Health

There are no national statistics on the health of Nigerians. Statistics have been collected systematically in Lagos, but elsewhere conclusions have to be based on a somewhat *ad hoc* set of particular studies. This, together with the considerable diversity in ecology and culture, must make any conclusions somewhat tentative. But all the indications are that the general state of health in Nigeria is very poor, and has not changed much in recent years. As a recent UNFPA study put it, 'The nation's health status is perceived to be very poor with the prevalence of largely preventable and communicable conditions with high levels of infant and general mortality and morbidity.'[9]

Life expectancy

Although estimates vary, as Table 6.1 shows, it is generally agreed that life expectancy in Nigeria is currently somewhere between forty-two and forty-five; that it has risen over the past quarter of a century, but not much in the last decade.

Infant and child mortality

Surveys show rates of infant mortality of well over 100, and similar rates for child mortality (age 1–4). As Table 6.2 shows there are considerable variations in different parts of the country, and between

TABLE 6.1   *Life expectancy at birth*

UNFPA estimates[1]	Total population	Male	Female
1950–55	31.3	30.0	32.6
1955–60	33.5	31.9	35.1
1960–65	36.0	34.4	37.6
1965–70	38.5	36.9	40.1
1970–75	41.0	39.4	42.6
Other estimates[2]			
1964[3]	41		
1965/6[4]	37 (rural only)		
1971[5]	44 (S.W. Nigeria only)		

Sources
[1] UNFPA (1979), table 5, p. 82 from *World Population, Trends and policies*: 1977, Monitoring Report, Vol. I, U.N., New York.
[2] ILO (1981), Technical Paper 1, table 3.
[3] *Population Growth and Socio-economic Change in W. Africa* (ed. Caldwell *et al*).
[4] Rural Demographic Survey of Federal Office of Statistics, 1965–6.
[5] *National Survey of Fertility Family and Family Planning*, DSS Monograph, no. 1, ed. Adeokun, University of Ife, Nigeria, 1979.

TABLE 6.2 Rates of infant and child mortality, per 1000

Place	Date	Infant mortality (0–1)		Child mortality (1–4)	Total (0–5)
Nigeria, rural[1]	1965–6	175			322 (M) 306(F)
Lagos (former W. Region)[2]	1967–8	143			
Lagos (former Federal territory)[2]	1967–8	79			
S.W. Nigeria:[3] of which,	1971	urban	rural		
		83	109		
		total			
		87			
Lagos		73			
West		77	109	91	
Kwara		125	113	116	
Midwest		148	107	112	
Village Ebendo, Midwest[4] State	1974	180		100	280
Villages in Western[5] State	1973				
Village A		99		99	198
Village B		288		171	459

Sources
[1] Rural Demographic Survey, Federal Office of Statistics, 1965–6 (sample of 200 rural villages).
[2] Sample survey of Lagos: former Federal territory has more medical facilities, piped water and sewage than former Western Region.
[3] 1971–4 National Survey of Fertility, Family and Family Planning.
[4] F. L. Mott (1974) *The Dynamics of Demographic Change in a Nigerian Village*, Human Resources Research Unit, University of Lagos, Monograph No. 2.
[5] I. O. Orubuloye and J. C. Caldwell (1975) 'The Impact of Public Health Services on Mortality: A Study of Mortality Differentials in a Rural Area of Nigeria', *Population Studies*, Vol. 29.

villages within the same area. One study showed deaths of under-fives to be around 460 per 1000 in a village without any medical facilities; a nearby village with a clinic had a rate of 200. Under-reporting, which is thought to be common for various cultural and psychological reasons, is likely to mean the figures are underestimates. Rates of infant and child mortality usually appear to be higher in the rural than urban areas, and lower in Lagos than in the rest of the country. In Lagos the infant mortality rate is around seventy; in the rural areas in general it is probably over 150, with much higher rates in particular areas as suggested by Table 6.2.

International comparisons

Health in Nigeria is poor by international standards. Nigeria's per capita income puts her among the middle-income countries, according to the World Bank classification. On average, low-income countries' life expectancy in 1979 was fifty-seven, while that of middle-income countries was sixty-one.

While international comparisons should not be taken too seriously, since the basis for the statistics of other countries may well be as weak as those of Nigeria, it seems that despite the higher per capita income, the health situation of Nigeria's rural areas appears to be much the same as that of the rural areas in some of the poorest areas in the world.

TABLE 6.3 *International comparisons*

Country	Per capita income $ 1979	Life expectancy 1979
Bangladesh	90	49
Mali	140	43
Malawi	200	47
Tanzania	260	52
Sri Lanka	230	66
Kenya	380	55
Egypt	480	57
Nigeria	670	49 (42–45)*

Source: *World Development Report, 1981.*
*49 is figure in *World Development Report*; 42–45 'best' guess on basis of surveys.

Disease/morbidity

The pattern of disease in Nigeria is similar to that of other tropical countries with low incomes and poor health services. Malaria leads as the major notifiable disease followed by dysentery and measles. There was an increase in the number of reported cases of the three main diseases between 1968 and 1977, possibly due to improved reporting. The figures indicate a continued high incidence of disease.[10]

Statistics based on notified diseases understate the total prevalence of disease. A study of parasitic disease in one community showed a level three times those reported by hospital statistics. Two surveys among children under five in Ife found that only 12 per cent and 19 per cent respectively of the children examined were clinically fit.[11] In the rural areas, parasitic diseases are prevalent.[12] Leprosy is widespread in the north. There are high rates of maternal deaths. For Lagos (where medical facilities are most accessible) the maternal death rate is reported to be 2.5 per 1000 total births in 1970 rising to 5.2 per 1000 in 1973.[13] Water-related diseases are particularly significant in the North. In 1977 there were a total of over 1½ million notified cases.

For Lagos, statistics for mortality and morbidity are available by age group.

Nigeria's very low life expectancy is largely due to the high rates of death among children under five. These accounted for over half the deaths in Lagos in 1969. While precise information is not available, the overall rate of mortality for children under five probably ranges between 150 per 1000 (Lagos) and over 400 (in the most remote rural areas). In contrast in developed countries deaths of children under five typically account for 3 per cent of total deaths; and infant and

TABLE 6.4 *Percentage of deaths by age, Lagos, 1969*

Under 5	55.9
5–14	4.7
15–54	21.1
55–64	5.8
Over 65	12.8

Source: *Annual Abstract of Statistics*, 1975, table 15.5

child mortality rates are 15 per 1000 for industrialised countries (1977). In Sri Lanka deaths of children under five are around 55 per 1000; in Thailand they are 74; in the Philippines 72; Malaysia 35; Jamaica 25; and in Cuba 24. Generally rates of child and infant mortality in Africa tend to be higher than elsewhere. Rates of infant mortality (deaths per 1000 under one year old) were 163 in Nigeria in 1975, similar to Senegal (158), and Niger (162), but higher than Mali (120), Rwanda (133) and Malawi (142) and much higher than Kenya (51) and Ghana (63).[14] Figures for the age distribution of the main registered diseases in Lagos again show the preponderance of diseases among children under five (Table 6.5). Over 80 per cent of all cases of measles, pneumonia, gastro-enteritis and diarrhoea were for this age group. Very high fatality rates for pneumonia and gastro-enteritis (over 40 per cent) make them the two leading killers among notified diseases. While the diseases as reported are the proximate causes of death, it is well known that malnutrition (see below) is a major contributory factor in many cases, causing a predisposition to infection and reducing the chances of recovery. The survey of health in Nigeria by the UNFPA concludes that, 'Of all the major causes of mortality and morbidity, the major one is the prevailing poor level of nutrition.' (p. 89)

This brief review of the rather scattered and uncertain evidence of mortality/morbidity in Nigeria points to three significant conclusions:

1. There is a marked difference between the situation in Lagos and other areas, and although the situation is very bad everywhere it is worst in the rural areas.
2. The worst manifestations of disease and of mortality are concentrated among children under five. If rates here could be reduced substantially – as they have been in countries with similar income levels – this would go a long way to raising life expectancy and reducing the disparity between Nigeria and other countries which have much better levels of health.
3. Neither complex research nor expensive medical facilities are necessary to reduce the devastation caused by the main killers – gastro-entritis, pneumonia and measles. Such diseases could be radically reduced by improved nutrition, health education, and access to simple medical care.

TABLE 6.5 Diseases among children under five, Lagos, 1973

Disease	Total no. of cases, children 0–4	% of cases notified, estimated	Fatality rate among children 0–4	% of all diseases notified 0–4	% of deaths from notified diseases 0–4
Measles	4 993	90.4	6.3	44.1	11.5
Pneumonia	1 863	81.5	46.6	16.5	31.6
Gastro-enteritis	1 756	83.0	40.5	15.5	45.5
Malaria	1 292	38.5	17.2	11.4	8.1
Diarrhoea	1 206	83.2	2.3	10.7	1.0
Meningitis	212	66.1	29.2	1.9	2.3

Source Calculated from UNFPA (1979), table 7.

Health services in Nigeria

There were very low levels of expenditure on health services in Nigeria during the first three Five Year Plans:

TABLE 6.6 *Expenditure on the health sector*

	Current expenditure[a]		
	1963/4	1969/70	1975/6
GDP arising in health sector, Nm, current prices	18.2	24.1	127.9
As % GDP	0.6	0.7	0.9
N per capita,[15] current prices	0.4	0.4	1.9
N per capita, 62–3 prices	0.4	0.4	1.1

	Capital Expenditure[b]		
	1962–8	1970–4	1975–80
Public sector investment in health as % total public sector investment			
Planned	2.5	5.2	2.3
Actual	1.4	4.6	n.a.
Capital expenditure p. head p.a. (approx), N	.02 (actual)	0.6 (actual)	1.2 (planned)

Sources:
[a] *Economic Indicators*, Vol. 13, June 1977, tables 10.1 & 10.2.
[b] Second and Third National Development Plans.

The expenditure (current and capital) of around $1.75 in 1975/6 is low by international standards. Out of nineteen countries with GNP per capita of between $300 and 599, government expenditure on health per head exceeded $2 in eighteen countries and exceeded $6 in eleven countries.[16]

Despite lip service to the importance of preventive services, each of the Plans has been heavily biased towards curative medicine. In the Second Five Year Plan (1970–4), 80 per cent of Federal capital expenditure was planned to be devoted to teaching hospitals; the states planned to spend 16 per cent of their capital expenditure on public health services. In the Third Plan capital allocations were:

TABLE 6.7 *Planned capital expenditure, 1975–80*

	Hospital programmes	Basic health service programmes	Training programmes	Supporting health programmes
Federal ₦m	212	51	24.2	27.0
% of total Federal	67.5	16.2	7.7	8.5
States ₦m	194.4	168.2	45.9	37.3
% of total states	43.6	37.7	10.3	8.4
% of Federal and state	53.5	28.8	9.2	8.5

Source: *Third National Development* Plan, 1975–80, p. 271.

Over the five year period then approximately ₦3 was planned to be spent per person on capital programmes for basic health services. Taking these capital allocations as a rough guide, we can conclude that in 1975-6 approximately ₦0.5 was spent per person on basic health services (which is rather more than 25 US cents).

There was also an acknowledged bias in expenditure towards the urban areas – in part a natural by-product of the bias towards expenditure on hospitals. For example, in 1973, Lagos municipality, which accounted for 45 per cent of the population of the state, had more than 90 per cent of registered medical practitioners, 67 per cent of all state hospitals and clinics and 72 per cent of all private clinics.[17] However, Lagos does serve as a health care centre for much of the surrounding area.

In aggregate the doctor/population ratio in 1978 was 1:11 000 which represented a substantial reduction compared with previous figures. The ratio of registered nurses to population was 1:3 600. These aggregate ratios are roughly 'normal' for countries of similar income levels. But the strong curative/urban element has meant that a very large proportion of the rural population is without access to medical services. It was estimated that in 1975 the health coverage of the population 'was at most 25 per cent and this was largely biased in favour of the urban population'.[18] While there has been strong verbal emphasis on basic health care since 1975, very little has been achieved.

Effective coverage by health services depends on their location and the distance people can be expected to go to get to them. It has been estimated for one part of Nigeria that 4.0 km is the outside limit, beyond which people will not go in significant numbers. On this assumption, one study suggested only 1.6 per cent of the population were covered by maternity clinics and 1.8 per cent by dispensaries.

TABLE 6.8 *'Iso-care coverage': per cent of population*

	Maternity Clinics		Dispensaries	
	Iso-care coverage %	Max. distance to clinic km.	Iso-care coverage %	Max. distance to dispensary km.
North	0.1	68.4	0.6	25.4
East	8.1	6.9	6.5	7.8
West	5.9	8.1	6.9	7.5
Midwest	4.7	9.1	5.2	8.7
Lagos	100.0	0.4	100.0	1.0
Nigeria	1.6		1.8	

Source: L. Adeokun and A. Odebiyi (1977)

Other studies suggest greater coverage, for example a study in Oyo State showed coverage of antenatal care ranging from 6.6 per cent to 38 per cent.[19] Coverage of the population at risk by measles vaccine varies from 6 per cent in Rivers State to 41 per cent in Kwara.[20]

Nutrition

All the evidence suggests that there is considerable malnutrition in Nigeria; there is no indication that the situation has been improving over the last decade and some suggestions that it may have been worsening. In 1977 the FAO listed Nigeria as amongst the thirteen nations facing the most serious problems of inadequate food. The FAO calory requirement is 2 200 per day, while the WHO protein requirement (now agreed to be somewhat high) is 67 grams per day. A National Survey in 1965, differentiated between three geographical areas, the north, a rural coastal area and Port Harcourt. It also distinguished between different socio-economic groups within Port Harcourt. The survey found a general – and in some areas a substantial – deficiency in calories and proteins:[21]

TABLE 6.9

	Rural			Port Harcourt	
	North	Coast	Operatives	Junior clerks	Senior staff
Calories	1868	1377	1510	2353	1718
% requirement	82	63	71	106	87
Protein % requirement	84	53	49	73	146

Source: *Nutrition Survey*, Feb–April 1965, US Department of Health, Education and Welfare, March, 1967.

A number of estimates have been prepared for Nigeria as a whole; some of them suggest that on average requirements are just met; others that there is an average deficiency.[22]

The national estimates do not suggest any trend over time; agricultural production figures show declining per capita food production for the nation as a whole. While these may understate the production of food, the evidence from micro-nutrition studies, from hospitals and from the impression of well-informed observers (for example, Professor Omolulu[23]) is that the food and nutrition situation has not improved over time.

Unequal distribution across seasons, among households and within families means that even where *average* calory/protein availability is just sufficient there will be substantial malnutrition.

There is considerable seasonal variation in Nigeria. For example, a study of three villages in Zaria found that calory intake varied from 86 per cent of average in December/January to 109 per cent (April/May), while the protein variability was somewhat greater.[24] The study found that average calory consumption per villager over the year as a whole was nearly 30 per cent greater in the richest village as compared with the poorest. Thus while for the three villages average calory intake just about reached the required miniumum, the poorest village showed an average deficiency of 13 per cent. Within each village calory intakes varied according to income, as shown in Table 6.10, such that calory consumption per head of the high-income group was 126 per cent, 139 per cent, and 182 per cent of calory consumption of the low-income households. This unequal distribution between households within the village

TABLE 6.10

	Daily calory intake	Daily protein intake	No. of consumers
Doka	2 467		
Low	2 319	63.5	155
Middle	2 499	67.5	105
High	3 108	89.1	38
Dan Mahawayi	1 907		
Low	1 604	44.9	54
Middle	1 701	49.3	95
High	2 231	63.5	144
Hanwa	2 385		
Low	1 472	39.2	72
Middle	2 601	66.2	109
High	2 674	69.3	190

Source: Simmons (1976), Appendix Tables C5.

meant that in one village where average calory availability was greater than requirements, the low-income consumers (19 per cent of the total) had a very major calory deficiency, meeting only two-thirds of requirements. In the village where average availability was 87 per cent of requirements, the low-income households had 72 per cent and the middle-income households 77 per cent of requirements, together accounting for 51 per cent of consumers in the village. Taking the three villages together 30 per cent of consumers have a substantial calory deficit, despite the fact that on average calory availability exceeds requirements.

Intra-household distribution introduces another source of malnutrition. There is very little hard evidence on intra-household food distribution. But observers have suggested that the head of household is given priority in food allocation and consumes most of any meat or fish. There is abundant evidence that young children are the group worst affected by malnutrition.

Specific studies of the nutritional status of particular groups supplement the evidence on average calory availability:

1. Studies in the West of Nigeria in the 1960s found that three-

quarters of village children were below the 25th percentile international height/weight standard.[25] Another study of a similar village found that at age four children were 6 inches shorter and 4.5 kg lighter than well-to-do children in Ibadan;[26] in Katsina in Kaduna State, 1.6 per cent of children were severely malnourished and 11.7 per cent moderately malnourished in 1977–8.[27]
2. The incidence of severe malnutrition was found to be 7.6 per cent in a remote Northern community, south of Katsina; 39.6 per cent suffered from moderate malnutrition.[28]
3. A study in Cross River State found 4 per cent of children with signs of severe malnutrition, but the general state of nutrition was adequate.[29]
4. A survey of children under five in Ife reported signs of clinical malnutrition in 30 and 70 per cent of children in two villages.[30]
5. A study based on blood samples found low or deficient thiamine intake among 21–40 per cent; the majority of the sample had low values of riboflavin; vitamin A deficiency was found among pregnant and lactating women and young children; a moderate degree of anaemia; deficient iodine among 19 per cent of adult males and 8 per cent of adult females.[31]
6. A study in Western State found that one out of seven child deaths were due to malnutrition while it was a contributory cause in half the remaining deaths.[32]
7. One-third of the Nigerian athletes in the 1972 Olympics were found to be borderline anaemics.[33]
8. A survey of nutrition status among children in Lagos in 1969 found that between 3.5 per cent and 18.8 per cent of the children suffered from severe malnutrition, while between 6.1 and 17.1 per cent were undernourished, the proportions varying according to the district, with the district with the lowest earnings and worst health facilities having 34.1 per cent of the children malnourished.[34]

Causes of malnutrition

Two of the critical factors determining nutrition are levels of incomes and availability of food. In Nigeria, as elsewhere, there is abundant evidence that expenditure on food increases with incomes, and the better-off are better fed. The question of incomes and food consumption will be discussed in the next chapter, which concludes that a very large proportion of households in Nigeria – nearly half – have inadequate incomes to meet BN in food. Food availability is the second critical factor; this encompasses not only food production (and imports) but also storage and distribution. Nigeria has had a poor performance on both; production has been fairly stagnant, while very large losses are recorded as a result of poor storage facilities (e.g. a 10 per cent loss in cereals and grain legumes; 25 per cent in fish). Apart from these macro-factors, which will be discussed later, household behaviour is often a critical element determining nutritional standards. In Nigeria, a fundamental element is weaning practices. Malnutrition is particularly acute in the months and years immediately following weaning. In many cases, babies of around eighteen months are weaned very abruptly – often within a week – and are then fed food which is very bulky, and sometimes peppery. As a result many children do not eat enough. Acute malnutrition sometimes follows especially if the children's appetite is further diminished by some infectious disease like measles.[35] Taboos against feeding small children various nutritious foods are an additional factor. In a study of the causes of malnutrition in Lagos taboos were found to affect the consumption of milk (8%), fish (2%), eggs (3.5%), groundnuts (27.5%), meat (10.5%), beans (10.5%), okra (6%) and green vegetables (6%).[36] Less than a quarter of the mothers of malnourished children had no taboos. The general level of education among the parents of malnourished children was very low: 58 per cent of the mothers had had no formal education and 40.5 per cent of the fathers. The study found that little cooking was done; food was mostly bought from street hawkers, which was an expensive source. The study concludes that health and nutrition education has an important part to play. Over half the sample of mothers believed disease was an act of God; but all those who believed it was due to lack of food had attended an Infant Welfare Clinic or the Lagos Teaching Hospital.

Another study of malnutrition in Lagos also emphasised the role of education; it found *no* cases of malnutrition among the children of mothers with formal education, even when their incomes were low. Among children with illiterate mothers there was a substantial incidence of malnutrition.[37]

A health programme in Katsina reduced the rate of malnutrition among children from 1.6 per cent (severe malnutrition) to 0.4 per cent after one year. The infant mortality rate fell dramatically.[38]

Health and nutrition interact. As stated disease often precipitates borderline cases into severe malnutrition. Okungbowa and Akesoda found that infection was a dominant factor in the development of malnutrition; 62 per cent of the malnourished had not been immunised. Half of the mothers had never heard of immunisation programmes. The diseases responsible were gastro-enteritis, measles and upper respiratory diseases.

The relationship between disease and malnutrition means that hygiene, sanitation and water facilities also play a role. The Ransome–Kuti study of Lagos found extremely low levels of hygiene/sanitation among the families of malnourished children:

> Sanitation was very poor. There was not a single water closet in any of the houses visited. The pail system was used and the stench can be almost unbearable. A few had no lavatory at all. Stools were thrown in the bush around. Generally children's stools are commonly found around the houses. Leaves used for wrapping food, waste food products, rags and even human and animal stools littered the surroundings and gutters.

Food was stored in the bedrooms generally under the beds. The growing practice of bottle-feeding, especially in the cities, also contributes to malnutrition directly and through the infection it tends to generate. In the Ransome–Kuti Lagos study a large proportion of mothers had introduced bottle-feeding at a very early stage, but most of them soon dropped it. Another study found that nearly three-quarters of the mothers had introduced bottle-feeding in the first month. Of these one-third read the instructions on the milk tin; two-thirds did not (70 per cent of the sample had not completed primary education). Fifty-five per cent of the mothers sterilised the bottles properly; 44 per cent did not.[39]

Diseases also contribute to malnutrition by reducing the nutritive value of a given amount of food. This is particularly the case for diarrhoea/gastro-enteritis, and for infestations of parasites. In both the cities and the rural areas, these diseases are prevalent at very high rates (see section on health). Cooking methods are another way in which household behaviour affects nutrition. One study has established quite substantial losses in nutrients through food preparation: these result from cutting and storing hours before cooking, extensive washing and rubbing, squeezing and discarding washing water and long cooking periods. Losses were recorded of 40–100 per cent of ascorbic acid, 3–49 per cent of D-carotene and vitamin A, 29–48 per cent of thiamine and pyridoxine, 1.2–30 per cent of riboflavin, 5.9–30 per cent of niacin and substantial amounts of calcium, iron and phosphorus, as well as important trace elements.[40]

Water supplies[41]

Water is one of the most fundamental human needs. A certain minimum amount is necessary for survival; but for health and hygiene, clean water needs to be available in fairly abundant quantities. It has been estimated that 112 litres per person per day is a desirable quantitative target;[42] while purity/quality is important, it is now generally accepted that quantity is the priority dimension for health. For rural households, particularly, distance between dwellings and water supplies is a further important dimension.

In Nigeria – in both cities and countryside – supplies of water are extremely poor with respect to all three dimensions – quantity, quality and access.

Urban water schemes covered about 63 per cent of the urban population in 1978, according to Ministry estimates, with wide variation between states (see Table 6.11). But most of the towns served fell well below the minimum desirable level, both in quantity and quality. In 1977 in only three states was the minimum target for urban water supply exceeded; most fell well below the minimum; eight states had less than half the target, while four had less than a quarter.[43] Maldistribution within each area – with some consumers receiving above average supplies and others below average – means that the proportion of the population receiving adequate supplies in quantity is probably less than half in the urban areas.

> Lagos (metro) provides an example where reported coverage is supposed to be high (94%) but water shortages are very common. Many families rely on substandard wells alone, while others rely on purchasing water from private contractors. Many housing developments still lack water even in the middle or high-income category. (ILO, Technical Paper 3, para. 22)

The quality of much urban water is poor; in Lagos about 30 per cent comes from ground water which is subject to pollution from septic tanks and pit latrines. Even pipe-borne surface water is often inadequately treated.

TABLE 6.11 Coverage of water supply by fifteen States, 1978.

	Area km² ('000)	Total population (m)	Number of centres (urban)	Urban % served	Rural[a] % served	Rural %[b] served by piped water	Population served by piped water (m)
Anambra	17	5.69	32	37	64	9	1.0
Borno	117	4.53	18	70	0	n.a.	0.5
Benue	43	3.53	8	80	8	n.a.	0.2
Cross River	28	5.08	19	85	8	5	1.1
Gongola	100	3.50	17	31	2	n.a.	0.2
Imo	12	5.00	9	100	20	1	0.7
Kaduna	70	6.40	22	31	13	4	0.7
Kano	43	8.36	20	n.a.	n.a.	n.a.	n.a.
Kwara	154	2.70	21	85	13	2	0.8
Lagos	34	4.53	4	94	4	n.a.	2.2
Oyo	22	7.60	24	79[c]	n.a.	n.a.	6.0
Ogun	16	2.60	10	100	14	10	0.8
Plateau	53	3.19	19	83	0.0	n.a.	0.6
Rivers	28	2.02	13	66	35	1	0.3
Sokoto	64	6.55	16	100	39	n.a.	0.9
Total		68.13	239	68	18	2	16.0[d]

Notes
[a] Rural population served by all types of 'improved' water supply sources including protected shallow wells.
[b] Rural population served by urban water supply.
[c] Oyo state claims to supply 79 per cent of total population (6.0 million)
[d] Piped supply in fourteen states with a total population of 59.77 million (i.e. 27 per cent).

Sources
Ministry of Water Resources.
  (The population estimates are very rough.)
  ILO Technical Paper 3, table 25.

Rural water

According to Ministry estimates only 2 per cent of the rural population are served by piped water. Around 20 per cent have access to 'improved' sources, including modernised wells. The remainder rely on traditional sources of water. In the Northern savanna zone with limited rainfall, the main source is hand-dug wells, which are not capped. There are high health hazards associated with traditional wells, which could be reduced by providing concrete lined walls with raised headworks. However, wells sometimes dry up and are also subject to pollution from nearby pit latrines. Boreholes with small handpumps are preferred on health grounds, but these too often dry up and the pumps are frequently out of order.

In the south with abundant rivers, most villages have access to sufficient supplies within 5 km. But quality is a major health hazard.

Nigeria aims to introduce modern waterborne sewage disposal systems in all towns. But at present no town is adequately served; pit latrine and pail systems are dominant. Refuse collection is poorly organised in most cities and non-existent in the rural areas.

Water supplies and sanitation have received a very small proportion of investment funds during the first three Plans:

TABLE 6.12 *Capital expenditure on water and sanitation*

	Total sector exp. (M₦)	% of plan total expenditure	Water share %	Sanitation share %
Plan I (1962–8)				
Planned	43.6*	4.6*		
Actual	49.4	4.4		
Plan II (1970–4)				
Planned	103.4	5.0		
Actual	129.1	5.8		
Plan III (1975–80)				
Planned (orig.)	1358.5	4.1	2.7	1.4
Revised	1247.6			

*Water only, sanitation very small.
Source: First, Second and Third National Development Plans.

Education

The colonial era left Nigeria with a very weak formal Western educational structure.[44] In 1966 the primary school enrolment ratio was estimated to be 30 per cent, while the secondary school ratio was only about 3 per cent.[45] These averages conceal strong regional variations, with the North having much lower levels of education than the rest of the country. Primary school enrolment ratios in 1966 varied from 4 per cent in some parts of the country to 90 per cent in others. There were also marked differences between the sexes, with female education lagging far behind male.[46]

The National Plans have given a high priority to education.

In 1977, education absorbed well over 40 per cent of the recurrent budget of the Federal Government and over 55 per cent of the recurrent budgets of state governments. These levels of expenditure are high in relation to Nigeria's per capita income.[47]

The heavy expenditure on education in recent years is a reflection of expansion of activity at all levels; a high priority has been given to primary education. Universal Primary Education (UPE) was made a major objective in 1976 giving every child the right to receive free primary schooling. But both recurrent and capital costs of primary education are far lower than that of other levels,[48] so that primary education received less than a quarter of the (planned) capital expenditure in the Second Plan and only 12 per cent of the planned expenditure in the Third Plan. It is estimated that primary education received 30 per cent of total educational expenditure in 1976/7.

The introduction of UPE saw a massive increase in primary enrolment – far in excess of that expected.[49] In 1976/7 it was estimated that about 60 per cent of the age group were enrolled; it is

TABLE 6.13 *Capital expenditure on education as proportion of total public capital expenditure*

	Per cent 1962–8	1970–4	1975–80
Planned	10.3	13.5	7.5
Actual	8.5	11.0	
N p. head, approx. p.a.	0.2 (actual)	1.4 (actual)	4.2 (planned)

Source: Second and Third National Development Plans.

expected that virtually universal primary education will be achieved by 1985. The speed of the expansion in primary education has been associated with very severe quality problems: primary school enrolments rose from about 3.5 million in 1970 to 9.5 million in 1977–8. An estimated 170–180 000 primary school teachers are unqualified, or about two-thirds of the total number of teachers. High rates of absenteeism and drop-outs are recorded; an average drop-out rate between Grades I and II was estimated to be 27 per cent, with considerable variations among the states.[50]

Secondary education which currently serves only a minority of the age group (around one quarter) has also expanded rapidly in recent years, from 380 000 pupils in 1970 to an estimated 854 000 in 1976–7. A further massive expansion will be required over the next decade following UPE if the targeted transition rate from primary to secondary education of 40 per cent is to be reached.[51]

The present state of education among the adult population in Nigeria reflects the extremely low levels of (Western) education available to the population in the past. Overall 60 per cent of the adult population is estimated to be totally illiterate, while a further 20 per cent are semi-literate or literate only in the Arabic script.[52] There are marked imbalances in educational levels between the sexes and regionally.

Surveys in the late 1960s showed that 23 per cent of adult males and 58 per cent of adult females in Lagos had received *no* education, compared with 46 per cent of males, 63 per cent of females in Ife and 71 per cent males, 92 per cent females in Oyo.[53] In a village survey in the north[54] only 5.5 per cent of the sample of males had attended elementary school, although 93 per cent had attended Koranic school. Whilst UPE may eventually eliminate much of the imbalance in primary school access, quality differences and differences in parental support are likely to persist.[55]

Imbalance in educational levels between the sexes tends to follow regional imbalances being greatest where access is most deficient. In Kano, which is an educationally deprived area, for example, girls formed only one quarter of the primary school population and 18 per cent of the (general) secondary school population in 1973, whereas in Lagos, where universal primary education is more or less a fact, girls accounted for half the primary and 44 per cent of the secondary school population.

The very low level of female education in the north is due to a combination of economic, cultural and religious factors. However, surveys of attitudes[56] show a very strong support for universal primary education here as elsewhere. But in practice it is reported that males outnumber females even in primary schools by about 2:1,[57] while the difficulties associated with the introduction of UPE have been greatest in the north. Seventy per cent of teachers are estimated to be untrained.[58] High rates of absenteeism are reported. One study found absenteeism as high as 60–70 per cent during peak farming months.[59]

Adult education

Adults in Nigeria, especially women, have been largely left out of the educational system. Yet expenditure on adult education is very low – receiving about 2 per cent of capital expenditure on education – so that 'there is little by way of infrastructure or curricula from which to develop, or suitable teaching materials, and there are few adequately trained personnel.' (*Blueprint*, p. 113.)

Content of education

The content of education is highly relevant to the question of how successfully the basic need for education is being met. This is true whether education is regarded as an important objective in itself, or as instrumental in achieving other objectives. From both points of view, a few years of schooling with little relevance to the rest of a person's life may make little positive contribution. From an instrumental point of view, education needs to be related to work-life and to the better fulfilment of BN. In Nigeria there is some BN content to primary education – i.e. education on health and hygiene and nutrition – although more could be done as indicated by the special Child to Child programme organised in Lagos.[60] Moreover, more or less irrespective of the content, formal education, especially of women, does seem to lead to quite marked improvements in family health.[61] These effects may flow from the different orientation that formal education bestows. Formal primary education also provides an essential stepping stone to modern sector activity. But the 'vocational' content of education for those who will work in agriculture or many parts of the informal sector is very deficient.

SUMMARY OF FINDINGS ON THE STATE OF BASIC NEEDS PERFORMANCE IN NIGERIA

Despite the dearth of good statistics, enough can be deduced to be confident about the broad picture of BN in Nigeria. All the indicators of health – life expectancy, infant mortality and morbidity – show a very poor state of health among most Nigerians.

Nigerian health compares badly with some other African countries such as Kenya and Tanzania whose per capita income is significantly lower. All studies of nutrition in Nigeria suggest that Nigeria is on the margin of suffering a protein and calory deficiency *on average*. Such an average situation, suggests that there must be many people suffering from malnutrition, some of severe proportions. This is borne out by more micro-studies. Food production appears not to have kept pace with population increase during the past fifteen years or so; nutrition certainly has not improved over this period; the most optimistic interpretation of the figures is that nutritional standards have not deteriorated. Educational achievements among the adult population are very poor, with perhaps as few as 10 per cent literate. But education has expanded rapidly recently and among the young achievements are much greater.

The education sector is the one BN sector which has received substantial resources in recent years. Nigeria has spent rather little on health in relation to her income; within the health sector there has been a strong bias towards curative medicine and towards the urban areas. The Guidelines to the Fourth Plan conclude that only 25 per cent of the rural population is covered by medical services. Water has received a negligible quantity of funds; throughout Nigeria water supplies are very poor in both quantity and quality.

7 A Macro Approach to Basic Needs in Nigeria

The BN of any economy is dependent on the macro-setting. Achievements in relation to particular BN and performance in the individual BN-sectors, as described in the last chapter, cannot be understood separately from it, nor can policy measures be properly devised without understanding the macro-context. Earlier, Chapter 2 suggested the need for a framework that would encompass three aspects: a production aspect describing resource allocation at the macro-level; an organisational aspect showing the organisational form in which this resource allocation takes place; and an incomes aspect describing the determinants of the distribution of income and of basic needs consumption among households.

The production and organisational aspects deal with the supply of BN-goods. The level of consumption also depends on demand. The incomes aspect of a BN-approach shows how the level and distribution of incomes in economy – together with consumption propensities – determine the level and distribution of some BN-goods.

Together the three aspects of a macro-framework trace the major determinants of consumption of BN-goods. But actual achievements in relation to the major BN objectives are not so much a matter of the consumption of certain amounts of particular goods and services but the way in which such consumption improves the lives of individuals in terms of their physical health and their mental capacities. Thus the approach requires one to go a step further from the actual consumption of a particular bundle of goods to the effects such consumption has on the ultimate objectives of a fuller life. This additional step – which applies to each of the approaches – we have described as the 'meta-production function', which relates the consumption of BN-items to improvement in the quality of life.

The aim of this chapter is to try to apply such a framework to the Nigerian situation, however, limitations of time and data have prevented the complete development of such a framework for Nigeria. In particular, while it has been possible to look at BN in Nigeria from the point of view of production and of incomes, the organisational framework is limited to qualitative presentation.

While there are departures from the theoretical model and other omissions and deficiencies, the macro-analysis, as it stands and with all the limitations, does achieve its main objective – of permitting an identification of the major obstacles to BN-achievement and of the main changes required.

PRODUCTION

The four most important BN-sectors are those producing food, water supplies, education and health services. Domestic production of these sectors plus net imports gives the availability of BN-goods, from the point of view of production.

Table 7.1 shows the proportion of GDP devoted to the four main BN sectors and net imports of agriculture products. It is assumed that agriculture production plus net imports provides some indication of food availability – to the extent that agriculture production goes to production of raw materials for domestic industrial processing, these figures will overstate food availability.[1] It is assumed that there is no trade in health, education or water services.

Between 1965 and 1975,[2] there was a marked drop in the proportion of GDP arising in agriculture, from nearly half to under one quarter of GDP. The effect on food availability was less marked than this because of the decline in exports and the growth in food imports, but this only alters the position slightly. The other sectors maintained their share of GDP (while education dropped its share at current prices, it rose in constant prices). However the total share of these sectors was low, with education around 3 per cent, health services under 1 per cent, and water 0.1 per cent. Table 7.2 shows the trends

A Macro Approach to Basic Needs in Nigeria

TABLE 7.1 *Production in BN-sectors: as % GDP, current factor cost*

		1965–6	1970–1	1975–6
1.	Agriculture, livestock and fishing	49.6	41.3	24.4
2.	Water supply	0.1	0.1	n.a.
3.	Education	3.2	2.9	2.2
	(Universities)	(0.3)	(0.4)	
4.	Health	0.8	0.8	0.9
5.	TOTAL	53.7	45.1	27.5
6.	Net imports of agricultural products	−3.3	−2.7	+0.5
7.	Agriculture, forestry, fishing plus net imports	46.3	38.6	24.9
8.	TOTAL plus net agricultural imports	50.4	42.4	28.0

Source: *Annual Abstract of Statistics* 1975, table 8.2 *Economic Indicators*, Vol. 13, nos. 1–6, June 1977, table 10.1

in availability of these BN-goods. On these figures, and assuming a population growth of 2.7 per cent per annum,[3] food availability per capita *fell by nearly one quarter* between 1965 and 1975, despite the fact the GDP per head rose by nearly one half during the same period. Education and health services (at constant prices) rose more rapidly than GDP per capita.

TABLE 7.2

Index of	1965–6	1970–1	1975–6
1. Food availability*	100	110.0	100.4
2. Education services	100	137.2	241.0
3. Health services	100	152.9	261.8
4. Population**	100	114.3	130.5
	Per capita		
5. Food	100	96.2	76.9
6. Education services	100	120.0	184.7
7. Health services	100	152.8	261.8
8. GDP	100	131.1	148.6

* index of value-added in agriculture, livestock and fishing plus net imports at 1962–3 prices.
** assuming growth in population at 2.7% per annum.

There is considerable doubt about the reliability of the figures for agricultural production. It is generally agreed that official figures understate total production, probably to a greater extent towards the end of the period. Hence the real drop in food availability per head was almost certainly less than that shown in Table 7.2. But the sharp rise in food prices over this period suggests that food supplies did not keep pace with demand. While the per capita drop was probably not as great as shown, it is very unlikely that there was any rise; the most 'optimistic' view would be that food availability remained constant, and this at a time when real GDP per capita was rising rapidly.

Table 7.3 estimates the absolute per capita availability of BN-goods compared with other items in GDP for 1975–6. At around ₦80, estimated food consumption per capita accounts for about 40 per cent of total private consumption.[4] Current expenditure on education,

TABLE 7.3 *Disposal of national income 1975–6*

		Value per capita ₦	%
1.	GDP per capita of which:	324	100
2.	Private consumption	203	62.5
	– food per capita	83[a]	25.6
3.	Government final consumption	34	10.4
	– Education services[b]	5 (7)	1.5 (2.2)
	– Health[b]	2 (3)	0.6 (0.9)
	– Water[c]	0.3	0.1
4.	Gross fixed investment	77	23.7
5.	Increase in stocks	7	2.3
6.	Net exports	5	1.6
7.	Total 'Basic Needs'[b]	90.3 (93.3)	27.8 (28.8)

Sources: Ittah: 'National Accounts of Nigeria' (1980)
Economic Indicators, June 1977, table 10.1;
Annual Abstract of Statistics, 1975, table 13.1.

[a] Value of agriculture, livestock + fishing output + net imports of food per capita.
[b] Value of education and health services (unbracketed) are those given in table 10.1, *Economic Indicators*. In new (supplied figures) this category is omitted. Bracketed figures show value if *Economic Indicator* figures are revised upwards in line with upward movement in GDP estimates.
[c] No values given for 1975/6. This value is same proportion of GDP as in 1973/4 according to *Annual Abstract*, table 13.

health and water services formed between 20 and 30 per cent of total government final consumption expenditure.

Table 7.4 shows past, actual and planned allocation of investment resources. Agriculture received a very low proportion of investment compared with its share of total gainful employment and GDP. In 1975, it is estimated that agriculture accounted for 65 per cent of gainful employment and nearly a quarter of GDP; between 1970–4 it accounted for 10 per cent of public investment; the Third National Plan allocated 8 per cent of total investment to agriculture (of which 48 per cent was to come from the private sector). In contrast, education received a substantially higher proportion of investment (both actual 1970–4 and planned 1975–80) than its share of output indicating that the share of education in GDP is likely to rise. Investment in health services was also a bit higher than its share of GDP, but was still only 1.7 per cent of gross capital formation in the 1975–80 Plan. Together the BN-sectors accounted for 25.7 per cent of public investment, 1970–4 and 15 per cent of total planned investment between 1975–80.

These production figures show the total output and investment in each of the sectors; but by no means 100 per cent of the output of each sector goes towards the fulfilment of BN. Where the output goes to people whose standards already exceed some defined minimum, then they do not contribute to the achievement of BN. For example, water supplies devoted to filling the swimming pools of the rich; or expensive curative medical care; or higher education. All these may contribute to someone's welfare, but they should not be defined as BN. Partly it is a question of the same sectors (e.g. health) producing other types of services as well as BN ones; partly of the distribution of the BN-type goods and services with some consumers receiving more than their minimum needs and others less. Where it is a question of different types of goods and services, proper accounting would exclude these from the BN-sectors; but where it is a question of distribution, then they should be included in the BN-production statistics and their distribution discussed separately. However, in practice it is difficult to draw the line between the two, and there is a dearth of sufficiently disaggregated data.

The earlier discussion of the health services showed that less than 30 per cent of capital expenditure on health in Nigeria was devoted to primary health care (1975–80); in education a similar proportion (30 per cent) of total expenditure goes to primary education. While in both sectors other services also make a contribution to BN, we would

TABLE 7.4 *Gross fixed capital formation sectoral distribution, per cent*

	Actual, 1970–4 Public sector	Planned, 1975–80 Public	Private	Total	1975 Share Employment	GDP
1. Agriculture, forestry and fishing	9.7	6.5	12.0	8.3	64.0	27.6
2. Mining and quarrying	0.9	7.0	11.0	8.3	0.4	31.5
3. Manufacturing and crafts	3.9*	19.0	20.0	19.3	16.8	11.5
4. Electricity and water	10.8*	5.0	—	3.3	0.1	0.5
5. Buildings and construction	n.a.	n.a.	27.0	9.0	0.9	5.8
6. Distribution	2.5*	0.5	14.0	5.0	12.2	11.3
7. Transport and communication	25.5	27.5	5.0	20.0	0.6	3.4
8. General government	21.3	15.0	—	10.0		7.1
9. Education	11.0	7.5	n.a.	5.0	5.0	2.2
10. Health	5.0	2.0	1.0	1.7		0.9
11. Other services	10.3	10.0	10.0	10.0		1.7

Share of public in total investment = $\dfrac{2}{3}$

Source: Third National Development Plan, 1975–80, table 2.11, 5.10.
*Some of the classification differs for 1970–4 from that given: hence the division is somewhat arbitrary

A Macro Approach to Basic Needs in Nigeria 137

be safe to conclude that less than half of the total production is of BN-type in both sectors.

This brief analysis of production of BN-goods in Nigeria suggests the following conclusions:

1. A poor performance on availability of food – at the very best no increase per head at a time of rapid growth in GDP.
2. Low level of expenditure on education, health and water. Expenditure on water services was almost negligible in the ten years preceding 1975, while expenditure on health was well below that of countries with equally low average incomes.
3. The trends in investment (past and planned) gave continued low priority to agriculture and to health; but investment expenditure on education (at 5 per cent of gross fixed investment 1975–80) was at a more substantial level.
4. The low proportion of private consumption accounted for by food, and of public consumption by health, education and water, show that substantially greater BN-achievement could be realised by reallocation within these totals, without affecting the overall investment rate.

'Productivity' aspects

From a dynamic point of view, an important link in the production framework is the way in which improvements in BN increase the economy's productive capacity and hence its ability to produce goods in the next period. While common sense suggests that improved health and education would add to the productivity of the workforce, it is difficult to establish concrete evidence of the relationship. In Nigeria it was not possible to find evidence on the health/productivity link, but there is more evidence on the relationship between education and productivity. At a macro-level it is clear that shortages of trained manpower are in part a constraint on the growth of the economy and in part on the rate of indigenisation possible. According to Ozgediz: 'There is little question that the unavailability of skilled manpower in sufficient quantities across the country constitutes one of the most binding constraints to Nigeria's development.'[5] Within the basic needs sectors shortages of the right sort of manpower are a major factor slowing down expansion and reducing the quantity/quality of the output.[6] In the education sector itself the very large numbers of untrained teachers are one example. In health, shortages of auxiliary health workers are an important constraint on the development of primary health care. In agriculture, there is a major deficiency of extension workers. Thus the education sector has a large role to play in the provision of BN.

In addition to the training of specialised workers, the education sector influences the aspirations and productivity of the workforce in general. It is widely believed that the spread of primary education in Nigeria influences aspirations, turning students against agriculture and towards further education or modern sector urban employment. Although there is little systematic evidence on this, which in any case may change as primary education becomes universal, it is the firm view of everyone asked about it.[7] This effect on aspirations could be of critical importance to the development of the Nigerian economy and the fulfilment of BN. The relative failure of agriculture in recent years – in part due to the movement of labour, especially the young and dynamic, away from the agricultural sector – has been responsible for the stagnation in per capita food availability. It is not just a question of education-induced aspirations; income earning opportunities in agriculture are also important. But given the necessity for a rapid expansion in agriculture it is important that the achievement of universal primary education does not herald a stampede out of agriculture, but rather lays the foundation for higher incomes and productivity in agriculture.

The few systematic studies that have been conducted give conflicting evidence as to the contribution of education to agricultural productivity; the most positive effects are shown for functional adult literacy programmes. For example, the Nigerian Tobacco Company introduced a functional literacy programme in Bendel State which was associated with adoption of improved farming practices and increases in productivity. But it is difficult in this case to distinguish the effects of literacy as against the other changes which were simultaneously introduced. Some of the studies of innovation in agriculture have not found education of the farmers to be a significant factor.[8] But others have found education and/or literacy to be a significant variable explaining adoption of recommended practices.[9]

One study found that education of the farmers was one of the factors associated with contact with extension workers, while knowledge of modern cocoa farming practices was significantly greater among those with high contact with extension services.[10] Another study established extension workers as a major source of information.[11] Thus the (limited) evidence from micro-studies is somewhat conflicting: it does not show that primary education is an important determinant of agricultural productivity in Nigeria, while as far as the agricultural sector is concerned it tends to have a negative effect on aspirations.

These studies look at education as such, irrespective of its content. In general, there is virtually no agricultural content to primary education in Nigeria. More 'vocational' education might have more marked effects.

ORGANISATION AND BASIC NEEDS

Identification of the organisation of production of BN-sectors is important in determining appropriate interventions. Figure 7.1 below describes the main organisational features of the BN-sectors in Nigeria. Organisational responsibility is divided mainly between the state (at various levels) and the household sector, with the large-scale 'formal' private sector playing an insignificant role. In food production the household sector is dominant, with the state of significance in providing infrastructure, subsidising inputs, credit, etc. In the remaining sectors, the state is the major source of modern services, but their activities are quite substantially supplemented by traditional activities of the household.

Within the public sector, formal financial and organisational responsibility varies between the sectors and also according to the level of services. Although in many cases the Federal Government takes the major financial responsibility, in many areas state initiative and support is essential for effective action.

The role of women

Within the household the role of women is quite distinct from men in their role as *producers* of BN. (Their role as consumers of BN is discussed below). The precise sexual division of labour varies quite markedly across the country. In the Muslim north women play only a minor role in agricultural production. For example, a survey of occupational patterns among the Hausa in Northern Nigeria[12] found *no* cases of farming being a 'first' or 'second' occupation. But women did help their husbands pick peppers, groundnuts and cowpeas, and also in other farming occupations. Village studies of farm labour

FIGURE 7.1 Organisation of production of basic needs

Oranisational alternatives	BN sectors: Health services	Education services	Water sanitation	Food
Private sector				
Foreign	Drug supplies	—	—	Inputs; being encouraged to enter production
Large scale, local 'formal'	Some, not in basic health; chemists	Some	—	Small
Public sector				
Federal	Major responsibility Curative (hospitals)	Major responsibility	Major responsibility	Provides infrastructure fertiliser, credit, etc. extension
State	Preventive	Higher	⎱ Main responsibility	
Local govt.	Preventive Rural clinics	Secondary Primary	⎰	
Foreign	—	—	—	Increasing role organising production and providing finance, esp. World Bank
Household sector				
Men	Traditional healers Informal sector chemists	'Koranic' schools, traditional education	Organise distribution in informal urban sector	Most significant element in production
Women	Traditional and household remedies	Informal education esp. of girls	Fetch water	Some production. Most marketing
Co-operatives	—	—	—	Active in marketing

show that women contribute less than 2 per cent to total hours[13] in Hausaland. Elsewhere in Nigeria women play a more active role in farming. Berry found that in one cocoa producing area in Western Nigeria, 20 per cent of women's main occupation was farming; in another area, where farming was not listed a major occupation nearly all the women said they helped their husbands with farm work.[14] In general in Western Nigeria women play a more active role in farming than in the north, but still a generally subsidiary one.[15] Throughout Nigeria, women play a dominant part in food processing, cooking (often for sale) and have a very significant trading role.[16] Preparing food for sale and other food processing accounted for 65 per cent of the 'first occupation' of Hausa women, while trading accounted for a further 10 per cent.[17]

Co-operatives

There is a long (and checkered) history of co-operatives in Nigeria. In 1970 there were nearly 8000 separate societies with nearly half a million members.[18] They handle a considerable share of the marketing of agricultural produce. Under the 'Operation-Feed-the-Nation' programme introduced in 1976 a number of states encouraged co-operatives to provide storage for food to prevent seasonal scarcities. Co-operatives also play a part in credit and banking. In places they have launched adult literacy programmes; in others they have built clinics and hospitals.[19] Women's co-operatives give credit, advice and support to women's trading activities.[20]

Appropriate BN-interventions are clearly dependent on the dominant form of organisation; in so far as women play a dominant role, interventions aimed primarily at men will be ineffective; where peasant agriculture dominates, interventions whose effects are confined to the large scale and the 'progressive'[21] may increase production, but do little to raise the consumption of those whose BN-standards are most deficient. The form of organisation influences the distributional consequences of BN-production: for example, credit institutions which successfully steer credit to the poorest farmers may succeed in raising food production *and* incomes and consumption of those most in need. In contrast, where credit is channelled to large farmers, production may increase but BN-satisfaction may be unaffected because those most in need do not increase their production or incomes. Indeed in extreme situations, the additional production from the large scale may actually depress incomes among the poorest. Similarly for publicly provided services, the organisational form often influences the distribution. Co-operatives tend to be thought of as distributionally beneficial. Yet a study in Nigeria has shown that they are often dominated by local élites and their major benefits monopolised by them.[22] Consequently, they do little to change the initial distribution of income and power, although if they raise incomes (even if mainly of the relatively well-off) in very poor areas, they may improve BN.

While this has only been a very sketchy summary of organisational forms in Nigeria, it suggests certain (tentative) conclusions:
1. The distinction between production and income distribution can only be maintained up to a certain point because *how* extra production is organised determines *who* benefits and consequently the effects on BN.
2. In Nigeria in BN the dominant organisational forms are the public sector and the household.
3. Within the household it is necessary to differentiate between men and women – this conclusion is substantially strengthened by the discussion below of the different roles of men and women as consumers of BN-services. Within the public sector it is necessary to distinguish between levels of government.

INCOMES AND BASIC NEEDS

The level of real income among households determines their ability to buy those BN-goods which are marketed – notably food. Whatever the availability of such BN-goods, households must have enough income to acquire adequate quantities. Moreover, many of the non-marketed BN-goods (such as education and health services) involve quite heavy indirect expenses on the part of their consumers (for example, costs of school uniforms, opportunity cost of child labour), so that the ability to acquire non-marketed BN-goods also depends on the level of real incomes among households. Thus while production and availability of BN-goods is a necessary condition, the need for a sufficient level of income among poor households is critical to BN-achievements. The same production situation may be associated with a very different situation in relation to BN according to the distribution of the BN-goods and services. For marketed BN-goods, this distribution depends largely on the distribution of incomes. But the actual minimum level of income necessary to ensure that any specified BN-target is achieved (for example, a minimum calorie consumption per capita), depends not only on income and price levels, but also consumption patterns (i.e. how much of any income, households spend on BN).

In Nigeria, food is the main marketed BN-good and we shall concentrate discussion on this item. However, two elements in the Nigerian situation make the sharp distinction between production, incomes and consumption rather misleading. First, there is a large subsistence element in agricultural production. The 1975 household survey showed 'production for own consumption' to be 12 per cent of *total* rural incomes; production for own consumption together with income in kind was equivalent to 30 per cent of total cash expenditure on food among rural households. Matlon's study of three villages in Northern Nigeria found that, on average, 53 per cent of income per household was converted into cash, in one form or another. The subsistence element means that any measures which affect production may also affect consumption. But this subsistence element – however large – may not be as important as it appears in determining consumption patterns since farms of all sizes appear to participate in the cash economy (producing cash crops and buying food), while all farms have quite substantial sources of non-farm income.[23] Of greater significance is the very heavy dependence of the rural economy on agricultural output as a source – direct or indirect – of income. This dependence means that the level of rural incomes is directly related to the level of food production (for any given level of prices). Thus the determinants of the production of this major BN-item is also a major determinant of levels of income among rural households. As we shall see, the factors which depressed agricultural production have also depressed rural incomes. Consequently, because of the coincidence the production of a major BN-item – food – is also the source of income for the majority of the poor, the sharp distinction between production/availability of BN-goods, and the generation of adequate incomes turns out to be false for food and agricultural incomes in Nigeria.

As far as achievement of BN is concerned, it is the level of incomes among those whose consumption of BN-items is at or below what is considered to be the desirable minimum that are relevant. In Nigeria, where *average* nutrition standards are probably below the FAO determined minimum, and where per capita food availability has been falling, the relevant income categories include as much as 60 per cent of the population. But the bottom 60 per cent is a highly differentiated group: while standards of all may in some sense be inadequate, BN-deficiencies are likely to be much greater among some groups than others. Hence ideally one needs a detailed analysis of trends in real income and consumption among different groups. In aggregate terms, per capita incomes rose by around 3 per cent per annum in the 1960s, and by about 4½ per cent per annum in the 1970s. Evidence for income distribution is weak and scattered. But all observers agree that by any of the usual measures of inequality, income distribution was getting more unequal over this period, and is now quite markedly unequal, with a Gini co-efficient of around 0.6.[24] However, detailed evidence for changes in household income distribution over time is non-existent, and while there is agreement about trends there is not enough reliable evidence about actual shares over time to use this approach for deriving trends in incomes among the lower 60 per cent. In any case, from an analytic and policy point of view it is more helpful to analyse trends in income of particular categories, rather than changes in aggregate household income distribution.

Sectoral income distribution

Incomes among households are derived from their activities in different sectors: the sectoral division of national output, combined with information about the numbers gaining their incomes from the different sectors, thus shows average incomes in each sector. Moreover, since those in the rural areas are primarily engaged in agriculture while those in the urban areas are mainly outside agriculture, the ratio of incomes per head in agriculture to those in non-agriculture gives a first approximation to rural–urban incomes. To find the distribution of income among households – and particularly the income levels among the lower 60 per cent of the population – two further steps are necessary: first to amend this ratio to allow for non-agricultural sources of income in the rural areas, and agricultural income in the urban areas; secondly, to consider the distribution of income *within* the rural and urban areas.

Table 7.5 estimates urban and rural incomes per capita for 1977–8. On the assumptions in that table, rural per capita income was ₦199 compared with ₦694 for urban areas excluding petroleum, and ₦1017 including petroleum. (It probably makes more sense at this stage to exclude petroleum since the income is highly concentrated in the first

TABLE 7.5 *Rural–urban income levels*

Rural	1977–8
1. Income from agriculture, forestry, fishing (₦m)	7 474
2. Assumed non-agricultural income (30%) ₦m	2 242
3. Total rural income (₦m)	9 716
4. Nos. in rural areas (m)	48.8
5. Income per head in rural areas, ₦	199
Urban	
6. GDP minus agriculture, forestry and fishing, excluding petroleum ₦m	17 447
7. Assumed rural share ₦m (see 2, above)	2 242
8. Urban income excluding petroleum ₦m	15 205
9. Urban income, including petroleum ₦m	22 276
10. Nos. in urban areas (m)	21.9
11. Income per head excluding petroleum in urban areas	694
12. Income per head including petroleum in urban areas	1 017

Source: Ittah (1980).
Notes
Non-agricultural income has been *assumed* to be 30% of total income. Village studies show non-agricultural incomes to amount to between 20 and 30% of agricultural incomes.
Population is assumed to be 70.75m with 69% rural, 31% urban.

instance, going to a very small number of employees, to various companies, local and foreign, and to the government).

There are marked differences in prices paid by rural and urban consumers particularly for food, but also for rent, transport, etc. One study of Northern Nigeria shows marketing margins for food of 43 per cent for sorghum and 47 per cent for millet.[25] A comparison of urban and rural wholesale prices showed that for six major food items the price differential was 40 to 60 per cent.[26] If we adjust urban incomes downwards by one-third to allow for this price differential we get urban income per capita of ₦463, or a ratio of 2.3 for urban to rural per capita incomes, excluding petroleum.[27]

These estimates depend on all sorts of unknowns, including the size of the population, its division between rural and urban areas, price differentials between rural and urban areas, the size of non-agricultural rural income as well as the real value of agricultural production. If agricultural production were understated in the official figures by, for example, 20 per cent, then rural per capita incomes would be just half of those of urban incomes. On the other hand, if the ratio of rural to urban population is 75:25, then the urban–rural per capita income ratio would be 3:1, with rural incomes per capita at ₦183, and adjusted urban incomes at ₦573. However, the estimated rural–urban differential is in line with the results of the 1975 *Household Income and Expenditure Survey* which showed an average differential per household of about two.

Income distribution within the rural areas

There are differences in per capita incomes between different regions and within regions. There are no recent estimates for GDP by State. Figures for 1965[28] are shown in column (1) of Table 7.6. But these figures include the urban areas, and a good deal of the difference in per capita incomes between regions is due to differences in incomes between the urban and the rural areas, not differences in rural incomes. This is illustrated by the figures in column (6) of Table 7.6 which show what per capita incomes in different areas would have been if the only source of differential were the urban–rural income differential, and per capita urban incomes were two and a half times rural incomes throughout the country. The similarity in ordering between the figures in column (1) and column (6) suggests that differences in average income per head among the *rural* population are much smaller than those shown on a regional basis. There are a number of other indicators of differences between regions/States, some of them much more up to date than the Teriba–Phillips figures. But they all fail to separate urban from rural population: thus, while they are valuable as indicators of regional inequalities, they do not tell us much about disparities between rural incomes in different regions. In Usoro's travels around Nigeria in 1974, he found areas of acute poverty, but these were widely distributed throughout the country.

There have been a number of micro-studies showing income distribution in particular areas.[29] In general they find rather equal distribution of both income and land, as compared with the situation in many other countries. On the whole, agricultural incomes are distributed more equally than land; off-farm activities tend to have an inegalitarian effect, being higher among those whose agricultural

TABLE 7.6 *Regional disparities, 1965*

	(1) GDP per capita by regions 1965	(2) Share of manufacturing employment 1964 %	(3) Estimated population 1963 m.	(4) Estimated urban population m.	(5) Estimated rural population m	(6) Per capita income assuming urban income = 2.5 × rural
Northern	100	22.3	28.9	2.5	26.4	100
Eastern	105	21.4	12.4	2.4	10.0	114
Western	132	19.9	10.3	2.2	8.1	129
Mid-Western	163	12.2	2.5	1.4	1.1	132
Federal territory of Lagos	647	24.1	0.7	2.9	—	163
TOTAL	116					

Source: Teriba and Phillips (1971). cols (1), (2), (3). Remainder are estimates.

incomes are higher. In Matlon's study, female earnings had a markedly equalising effect.[30] Studies of cocoa production in the west show more inequality than studies of agriculture in the north. Studies conducted between 1966 and 1975 in the Northern states of Kano, Sokoto and Kaduna found that the bottom 40 per cent of the residents/households accounted for between 11 and 34 per cent of the total income – most between 20 and 30 per cent. The top 10 per cent of households/residents accounted for between 11 and 52 per cent with something near 20 per cent being typical. Studies on the earnings of cocoa producers in Ondo, Oyo and Ogun States conducted between 1948 and 1969 showed that the bottom 40 per cent accounted for between 6 and 14 per cent of total earnings, while the top 10 per cent accounted for 31 to 60 per cent of the total.[31]

Studies of land distribution among cocoa growers around 1950 showed a marked degree of inequality, with 40 per cent of the farmers holding only 10 per cent of the land, and the top 10 per cent holding 40 per cent of the land. But over the next two decades there seems to have been some reduction in inequality in land holding in the cocoa area. In contrast, in the north some of the early studies showed relatively little inequality in land holding – with the poorest two-thirds of the households holding at least one-third of the land; a significant part of this inequality was due to differences in size of household. But in the north it appears inequality has been increasing over time. In studies in the 1970s, the bottom 40 per cent of the farmers hold between 6 and 15 per cent of the land, and the top 10 per cent between 32 per cent and 40 per cent.[32]

In general it appears that the distribution of land is less unequal than the distribution of earnings. This is borne out by individual village studies showing that part of the differences in earnings are due to differences in the quality of land and part to differences in labour-input.[33]

Table 7.7 shows the level of income among different rural groups, based on assumptions derived from these micro-studies. It is assumed that average incomes in the cocoa producing areas are above those of the Northern farmers. However, because of the greater inequality in the cocoa areas, the average incomes of the lower 40% are substantially below those in the north.

Urban income distribution

The distribution of income in the urban areas is far more unequal than that in the rural areas. In the formal sector, the wage and salary

TABLE 7.7 *Hypothesised level of income in rural areas, 1977*

	Per Capita income	
	North	Cocoa production (West)
Average	175₦	250₦
Share of bottom 40%	20%	10%
Share of top 10%	20%	40%
Average income of bottom 40%	88₦	62₦
Average income of top 10%	350₦	1,000₦
Average income of middle 50%	210₦	250₦

Source: Guesstimates based on microstudies and calculations of average rural income (Table 7.5).

bill forms about 26 per cent of value added. Among wage and salary earners there are large differentials according to size of establishment (establishments of 500 plus pay 3.4 times average earnings of establishments of 10–19),[34] skill and education,[35] (the average incomes of those with primary education is 1.7 times those with no education, workers with secondary education earn 2.7 times those of illiterates and university graduates earn 12 times those with no education; the skill differential among public sector employees between the highest and lowest was 10:1 in 1975).[36] Earnings in the informal sector, which is estimated to account for about 70 per cent of the urban population, are in general well below those of the formal sector: in 1975 the low income self-employed had an average income of 62 per cent of the *lowest* paid workers in the formal sectors.[37] However, this may not allow for under-recording of informal sector earnings. Bienen and Diejomaoh (1981) give the following differentials among various urban groups:

Market traders:	1	Informal sector
Street traders:	2	
Shop keepers:	3.3	

| Skilled and unskilled workers: | 3.2 | Formal sector |
| Clerical workers: | 5 | |

150 Planning to Meet Basic Needs

The *Household Income and Expenditure Survey* gave the following distribution of income:

TABLE 7.8 *Average monthly income of urban household*

Wage earners	N per month 1974	1975	% of households 1974	1975
Lower	110.7	119.7	33.2	27.8
Middle	276.6	251.3	4.9	9.7
Upper	491.9	578.7	3.4	3.0
Self-employed				
Lower	66.7	74.7	52.8	52.7
Middle	288.6	262.7	3.6	5.0
Upper	653.5	682.7	2.1	1.8

Source: Tables 2.2 and 2.4, Aboyade and Sipasi, in O. Aboyade (1979) Vol. II.

Since 1974–5 average wages have risen by 20 per cent. Thus we can assume that incomes in 1978–9 were roughly 20 per cent above those shown.[38]

Basic needs minimum income

The minimum income necessary to meet basic needs in food depends on the particular standards set, the price of foods and household consumption habits as to the proportion of income spent on food, the nature of the foods, and distribution of food within the household. Because the standards are somewhat arbitrary and because of lack of knowledge about the other factors, any conclusions are inevitably tentative but it is worth trying to make approximate guesses.

Two independent estimates of the cost of an adequate (by FAO standards) diet in Nigeria came to very similar conclusions. One estimated the monthly cost for a household of 5.6 as ₦80 for Lagos and ₦66 for Kano.[39] Another[40] showed a range according to the nature of the diet selected. An intermediate quality diet costs ₦83 in Lagos and ₦79 in Kano.

TABLE 7.9 *Caloric composition and cost of a basic daily diet per capita and by cities, 1978*

	Lagos		Port Harcourt		Ilorin		Kano	
	Calories (%)	Cost (Kobo)	Calories (%)	Cost (Kobo)	Calories (%)	Cost (Kobo)	Calories (%)	Cost (Kobo)
Maize	7	1.46	7	2.04	14	2.36	—	—
Millet	—	—	—	—	3	0.56	40	9.42
Sorghum	—	—	—	—	25	4.39	35	6.85
Gari	60	16.23	50	8.62	20	5.14	—	—
Yam	5	4.48	16	13.23	20	11.58	—	—
Beans	2	0.87	8	4.15	—	—	5	1.46
Meat	2	7.18	—	—	2	5.23	5	16.46
Fish	3	9.45	5	20.39	2	7.80	—	—
Palm oil	15	5.13	10	2.86	10	3.57	10	3.06
Total	94	44.80	96	51.29	96	40.63	95	37.25
Adjusted	100	47.65	100	53.42	100	42.32	100	39.21
Cost per month per household (5.6) N		80.1		89.7		71.1		65.8
Jamal estimates, N		54–112						42–118

Sources: Rouis (1980), table 4.
Jamal, Background Paper for ILO Mission, 'Incomes, Inequality and Basic Needs'.

The 1974–5 Household survey showed the proportion of income spent on food as follows:

TABLE 7.10 *Expenditure on food and income in kind and consumption from own production as per cent of total income*

	1974	1975
Urban		
Wage earners		
Low	29.1	39.5
Middle	28.6	29.8
Upper	18.3	24.3
Self-employed		
Low	46.6	49.3
Middle	27.8	34.6
Upper	17.0	17.7
All urban	28.1	34.9
All rural	—	46.1
All households	—	42.5

Source: O. Aboyade and O.N. Sipasi, in O. Aboyade (1979) vol. II.

This data may be atypical, however, because of the large rise in real incomes among wage-earners in 1974 which may have resulted in a (temporary) decline in the proportion of income spent on food. Household surveys in Enugu, Kaduna and Sokoto/Gusau in the 1960s showed some poor households spending more on food as a proportion of income, as shown in Table 7.11.

A survey of three villages in the Sokoto area in 1967 found that 58.6 per cent of family income was spent on food. A survey of three villages near Zaria in 1970–1[41] found that 45.4 per cent of total expenditure (including imputed expenditure) was devoted to food, drink and tobacco. If we assume – on the basis of these surveys – that

TABLE 7.11 Per cent of total income spent on food

	Enugu 1961–2	Kaduna 1962–3	Sokoto/Gusau 1964–5
Households of:			
1. Low income wage earners			
under 150/- per month	43.1	64.0	69.3
150 – 249/11	36.3	38.7	46.7
250 – 349/11	30.6	31.9	44.4
350 – 449/11	24.6	25.4	39.6
2. Self-employed			
under 150/-	51.2	78.6	66.9
150 – 249/11	49.2	60.3	62.2
250 – 349/11	41.8	40.8	46.6
350 – 449/11	49.4	45.2	43.5
Average no. persons per household	3.9	3.4	5.1

Source: Urban Consumer Surveys, Kaduna and Enugu Sokoto/Gusau Federal Office of Statistics

the lowest income groups may spend around 60 per cent of their income on food, then using the estimates in Table 7.9 for cost per diet per family, a minimum family income of ₦134 (Lagos) and ₦110 (Kano) would be needed.

From Table 7.8 we see that the lower income households in the informal (self-employed) sector in the urban areas fall *well* below this income level, allowing for some increase in incomes since 1975. While varying the assumptions would obviously alter the results, this would be unlikely to alter the conclusion that most of the households in the lower income self-employed category, who together account for over 50 per cent of urban households, fall below the minimum necessary to meet adequate nutrition standards. The lower income wage-earners seem to fall just on the margin; for this group then the correctness of the assumptions is critical to any conclusions. Some households in this group (together accounting for a third of urban households) are likely to have inadequate incomes for BN in food – in particular those with below average incomes.

In the rural areas, per capita incomes among the bottom 40 per cent are hypothesised to be between 60 and 80₦ per annum (Table 7.7), Expressed as monthly income per household (of 5.6 members) this comes to 28₦ to 37₦, while monthly average income per household of the middle 50 per cent of the rural population comes to 98₦ to 116₦. Assuming that food prices among rural households are half those for urban households, it would appear that the lower 40 per cent of rural households have inadequate incomes to meet a basic needs minimum in food, while the middle 50 per cent are probably somewhat above the minimum.

TABLE 7.11 *Households with inadequate incomes to meet BN in food*

	Per cent of households	No. households	No. people
Rural	40	3.5m	19.5m
Urban	50	2.0m	11.0m
TOTAL	43.7	5.5m	30.5m

The operation of market forces – in the form of rural-urban migration – make it likely that the marginal groups in both rural and urban areas have similar real incomes, despite the differences in average incomes between the areas.[42] In both cases it appears that most of the bottom half of the income distribution have inadequate incomes for BN in food – this conclusion is in line with the nutritional evidence and the evidence on food production (see above). According to these calculations the income deficiency is quite substantial. An increase of the order of 50 per cent of real income among the lowest half of the income distribution would be needed to ensure adequate nutrition from an incomes point of view. But in both rural and urban areas *average* incomes are sufficient, which means that, in theory, adequate incomes for the bottom half could be achieved either by redistribution or by economic growth in which the bottom half of the population participates.

Past trends

Trends in the incomes of different groups over the recent past are of significance both in indicating how BN-fulfilment has been changing over time, and in suggesting likely directions in the future. In particular, for the future, it is important to know whether we can assume that those whose incomes are most inadequate will participate automatically in the general process of growth, or whether special interventions will be necessary.

Over recent years, there has has been a fairly steady and rapid growth in aggregate incomes. Between 1966–7 and 1975–6 GDP per head grew over 5 per cent per annum in real terms. But the poorest groups did not fully participate in this process of growth—as indicated by the rising Gini co-efficient over this period. However, the evidence for changes in real income among different groups is sparse.

In the rural areas, aggregate incomes depend on aggregate production (agricultural and non-agricultural), the movement of agricultural producer prices and other prices and the level of net remittances. Changes in per capita incomes also depend on changes in the size of the rural population. There is considerable uncertainty about the values of each of these variables at any one time, and changes over time.

The official statistics show that agricultural production grew at less than 1 per cent per annum in real terms during the 1970s; this was roughly in line with the growth in rural population, so that on these figures agricultural production per man remained roughly constant. It is widely believed that these figures understate total production; but it is certainly the case that agricultural production grew much slower than GDP as a whole. Non-agricultural rural incomes may have risen somewhat faster than incomes from agriculture as a result of the road building, commercial activity, etc. associated with the oil boom. It is assumed that rural non-agricultural incomes formed 25 per cent of agricultural incomes in 1963–4 rising to 30 per cent in 1977–8. Unless trends in agricultural production are substantially understated, it seems likely that on average rural incomes rose very slowly during this period. The evidence on urban–rural remittances is meagre. One study shows quite substantial net *rural–urban* remittances.[43] There is evidence of a number of particular rural projects financed by urban remittances;[44] evidence from expenditure surveys in cities in the 1960s shows that migrants remit from 3 to 10 per cent of total expenditure to relatives. Remittances thus might add 3–4 per cent to rural incomes.

Taking the GDP figures, estimating rural population, and deflating by the GDP price index, shows per capita income in the rural areas rising a bit between 1963–4 and 1970–1 and falling a bit up to 1977–8, as shown in Table 7.11. It seems unlikely that there was any very significant change in average per capita incomes in the rural areas.

Although particular projects have been associated with increased rural differentiation,[45] there is no evidence of any systematic increase in rural inequality. The incomes of the poorest, therefore, probably moved in line with average rural incomes. Thus absolute levels of rural poverty probably did not increase: and allowing for

TABLE 7.11 *Rural and urban incomes*

Rural	1963–4	1970–1	1977–8
Income from agriculture, forestry, and fishing Nm current prices	1 674	2 576	7 474
Non-agricultural income as % agricultural	25	27.5	30
Non-agricultural income N	419	708	2 242
Total rural income	2 093	3 284	9 716
Nos. in rural areas (m)	39.4	46.2	48.8
Income per head in rural areas, current prices, N	53.1	71.1	199
GDP price index	100	125.2	378.7
Income per head in rural areas, constant prices	53.1	56.8	52.5
Urban			
GDP less rural income, Nm	663	1 997	22 276
GDP less rural income and petroleum	634	1 507	15 205
Nos. in urban areas, m	9.6	12.8	21.9
Income per head urban areas excluding petroleum, N, current prices	66.0	117.7	694.3
Income per head excluding petroleum, constant prices, GDP index, N	66.0	94.0	183.3

Sources: *Economic Indicators*, June 1977, and Ittah (1980).

underestimation in the statistics, incomes of the poorest may have increased, at most by 1 or 2 per cent per annum.

Average urban incomes rose much faster than rural incomes, as illustrated in Table 7.12. The rise was very marked if one includes income from petroleum; however, the rise was accompanied by increased differentiation. The index of real wages among unskilled workers fluctuated enormously during this period, but over the period as a whole it remained broadly constant.

TABLE 7.12 Government minimum wage

	Money wage index	Price index for low income Lagos consumers	Real wage index
1960	100	100	100
1963	100	109	92
1966	132	127	104
1969	132	136	97
1972	172	181	95
1975	344	287	120
1976	344	343	100
1978 (April)	377	429	87
1979 (April)	377	469	80

Sources: 1960–76, A.J. Pearce (1979), p. 186; ILO (1978, 1979) technical paper 7B, table 49. The ILO table also includes lower paid workers in the (large-scale) private sector.

There is very little evidence on movements in real incomes in the informal sector. Given the substantial mobility of labour, and the very rapid growth of this sector, it seems unlikely that incomes per head among the lower income groups in the sector can have moved very far out of line with agricultural incomes or the wages of unskilled workers. Any very substantial and systematic deviation upwards, for example, would have attracted workers from unskilled wage earning and thus put upward pressure on the real wage, while any substantial downward deviation, compared with agricultural incomes, would have halted rural–urban migration.

Thus it seems probable that real incomes among the low-income groups – rural inhabitants as a whole, low-income informal sector, and unskilled workers – have risen very little, despite the high aggregate growth rate. That this is so is also indicated by the evidence on food consumption per capita over time (see discussion of nutrition in the last chapter).

Nigerian development appears to be a clear example of failed 'trickle down', although a special one because of the position of oil. On past trends, therefore, one cannot rely on growth alone to generate the rising incomes among the poor necessary for the achievement of basic needs.

The distributional effects of taxation and public expenditure

Taxation

With the massive expansion of revenue from oil, taxation has become of less significance as a source of revenue. Revenue from oil rose from 26.3 per cent of total revenue in 1970 to 75.6 per cent in 1977. Among Federal sources of revenue other than oil the most significant are import duties (12.7 per cent), and company taxation (6.6 per cent) in 1977–8. The States receive the bulk of their revenue from the Federal Government: in 1972 Federal sources accounted for 84.6 per cent of all States current revenue. Federal taxes other than oil amounted to 9 per cent of GDP.

Studies of the distributional incidence of taxation in Nigeria have been confined to the effects of the personal income tax – which in theory ought to be the most progressive of Nigeria's taxes. A study in the 1960s[46] found that 'inequity in the after-tax income distribution was not significantly different from the pre-tax situation'. Another study of two States found that personal income tax 'has little or no effect on the redistribution of income'.[47] Very substantial evasion was reported.[48] This study found that personal income tax accounted for less than 2 per cent of pre-tax incomes.

From this evidence, it appears that the present tax system in Nigeria does not significantly alter the distribution of incomes, so the earlier conclusions based on analysis of primary (pre-tax) incomes remain valid.

Public expenditure

Public expenditure as a proportion of GDP grew very dramatically in the 1970s, largely as a result of the oil revenue. The government budget excluding parastatals accounted for about 44 per cent of GNP in 1979. A systematic analysis of the distribution of the benefits of public expenditure in Nigeria in 1977–8 came to the following conclusions:[49]

1. The distributional incidence of Federal *recurrent* expenditure among *urban* and rural households is 'by and large proportional and tends to maintain the *status quo* of income distribution'.[50] But at the upper end of the income distribution there is some tendency for expenditure to rise as a proportion of income.
2. Federal *capital* expenditure 'is unambiguously pro-rich in both sectors'. For urban households Federal capital expenditure is over 20 per cent of household income for the lowest income group, falls to 15 per cent for middle-income groups and rises to over 30 per cent of income for the highest group; for rural households it ranges between 18 and 12 per cent for the ten lower income groups and then rises sharply to 35 per cent for the top group.
3. For both the recurrent and capital Federal budget, expenditure is higher for urban than for rural households.
4. Both recurrent and capital Federal expenditure is progressive in terms of *State* distribution with the States with lower per capita income receiving more, as a proportion of income than States with higher per capita income.
5. Examination of the expenditure patterns of one State (Bauchi) shows benefits from State expenditure and local government expenditure are progressive in both rural and urban areas. Together State and local recurrent expenditure account for over 8 per cent of urban income for low-income households; the proportion falls to around 7 per cent for high-income households; in the rural areas, the proportion is nearly 25 per cent for low-income households falling to 13 per cent for high-income households. State and local recurrent expenditure thus show a rural bias, in contrast to Federal expenditure.
6. State (i.e. Bauchi) *capital* expenditure is mildly progressive comparing low and middle-income households but rises sharply (both in urban and rural areas) at the upper end of the income distribution. Rural capital expenditure, as a proportion of income, is substantially greater than urban.
7. Taking the whole public sector together, for Bauchi, recurrent expenditure is progressive in both urban and rural areas, more markedly so in rural areas; capital expenditure is mildly progressive in the lower part of the income range, but becomes sharply regressive at the upper end. The top income groups among urban

households benefit to the extent of over 80 per cent of their income; the lowest income groups benefit to just over 40 per cent of their income. Rural households show a similar pattern. 'In short, it can be concluded that Nigeria's recurrent budget is pro-poor and its capital budget is pro-rich.'[51]

We may conclude that with the present structure of taxation and public expenditure, the public sector does not markedly alter the primary distribution of incomes. On the public expenditure side, this in part reflects the relatively low expenditure on BN-sectors, already noted. A substantial expansion of the proportion of public expenditure devoted to BN-sectors would ensure a more progressive distribution. But even where the expenditure is apparently devoted to BN, there can be bias in access, preventing it fully benefiting those most deficient in BN. This is obvious, for example, if expenditure on education goes mainly to secondary schools and higher education. But even for expenditure on primary schools, disproportionate attendance by children of the middle and upper-income groups occurs. Similarly, use of health clinics is related to income and education levels. A study of the use of subsidised fertiliser and access to extension officers in a village in Northern Nigeria[52] showed that the 'élite' had received 145 kg of subsidised fertiliser compared with 22 kg in the sample as a whole, and had five contacts with extension officers in the previous five years compared with 0.3 for the sample as a whole. Another study of urban services[53] showed how access varies with class and income level: 'socio-administrative power ... determines access to urban resources – land, housing loans, infrastructure and social facilities'.

THE META-PRODUCTION FUNCTION

The previous sections of this chapter have described how production, organisation and income distribution leads to a certain pattern of consumption of BN-goods. To translate this into BN-achievements requires a knowledge of the meta-production function, or the relation between the consumption of BN-goods and the ultimate BN-objectives (see Chapter 2).

There are conceptual as well as empirical problems about putting values on the meta-production function which have been discussed earlier (Chapters 2 and 4). There is a certain distributional content to the objectives, which needs to be specified.

Apart from the conceptual problems there are severe deficiencies in empirical evidence in most countries. In Nigeria, evidence is limited to micro-studies carried out for different purposes and normally only representative of a small area, and some generalisations by 'experts'. While the micro-studies suggest the general direction of the relationships, they rarely give quantitative relationships. There are cases where quantitative evidence is available, but in most it is not possible to be confident about the results because of the methodology used. For example, some studies showing positive effects of maternal education on health do not control for other variables (e.g. incomes). Moreover in a society where only a minority go to school, the more innovative are likely to be school-goers, and hence this may be part of the explanation of some findings – for example, greater contact with extension officers among the educated. Furthermore, some studies report on the results of programmes which have combined a number of inputs – e.g. health services, improved water and education – showing that together the programme has had a marked effect on health, but not indicating the relative contribution of each input.

All these problems suggest that it is not possible to arrive at a properly defined meta-production function for Nigeria without substantial additional research. But the many micro-studies do suggest the general direction of the relations, which is itself important both for planning for BN and for suggesting directions for future research.

For example, studies have shown that integrated health programmes have had a marked effect in reducing infant mortality and raising life expectancy. One study showed the infant mortality rate falling from 295 per 1 000 to forty–eight and the child (1–4) mortality rate falling from sixty-nine to nineteen following the introduction of a health and nutrition programme.[54]

Another[55] showed a village with access to hospital had life expectancy of forty-five years, while a similar village with no access had life expectancy of thirty-four. Studies of health programmes in Katsina and Lagos show similar results.[56]

Many investigations have shown how formal education, particularly female education, appears to improve BN-achievements in raising standards of health and nutrition. A study of malnutrition in Lagos found no cases of malnutrition among children of mothers with formal education, but substantial incidence among children of illiterate mothers;[57] a comparison between two similar areas in Northern Nigeria which differed in educational facilities, found that the social indicators (health, mortality, nutrition) were substantially better in the educated area;[58] a study of the use of health services by mothers

FIGURE 7.2 Meta-production function – relationships in Nigeria

Basic needs inputs	Instrumental and planning objectives				Final objectives		
	Food	Water	Health services	Education services	Health	Nutrition	Education
Food	★	—	—	Higher attendance among better fed (Callaway).	Well nourished less disposed to disease – malnutrition major contributory cause of death. (Omolulu see nutrition section, Chapter 6)	★	Better attendance and more attentiveness among better fed (Callaway).
Water	—	—	—	—	Water borne disease and intestinal major cause of ill health. (See health section, Chapter 6)	Nutritional value of food reduced by intestinal diseases and caused by poor water.	Via effects on health.

Health services	—	—	—	Better health, better school attendance.	Various studies show significantly improved health from health facilities (Orubuloye and Caldwell).	Disease reduces nutritional value of food consumption and reduces appetite. Health programme (Katsina) substantially reduced malnutrition.	Better attendance at school. More attentiveness.
Education Female	Probably as male but less marked. No evidence available.	Improve quality of water used (boiling, etc).	Increased use of health services by educated mothers (Bamishaye; Caldwell).	★	Health practices taught, better attendance at clinics; improved nutrition.	Identification of malnutrition by teachers and by training children in nutrition education (esp. female).	★
Male	Improves use of extension, agricultural innovation, turns aspiration away from agriculture. (See Education sect.)	As female, much less significant (Caldwell).	★	★	Probably same direction as females – much less significant	As female	★

★ indicates positive relationship.

in Lagos found the level of use was positively related to the educational level of the mother especially for immunisation;[59] a study in Cross River State showed that 93 per cent of women with some education had attended a health centre, but only 63 per cent of women with no education.[60]

There is conflicting evidence as to the effects of education on fertility in Nigeria. Some studies have shown a decline in fertility as maternal education increases,[61] as is the experience in most parts of the world. But others have found no effects of education,[62] or even in some cases a positive effect, with fertility increasing with education level[63] – a fairly common finding for Africa. The most widely accepted view seems to be that in the short run education may actually increase fertility, but that in the long run, it is likely to reduce fertility particularly as the consequence of the fall in infant mortality which generally accompanies education.

Evidence for other aspects of the relationship between inputs and outputs are described in the last chapter. For example, many observers have noted a relationship between malnutrition and infection. The matrix above (Fig. 7.2) summarises the evidence showing the direction of relationship between the various planning variables and the final objectives.[64]

As shown each of the inputs affects (positively) each of the final objectives. In addition, female education has a marked positive effect on each of the other inputs, as well as direct effects on the final outcome. Male education has a much less significant effect on other inputs – and indeed an ambiguous one in the case of agriculture and food, in so far as it has a negative effect on aspirations, turning boys away from farming.

One set of studies in Nigeria comes closest to establishing empirical data for part of the meta-production function. These are the studies by Orubuloye and Caldwell, which aim to establish the impact of health services and education in determining mortality in Nigeria.[65] The first study compared health/mortality rates for two villages which were broadly similar in all relevant characteristics except the presence (or absence) of a hospital. This showed (a) that the village with a hospital had a life expectancy of approximately forty-five years, compared with one of thirty-four years for the village with no hospital. Most of this difference was due to different rates of infant and child mortality; (b) in each village, rates of infant and child mortality were related to the education of the mother, while no other personal characteristics were found to be significant.

The second study was intended to investigate further the effects of maternal education in comparison with other variables in determining child mortality. The table below summarises the results in two surveys, one of Yoruba women in Ibadan (1973) and the second of Yoruba women in Western and Lagos States (also 1973). As Table 7.13 shows maternal education is the characteristic associated with the largest differences in child mortality in each of the surveys. Further analysis – see Table 7.14 – showed that this remained true when the other apparently significant variables were held constant. Moreover the positive effects of maternal education increased with the level of education, being significantly higher for secondary than for primary education. Thus the child mortality of mothers in both traditional and 'modern' Ibadan was 30 per cent lower for mothers with primary education than mothers with no education and 60 per cent lower for mothers with secondary education. The effects of the other variables – holding maternal education constant – were shown to be substantially less than maternal education in each of the surveys. Father's education – in cases where the mother has no education – reduces child mortality by 10 per cent (primary education) and 20 per cent (secondary), whereas where the father has no education, maternal education reduces child mortality by 61 and 85 per cent.

It is not possible from this evidence to arrive at a complete meta-production function and therefore an appropriate set of targets for planning. But the evidence above does suggest priorities, with female education as a first priority and health services as second. Nigeria is already giving major priority to primary education – and this is likely to lead to significant expansion in female education. But from a BN point of view, the extension of female education at all levels should be an explicit priority. The evidence underlines the need to give greater priority to expenditure on provision of health services, especially in the rural areas.

From a planning point of view, this exercise has underlined the need to establish values in the meta-production function to derive appropriate BN planning targets. On the other hand, the richness of the relationships and the paucity of empirical data also emphasise the difficulties involved in arriving at such a function.

TABLE 7.13 Ratio of highest child mortality rate to lowest child mortality rate in socio-economic divisions, Nigeria, 1973

Source	Socio-economic division	Highest Child mortality (CM) Subdivision	Index value of CM	Lowest Child mortality (CM) Subdivision	Index value of CM	Ratio of highest to lowest
a. Dichotomised socio-economic divisions						
Survey 1						
	Mother's education	No school (NS)	1.29	primary school + (PS)	0.72	1.80
	Marriage type	polygynous	1.30	monogamous	0.87	1.50
	Area of residence	Old Ibadan	1.24	rest of Ibadan	0.86	1.45
	Birth control	never practised	1.18	have practised	0.73	1.62
	Conditions of last child's birth	no doctor or hospital	1.28	doctor and/or hospital	0.97	1.32
Survey 2						
	Mother's education	NS	1.38	PS+	0.74	1.86
	Father's education	NS	1.36	PS+	0.91	1.48
	Number of mother's marriages	2+	1.31	1	1.21	1.08

Whether children of school age sent to school	not all sent	1.30	all sent	0.97	1.34
Whether parents eat together	never or rarely	1.32	usually	0.87	1.52
Whether parents sleep in the same room	never or rarely	1.20	usually	1.20	1.00

b. Trichotomised socio-economic divisions

Survey 1

Mother's education	NS	1.29	secondary school + (SS)	0.51	2.54
Mother's occupation	housewife	1.20	white collar	0.45	2.56
Father's occupation	unskilled and trader	1.30	white collar	0.85	1.53
Maternal grandfather's occupation	farmer	1.15	white collar	0.84	1.36

Survey 2

Mother's education	NS	1.38	SS+	0.57	2.42
Father's education	NS	1.36	SS+	0.77	1.77
Urban-rural residence	village	1.43	city (Lagos and Ibadan)	0.72	1.98

Note: 'White collar' is used to mean working in the modern sector. It includes professionals, administrators, clerks, ministers of religion, police and army officers and those who work in offices and modern large shops.
Source: Caldwell (1979).

TABLE 7.14 *Relative child mortality by education of mother and one other characteristic: percentage CM in each group is of highest CM*

Characteristic	Subdivisions of characteristic	Mother's education		
		NS	PS	SS
Mother's occupation	white collar	–	–	32
	other	100	68	46
	(100=CM of 1.287)			
Father's occupation	white collar	84	59	32
	other	100	72	59
	(100=CM of 1.335)			
Maternal grandfather's occupation	white collar	96	68	32
	other	100	66	45
	(100=CM of 1.240)			
Area of residence	Old Ibadan	100	69	41
	Rest of Ibadan	80	55	33
	(100=CM of 1.367)			
Marriage type	Monogamy	79	54	33
	Polygny	100	70	50
	(100=CM of 1.405)			
Father's education	NS	100	39	15
	PS	89	70	–
	SS+	79	64	37
	(100=CM of 1.378)			
Area of residence	city[a]	110	37	25
	town[a]	90	74	43
	village[a]	100[b]	51	46
	(100=CM of 1.408)			

Notes

[a]City = Lagos and Ibadan; town = centres with 20,000 – 100,000 inhabitants; village = centre with fewer than 20,000 inhabitants.

[b]Chosen because all city CMs total less than village CMs.

Source: Caldwell and Caldwell (1978).

CONCLUSION

Examination of the three aspects of the macroeconomy of Nigeria has shown major deficiencies – as far as BN is concerned – with respect to each aspect, and has pointed the way to changes needed.

The next chapter examines policy changes for BN in the light of these deficiencies.

8 A Basic Needs Strategy for Nigeria

Evidence from the past decade in Nigeria strongly suggests that one cannot rely on the natural process of growth to lead to major progress on basic needs. It is true that Nigeria's progress was hampered in the 1960s by the civil war; and that the substantial impact of oil discoveries in the 1970s on measured economic growth has not really had time to affect the main BN-variables. Nonetheless, on present evidence it seems that Nigeria is a clear example of failed 'trickle down' and a substantial reorientation will be required for major progress on basic needs. The reorientation required needs to take place with respect to each of the three aspects of the macroeconomic analysis. As indicated in the last chapter, *production* of BN-goods has been inadequate both in the private sector (food especially) and in the public sector (especially health services and water to reach those most in need). Secondly, the process of growth in the past has not raised the real *incomes* of the bottom 40 per cent of the population; for progress on basic needs it is essential to achieve a pattern of growth which generates a sustained growth in the real incomes of the poor. Thirdly, *organisational* factors act as obstacles to progress at almost every level; a change in household behaviour in particular, could be a major source of progress.

But while changes are needed with respect to each aspect, it is plausible to argue, in the Nigerian context, that priority should be given to raising the real incomes of the bottom 40 per cent of the population. A sustained rise in their real incomes would enable them to buy those BN-goods which are directly marketed, such as food, some private medicine, education and water; it would also increase access to those BN-goods which are supplied free by the State but which involve heavy private opportunity costs, such as transport to schools and health clinics, time off work for getting education and medical attention, and so on. In one way or another every element in BN depends in part on the level of income. Studies show that, for various reasons, standards in each service rise sharply with incomes.[1]

There has been some tendency to emphasise the public provision of BN-goods, as the major thrust of a BN-approach to development. While the public provision of some services is essential, supply of public goods by itself is not sufficient; the poor must also have *access* to these goods. Yet access depends on incomes and power. The study by Sahota, described in the last chapter, showed that the distribution of public goods, has tended to be broadly in line with the distribution of incomes; if this relationship continues – and it is one that has been noted in many countries – then an increase in incomes among the poor may be a necessary aspect of increasing the level of *public* BN-goods they receive. In discussing 'income' of the poor, it is *primary* incomes that are the main issue – i.e. the incomes people derive from their own resources. In Nigeria, government interventions to change the primary distribution of income have been limited and ineffective. While in theory direct taxation is mildly progressive, in practice it has had little effect on the distribution of income.[2] Moreover, with the development of oil revenue it has become a very small element in total taxation. It seems unlikely that this will change in a significant way. Hence for sustained achievement on BN the main emphasis must be on securing a substantial rise in the primary incomes of the poor.

DETERMINANTS OF INCOME GROWTH AMONG THE POOR

Movements in real incomes among the poor can only be understood in the context of an analysis of development of the Nigerian economy as a whole.

It is estimated that about 64 per cent of those whose incomes fall below a BN-minimum are in the rural sector; the remainder are in the cities, mainly in informal activities.

The performance of the agricultural sector is the major influence on rural incomes. It directly affects all those employed in agriculture; it also has an indirect influence on non-agricultural earning opportunities in the rural sector (e.g. for trading, food processing and other services). Rural earning opportunities also have an important indirect influence on real incomes among the poor in the *urban* sector. Given the fact that most people in Nigeria can get access to land or employment in agriculture if they wish, those in the urban informal sector (a large proportion of whom form the urban poor) have the option of moving back to the countryside if they choose. Rural earning opportunities thus represent a floor of potential income for them, which tends to place a lower limit on incomes in the informal urban sector.[3]

There are numerous factors which determine the extent to which the lower 40 per cent of the income distribution participate in the process of economic growth. These include such factors as asset distribution (especially land), the rate of population growth, the nature (labour or capital-intensive) of the technology adopted in the industrial sector.[4] It is clear in the Nigerian context that, in addition to these factors, the performance of the agricultural sector plays a special role[5] This performance is bound up with developments in the economy as a whole and in particular with the impact of oil on the economy.

THE OIL ECONOMY AND INCOMES OF THE POOR

The advent of oil brought about a marked change in the nature of the Nigerian economy; the rise in national income accounted for by oil has been paralleled by agricultural stagnation. Agriculture, forestry and fishing accounting for 54 per cent of GDP in 1965–6, while mining and quarrying (which includes oil) accounted for 5 per cent. By 1977–8, agriculture's share had dropped to 24 per cent of GDP and mining and quarrying accounted for 25 per cent of GDP (of which oil was 22 per cent). Meanwhile, the share of manufacturing and of services remained broadly constant.

The dramatic decline in agriculture was even more marked in relation to trade, where from being a major exporting sector and the main source of foreign exchange for the economy, exports dropped to negligible proportions; by 1976, oil accounted for over 93 per cent of exports, and Nigeria had begun to import food in substantial quantities.

The decline in agriculture which accompanied the oil boom is of fundamental importance to both incomes and production aspects of BN. As far as incomes are concerned, the agricultural sector provides the main source of income for the majority of the poor, and, since it offers an alternative to urban employment for most people, it also helps to determine the level of urban poverty. On the production side, food is, of course, a major element in BN. The decline in agriculture was not due to deliberate neglect, although the successive plans did allocate proportionately small resources to the sector. In the third plan, agriculture secured only 8 per cent of planned investment. But in the context of an oil economy, the explanation is deeper and more pervasive. It concerns the relationship between tradables and non-tradables.

Tradable goods – which include agriculture, manufacturing and natural resources – are goods which may readily be bought and sold internationally. Such goods may be bought internationally so long as foreign exchange is available. Non-tradables are those goods and services which cannot readily be exchanged internationally, but for the most part are only available if supplied domestically. Transport and communications, distribution and many services, such as haircuts, education services, health services, are largely of this kind. While some elements may be bought internationally, domestic supplies are normally essential. There is a complementary relationship between tradables and non-tradables, such that most production/consumption of tradables requires some consumption of non-tradables. For example, to sell tradable commodities it is necessary to have a transport system, and a distribution system.

Oil, or any other substantial source of foreign exchange (e.g. workers' remittances), adds to an economy's tradable resources, but not to its non-tradable. That is to say, it provides foreign exchange which can be used to buy tradable goods, but it does not provide the non-tradable, domestic resources, necessary for the consumption of those goods – that is, the roads, ports and so on. If there is a sudden accretion of tradable resources, as with the expansion of oil revenue, then tradable resources expand out of proportion to the domestic capacity to supply non-tradables. The effect is considerable (and inflationary) pressures on the non-tradable sector – most visibly witnessed in the case of Nigeria by an eighteen-month queue at the port of Lagos around 1979–80. The relative rewards and opportunities of employment in non-tradables (services, construction work, etc) rise. This change in relative rewards for working in the tradable as against the non-tradable sector, which has its origin in the imbalance in resources brought about by the oil revenue, is reinforced by the exchange-rate effect. The effect of the addition to foreign exchange is to uphold or raise the exchange rate, unless expenditure on foreign goods rises as fast as the extra revenue accrues, or unless offsetting action is taken to hold the exchange rate down. But expenditure cannot rise as fast as the revenue accrues because of the bottle-necks on absorption caused by the relatively low capacity of the non-tradable sector. Hence there tends to be a marked upward effect on the exchange rate, which depresses the returns to traditional exports. In the Nigerian case, these were from the agricultural sector.

The agricultural sector in Nigeria therefore suffered in three ways: from the attractiveness of non-tradable activities, leading to a migration out of agriculture;[6] from the government giving priority to expanding the non-tradable sector (e.g. through road and port building) to eliminate the bottle-necks in the economy; and from the exchange-rate effect. The manufacturing sector in Nigeria did not suffer in the same way, continuing to receive considerable investment resources and support. This was because although theoretically a tradable sector, in practice it was *not* a tradable sector, being heavily protected and subject to government regulation, so that market forces did not operate to depress it, as they do in industrialised countries when there is a substantial build-up of oil revenue (as in the UK, Holland and Norway).

An effective BN-strategy in Nigeria requires as first priority a reversal of past trends in agriculture – that is, a rise in real incomes *extending to the poor in agriculture* is required. The policy changes to bring this about are not fully known, but the main elements are fairly clear. It is above all necessary to protect the agricultural sector from the adverse trends which accompany the development of oil. To a limited extent this may happen automatically with the weakening of the price of oil but this is not itself likely to be sufficient, and may be temporary.

Incomes in agriculture need to be protected against the downward pressure induced by the presence of oil. This may be achieved directly by subsidies/upholding producer prices, or indirectly by lowering the exchange rate. But it is essential to ensure that these changes are not offset by changes in internal prices brought about through the expenditure of oil revenue, with the consequent boom in non-traded activities. Therefore, in addition, a reduced rate of expenditure of oil revenues is necessary either by reducing the accumulation of oil resources and/or by accumulating foreign assets, while priority should be given to agriculture (and the rural sector) in public investment and in credit policies: it is also essential to ensure that any progress in raising agricultural incomes is not offset by an increase in differentiation within agriculture. This may occur if schemes to raise agriculture output concentrate on large/progressive farmers, or capitalist schemes using capital-intensive technologies. Although such effects might raise agricultural output and thus contribute to food targets at an aggregate level, to meet BN it is essential that they also raise the real incomes of the poor. Hence – from a BN point of view – it would be mistaken to place great emphasis on raising agricultural production irrespective of its distributional consequences. The experience of many countries which have done so have shown that rising agricultural production can often be accompanied by an increase in rural (and urban) poverty.[7]

According to the argument presented here, urban poverty can only effectively be tackled by measures which increase incomes among the rural poor. More direct measures to deal with low urban incomes (e.g. expansion of employment opportunities) may have short-run beneficial effects, but in the long run increased rural-urban migration is likely to depress marginal urban incomes to the level (with some margin to allow for the differential attraction of towns versus countryside) of incomes obtainable on the margin in the rural areas. However, food subsidies on low-income staples consumed by the urban poor (locally produced cereals) should accompany any sharp rise in agriculture producer prices, so as to avoid short-run deleterious effects on nutrition standards and an inflationary effect on minimum wages. Measures which increase non-agricultural opportunities in the rural areas are a further way to help raise rural incomes.

In Nigeria, the relative abundance of land plus the traditional forms of land tenure (although there is considerable dispute about how far these operate in reality) have put some kind of floor on rural poverty, which is indicated by fairly equal distribution of income (and land) observed. If either the land abundant situation ceased – as a result of population pressure – or new forms of land tenure precluded access for substantial numbers of people, it is likely that much worse forms of both rural and urban poverty would emerge. Thus even to preserve the existing situation in relation to BN, it is necessary that the present situation of more or less free and easy access to land for all continues.

Other elements of change would also contribute to a more equitable pattern of growth. One major aspect is technology. The lack of capital equipment in small-scale agriculture has been widely noted – and is due to a combination of lack of investment resources among small-scale farmers and a dearth of appropriate technology. In contrast, the large-scale modern sector takes very substantial investment resources to employ rather few people, thus indirectly depriving the majority of investment resources and creating a small privileged élite. The distribution of oil expenditure, combined with the pattern of industrialisation adopted, has created increasing inequality, with most of the additional incomes being confined to a rather small percentage of the population. Yet, as shown, the tax system does very little to offset this.[8]

PRODUCTION AND PUBLIC SECTOR PRIORITIES

An essential counterpart to policies which raise the incomes of the poor is a reorientation in production towards BN-goods. It cannot be assumed that these would occur automatically with a change in primary incomes, particularly with respect to publicly provided goods. Moreover, to some extent giving priority to BN-goods may improve the situation, even without a substantial increase in the real incomes of the poor. In the private sector, the main change in priority required is increasing the production of basic foods – if achieved this may raise incomes of the poor directly in agriculture and indirectly raise real incomes of those outside agriculture (both rural and urban) by moderating the rise in the price of staple commodities. In the public sector, the government has given very low priority to BN-goods in the past, with the exception of education. A substantial increase in expenditure on water and rural health clinics would in itself make a direct contribution towards BN.

While it is easy to see the direction of change required in production, it is extremely difficult to make sensible 'target' estimates, for a variety of reasons.[9] For one reason we know too little about the relationship between production/consumption of particular BN-goods and achievements in terms of improvements in the lives of the poor; for another, what is the appropriate target depends on the *distribution* of the relevant goods. If all extra health expenditures actually go to those most in need, then the total increase can be much smaller than if only a fraction do. Nonetheless, some rather arbitrarily defined targets are helpful for policy purposes, in illustrating the sort of resource reallocation required and alternative ways of achieving it.

Table 8.1 suggests some BN-targets, using 1975–6 figures. The target for food represents an addition of one-quarter of 1975–76 food consumption per capita, which is an (arbitrarily) selected target of the sort of order of magnitude required – given the current inadequacy of total supplies and the maldistribution of the total.[10]

TABLE 8.1 *'TARGETS' for basic needs production (1975–6 figures)*

	Actual p. capita output 75–6, ₦	As % GDP	Target % of GDP	Extra as % GDP
Food	83	25.6	33.3	7.7
Education	7*	2.2	3.1	0.9
Health	3*	0.9	2.0	1.1
Water	0.3	0.1	1.0	0.9
TOTAL	93.3	28.8	39.4	10.6

*Uses higher bracketed estimates of Table 7.3.
Source: Table 7.3

The share of education in GDP is raised to 3.1 per cent of GDP in the targeted estimate, which was the average for middle-income countries in 1970.[11] Health expenditure is raised to 2.0 per cent of GDP. This is a figure achieved by many middle-income LDCs.[12] In view of the major deficiencies in the Nigerian health services a higher figure would be justified in the medium term. The target selected for water is 1.0 per cent of GDP.

Taken together, the targets require that nearly 40 per cent of GDP be devoted to BN-production, as against the 1975–6 figure of nearly 30 per cent – a switch in production of over 10 per cent of GDP. The major switch is towards food, a private sector activity. Within the public sector, extra expenditure on BN-sectors of nearly 3.0 per cent of GDP is targeted. These figures are – as already stated – rather arbitrary. But they may provide a useful background for exploring the costs of a production reorientation towards BN.

TABLE 8.2

	Production 1975–6, %	Targets
GDP per capita of which:	100	
Private cons. of food, p. cap.	25.6	33.3
Other private consumption	36.9	
Govt. final cons. of BN-items (educ., health, water)	3.2*	6.1
Other govt. final consumption	7.3	
Gross fixed investment:	23.7	
Increase in stocks	2.3	
Net exports	1.6	

*Uses higher estimates in Table 7.3.

Source: Table 7.3.

This switch of over 10 per cent in GDP resource allocation could be achieved in one or other or some combination of the following ways:

1. At the expense of 'luxury' private consumption. Altogether the extra amounts to 29 per cent of non-food private consumption (see Table 8.2). Not all non-food consumption can be assumed to be 'luxury' in any realistic sense; a good deal of it in fact will be BN-consumption of one kind or another (e.g. private housing, etc.). If we assume that half the 'non-food' private consumption is luxury consumption, then a very severe cut (60 per cent) would be necessary if all the extra BN-production came from this. This would only be realistic with a rather different political system. Nonetheless, some of the extra should come from this element. A cut of one-fifth in luxury consumption as defined here would finance over one-third of the BN-target.
2. At the expense of 'luxury' government expenditure. Non-BN government final consumption amounts to over 7 per cent of GDP. Assuming again that half of this is essential, this leaves a potential 3.7 per cent of GDP which might be switched to BN – i.e. again one-third of the BN-target.

3. At the expense of investment. If the whole of the extra came from investment, a very substantial cut in investment would be involved (45 per cent). If one-third did, then the cut would amount to 15 per cent of investment.

It should be noted that the costs to the various sectors may appear less in a dynamic context, where additional resources resulting from economic growth may be devoted to BN. At growth rates of the 1970s, if all extra resources were devoted to BN, the targets would be achieved in about three years without any actual cuts in other sectors in absolute terms.

TRADE-OFF WITH ECONOMIC GROWTH

Whether or not there is a trade-off between BN-achievement and economic growth depends on where the resources come from. If the resources come from investment or government growth-related expenditure, then some trade-off in the short run is likely. In the longer run, this will be partially offset by positive effects on productivity of increases in health and education. Moreover, the reorientation towards agriculture is generally regarded as necessary for economic growth in Nigeria, with a switch in resources to agriculture being likely to raise the rate of growth. But to the extent that extra BN-fulfilment involves higher levels of consumption, then there are likely to be reductions in investment and therefore in economic growth. Any estimates are bound to be arbitrary given how little we know about the capital–output ratios and about the precise reallocation of resources. Assuming that one-third of the resource switch comes from investment, one-third from luxury private consumption and one-third from other government expenditure, then, as stated, a 15 per cent cut in investment could be expected. If we assume that this cut is likely to be investment of below average productivity then we might expect a cut in the growth rate of the order of one-tenth. Given that economic growth in the past has been concentrated on the better off, and has done little to improve BN, there is no reason to expect this to involve a decline in the growth of BN-fulfilment. In the longer run, positive effects on productivity of the greater expenditure on BN, might halve this loss in growth to one-twentieth (or roughly ¼ per cent of GDP per annum).

PRODUCTION PRIORITIES WITHIN BN-SECTOR

So far we have been concerned with increasing the total resources devoted to BN-sectors, but another important element of a BN-strategy (which could reduce the need for an increase in total resource, is to improve the allocation of resources within BN-sectors. For example, the expansion of rural health facilities as against urban hospitals; an emphasis on training para-medics as against buildings; within the agricultural sector, a change towards small rural activities as against large-scale irrigation and schemes which favour progressive and large-scale farmers; within education more emphasis on BN-related activities – more adult education with a health/nutrition and agricultural content; a change in syllabus within the primary schools in a similar direction; within water/sanitation emphasis on improving simple local facilities as against expensive 'modern' schemes which can only be confined to a small proportion of people; a strong component of training and education in such schemes, as against the present tendency to emphasise hardware.

Nominally, the Nigerian Government has already declared its intention of moving in the sort of directions proposed here. This is most obviously the case in health. But its declarations do not so far seem to have had much effect in practice. There are administrative and political problems which partly account for this. There is also the momentum of past decisions which make them difficult to reverse. For example, once new hospitals have been built they have to be staffed, thus pre-empting a good deal of recurrent expenditure. Moreover, there are serious manpower/training problems at every level. Health for BN requires a new type of manpower which at present scarcely exists) more agricultural extension officers are needed; to change the school syllabus in a BN-direction requires a major programme of retraining extending to all existing teachers. Thus there are undoubtedly severe problems which may limit the changes possible in the short run; while administrative and manpower problems can gradually be overcome, political obstacles to the required redirection may be a lasting problem.

THE HOUSEHOLD SECTOR

The household is the keystone of a BN-strategy. It is the household which makes use (or fails to make use) of BN-goods and services; it is the way in which the household uses the BN-goods it consumes that determines their effectiveness in improving health and wellbeing. While governments may provide free education for children and adults, they can rarely force children to go to schools. Absenteeism and drop-outs are of huge proportions in some parts of Nigeria. A similar situation holds for health clinics.

In the medium term, household behaviour need not be taken as a given of the situation, but can be affected in all sorts of ways. Discussions of the meta-production function showed that the performance of women is particularly important in determining BN-performance. This is so with respect to health practices, nutrition and hygiene, and the use of services. In each of these areas, formal education of girls has a significant and positive effect on BN-performance. This is so even where there is little formal BN-content to the education, but is likely to be greater if the BN-component were increased. It seems that the longer a girl has been at school, the greater the positive effect. Hence probably the single most important policy for improving BN in Nigeria is extending female education.

Present programmes will do much to extend primary education to girls, but efforts need also be made at the secondary level, and a greater BN content is needed in both female and male education. A special meals programme could be devised which would raise the children's nutrition, encourage school attendance and help learning while at school, while also teaching children about nutrition and the use of the local foods. Ideally such a programme would make use of the products of school farms and involve the local community.

One major problem about education at the moment is the way it is used as an escape from, rather than a preparation for, a life in farming. A major transformation is required to relate primary education to life in agriculture.

The extension of school education still leaves the vast majority of people in Nigeria uneducated. The education of adult women in health, hygiene, etc. could potentially have a major effect on BN in the short run – more immediate than the effects of primary education. Adult education receives a derisory quantity of resources in view of its significance; it should, however, be related to function (e.g. combined with agricultural education). Household behaviour can be affected by advertising, which could be used positively to promote BN rather than being negative or irrelevant.

Apart from formal adult education, which normally only reaches a minority, and tends to be especially weak among women, other experiments, such as plays, the use of radio, television, advertising and teaching children to teach their parents, perhaps offer greater potential for reaching adult illiterates.

CONCLUSION

Nigeria's performance on BN is not very different from that of many other African countries. The big difference is that oil, along with other factors, has provided Nigeria with far greater resources, a far higher growth rate, and now a much higher per capita income than her neighbours. Yet this has made little difference to BN. The main reason is the nature of the growth process, in which the benefits from growth have been almost entirely monopolised by those in the top half of the income distribution. The main element of a BN-strategy must be to reverse this process, so that the poor participate substantially in the growth process. To achieve this requires a substantial change in the nature of growth – in particular a successful insulation of the agricultural sector from the debilitating effects of oil. Without such a change in the macroeconomy, it is unlikely that much progress will be made on BN. The other essential elements of a BN-strategy are a radical change in government priorities towards BN, and a change in household behaviour which, at the moment, is not conducive, by and large, to effective use of BN-goods and services. It is not likely that a BN strategy – as outlined above – will conflict in a substantial way with economic growth. A strategy which raises agricultural production and productivity is not only essential for BN, but also for sustained long-run economic growth. A conflict could arise if agricultural growth were achieved by methods which led to marked differentiation within agriculture, however. A BN-approach also requires greater resource allocation to the other BN-sectors. Whether or not this reduces the overall growth depends on where the resources come from, and also the effects on productivity of improved health, education and nutrition – which are certainly positive, but the overall returns are unknown. However, at present the allocation of resources to these BN-sectors is so low that a substantial proportionate increase could be achieved with only a relatively small decrease in expenditure elsewhere. Moreover, reallocation of expenditure within sectors could produce major improvements without increasing overall resource allocation.

From a BN point of view, the most exciting prospect in Nigeria is the transformation likely as education is extended to all her people, and especially all her girls. This alone is likely to have a marked effect in improving performance.

9 Basic Needs and the International Crisis: A Case Study of Tanzania

INTRODUCTION[1]

The unfavourable international environment that followed the two oil price rises of 1973–4 and 1979 has tended to threaten BN-approaches to development among non-oil producing developing countries. Economic growth has slowed down, and very large current account deficits have emerged. The slow-down in economic growth, which was especially marked among African economies, itself reduces the resources available to meet BN. But the accompanying balance of payments problems have caused especial problems for developing countries. To finance these deficits, middle-income countries had recourse to the private international capital market, while many low-income countries needed International Monetary Fund assistance. Neither of these sources of finance is favourable to BN. Private borrowing requires a short-run commercial rate of return, while the pay-off from BN-programmes is more long term and often takes the form of social rather than private cashable returns. IMF conditionality has emphasised deflation, reduced public expenditure, and the elimination of consumer subsidies as part of the structural adjustment required to justify IMF loans.[2] If these prescriptions are followed, BN-programmes and achievements are likely to be threatened. The names of recent reports – for example, *Zambia: Basic Needs in an Economy under Pressure*, and *Basic Needs in Danger: a Basic Needs Oriented Development Strategy for Tanzania* – point to this vulnerability of the BN-approach at a time of international crisis. The implications for BN are beginning to be evident. In 1980, according to the World Bank estimates, for the first time there was *no* improvement in life expectancy compared with the previous year, and even some decline. Given the depth of the current crisis, the question of preserving BN may, in the short run, be more relevant than that of improving performance.

One response to the crisis – a correct one at the international level – is to consider how to eliminate it, and to restore the world's growth prospects. But this response is of little use to individual countries in their day-to-day activities, when they are forced to take the measures necessary to secure financial solvency. For them the critical question is whether adjustment programmes can be devised which preserve and promote BN, or whether the IMF-style package is the only viable alternative. The aim of this chapter is to examine this issue in the context of the particular country – Tanzania. Tanzania is a good example to use because it has a fairly good record on BN, the effects of the international crisis and domestic events have been such as to cause a crisis of major proportions, and it has had a prolonged debate with the IMF about the appropriate response.

THE CRISIS IN TANZANIA

The main symptom of the crisis in Tanzania in 1981 was a substantial deterioration in the balance of trade which led to a large trade deficit and major arrears in payments for imports. This deficit arose despite the existence of very stringent import controls. In 1980 exports were 4.4 b. Tanzanian shillings (TSh.), while imports were over 10 b.: imports financed only 43 per cent of exports and the trade gap was over 6 b. TSh. Yet this level of imports financed only a fraction of import requirements for full capacity operation. Import allocations were only 35 per cent of requests, for those imports not financed by foreign aid in 1980, while industrial capacity utilisation, constrained by import restrictions, was also running at around 35 per cent.

Table 9.1 gives more information about the deterioration which took place in the trade balance between 1977 (a particularly good year for exports) and 1980. First, there was a sharp deterioration in the terms of trade with import prices rising by 46 per cent while export prices remained more or less stable. In part this deterioration was due to a further rise in the price of oil which by 1980 accounted for over 55 per cent of export earnings and 23 per cent of imports. The rise in imports in volume terms was not large, 14.4 per cent over the period (but one should note that import restrictions were very relaxed in 1977 and very stringent in 1980). A major cause of the deterioration was the poor performance of exports, which fell by 9.0 per cent in volume. There were substantial falls in the officially recorded production of most of the major export crops – coffee, sisal, cashew nuts, tobacco and pyrethrum.

It is clear then that both worsening external environment, as indicated in the deteriorating terms of trade, and poor production performance on major export items, were responsible for the worsening trade situation. In terms of absolute magnitudes, the external deterioration was responsible for more of the worsening than export performance in these years. The precise balance between the two is not of particular relevance for future policy.

The crisis in Tanzania had two other important facets, both connected with the foreign trade position. First, as already noted, industrial capacity utilisation was extremely low because of the import restrictions. Estimates for 1981 were for capacity utilisation of between 20 and 30 per cent. Output of textiles, beer, cement, iron sheets, enamelware, blankets, fishnets, aluminium, pyrethrum extract, shoes, and chibuku in 1980 were below their 1979 levels, while preliminary evidence for the first six months of 1981 showed very sharp drops compared with 1980 in those industries for which data was available: for example, the production of shoes was running at 43 per cent of the level of production attained in 1978. For the first six months of 1981, import allocations of intermediate products (i.e. raw materials and finished products widely used in industry) were only 19 per cent of requests. The transport sector received only 5 per cent of its requests. Because of the low rate of output of local industry, those enterprises which used locally produced inputs or made use of local transport also met shortages and therefore had their output levels further constrained, below the level imposed by the import restraint. Acute shortages of consumer goods arose because of the low level of industrial output, while only a negligible amount of imported con-

TABLE 9.1 *Balance of trade 1977–80*

Imports	1977	1980	1977–80
Value of imports m. TSh. c.i.f. of which	6 161	10 308	+ 67.3
Oil	898	2 358[a]	+ 162.6
food, drink & tobacco	636	1 705	+ 168.1
other	4 627	6 245	+ 35.0
Import price index	100	146.3[b]	+ 46.3
Import volume	100	114.4	+ 14.4
Exports			
Value of exports, m. TSh. f.o.b.	4 464	4 166	− 6.7
Export price index	100	102.5[b]	+ 2.5
Export vol. index	100	91.0	− 9.0
Major exports:			
Cotton, vol. prod.	66.3	66.0	− 0.5
Value	541	399	− 26.3
Coffee[c], vol. prod.	52.7	48.0	− 9.0
Value	1 857	1 228	− 33.9
Sisal[c], vol. prod.	105.0	73.1	− 30.4
Value	228	256	+ 12.3
Cashew nuts, vol. prod.	68	43.4	− 36.2
Value	273	213	− 22.0
Tobacco[c], vol.	19.6	16.8	− 14.3
Tea[c], vol.	16.4	17.3	+ 5.5
Pyrethrum[c], vol.	2.6	2.0	− 23.1

[a] Provisional, estimate provided by Bank of Tanzania.
[b] Projected by World Bank.
[c] Volume of production of export crops, by financial year, 1977/8 and 1980/81.

Sources: Economic and Operations Report, Bank of Tanzania, June 1980 + updating supplied by Bank of Tanzania.
Export and import price index from World Bank.

sumer goods were permitted. These shortages were apparent throughout the country – indicated by queuing, shortages and the widespread escalation of prices in the parallel sector – but it appears shortages were most acute in the rural areas where, in places, there was a near complete absence of industrially produced or processed goods.

Another aspect of the crisis was the deterioration in the budgetary position, where large deficits on current account emerged. An estimate for 1980/81 was for a recurrent deficit of 1 372 m. TSh., i.e. nearly 16 per cent of recurrent revenue.[3] The deficit was accompanied, as would be expected, by heavy government borrowing from the domestic banking sector.

These deficits were another aspect of the trade and industrial crisis. Export duties had been more or less eliminated as a source of revenue in an effort to provide greater export incentives. Sales tax dominated Tanzanian revenue (see Table 9.2) accounting for over 60 per cent of it; this revenue is closely related to the level of sales. Estimates in the Treasury suggested that if industry were operating at full capacity, the revenue from Sales and Excise Tax would have doubled, adding a quarter to total recurrent revenue, eliminating the budgetary deficit, and making a healthy contribution to development finance.

Because of the growth in the significance of Sales Tax and Excise Taxes, which fall on industrial products, the revenue situation depended critically on the level of industrial output.

The BN-sectors involve considerable budgetary requirements: in education and health, especially, adequate expenditure on BN requires high levels of recurrent expenditure for salaries and materials. In the provision of water and sanitation, the major cost is for the initial capital expenditure, but here too maintenance involves recurrent costs. Buoyant revenue is therefore essential for expansion of BN-satisfaction in these areas, while the budgetary deficit threatened the maintenance of the levels achieved.

Tanzania was spending nearly 50 per cent of her recurrent budget on the BN-sectors, broadly defined (Table 9.3) in 1973/4 but the proportion subsequently fell when the economy faced substantial difficulties with the drought and oil price rise. An analysis of that period[4] suggested that although capital expenditure on social services was kept up, recurrent costs were hit so that many rural water supply facilities went out of use because of lack of maintenance and there were shortages of medical supplies. Tables 9.3 and 9.4 show that

TABLE 9.2 Changing significance of different sources of revenue

	% of total recurrent central government revenue contributed by:							
	1956/66	1970/71	1974/75	1977/78	1978/79	1979/80	1980/81 Approved estimates	1981/82 Estimate
Taxes on income and profits	23.8	26.6	24.9	27.3	28.4	31.2	23.1	18.6
Consumption and excise	11.6 ⎫ 39.3	26.0 ⎫ 46.6	34.6 ⎫ 47.4	36.8 ⎫ 51.5	39.1 ⎫ 52.5	38.1 ⎫ 48.6	54.4 ⎫ 62.0	60.7 ⎫
Import duties	27.7 ⎭	20.6 ⎭	12.8 ⎭	14.7 ⎭	13.4 ⎭	10.5 ⎭	7.6 ⎭	10.6 ⎭
Export duties	1.3	3.3	5.4	9.0	6.7	6.0	4.5	0.6
Dividends and income from Parastatals and other investment income	1.2	2.9	3.1	2.3	2.7	2.8	2.9	2.8
Other	34.4	20.6	19.2	9.9	9.7	11.4	7.5	6.7
TOTAL	100	100	100	100	100	100	100	100
Tax revenues % GDP	15.0	19.0	25.7	20.8	20.0	20.6		

Sources: *Tanzania Basic Economic Report* and Annex 1, World Bank Dec. 1977 for 1965/6 to 1974/5; *Financial Statements and Revenue Estimates*, various years, Dar es Salaam; Data from Ministry of Planning and Economic Development; *Economic Memorandum on Tanzania*, World Bank, January, 1981.

recurrent expenditure on BN-sectors in Tanzania has come under some pressure in recent years with a drop in the proportion of recurrent central government expenditure from 25.7 per cent (1977/8) to 18.5 per cent (estimates for 1981/2). These figures do not include regional expenditure, which is devoted to basic needs to a much greater extent than the central government expenditure. The economic crisis also depressed the share of total expenditure handled by the regions (from 27.2 per cent, 1977/8 to 22.5 per cent 1981/2). Hence the downward share of BN in total recurrent expenditure was to that extent greater.

For basic needs in Tanzania, an urgent requirement was to generate additional recurrent revenue: the most feasible way of doing this in the short run would be to raise the level of industrial capacity and the revenue from Sales and Excise duties.

The stringent import restrictions and low level of industrial output also adversely affected Tanzania's export capacity in both industrial and agricultural sectors. Industrial exports, which were quite sizeable in 1979, were affected by the limited imports, with some fall in industrial exports in 1980. Industrial exports made up of processed agricultural goods also suffered from the poor performance in agriculture. Agricultural exports were also adversely affected by the import restrictions and the low level of industrial capacity utilisation. Most obviously, restricting imports limited the quantity of inputs received (e.g. fertilizer and tools) by both agricultural and industrial sectors; there were major deficiencies in the transport system caused by fuel shortages, and vehicle deficiencies, as a result of lack of spare parts. Moreover, restrictions on government expenditure prevented adequate maintenance of roads.

There were other indirect effects of the crisis which limited the performance of agricultural exports. The absence of consumer goods in the rural areas, itself in large part due to the low level of output of consumer goods, restricted the incentive among peasants to produce for cash.

The Tanzanian situation in 1981 formed a type of vicious circle, in which the acute shortage of foreign exchange made it extremely difficult to raise the exports, both industrial and agricultural, essential for Tanzania to succeed in relaxing the foreign exchange constraint by domestic means. Some relaxation of the foreign exchange constraint was a necessary precondition of achieving sustained growth in either industrial or agriculture exports.

One important aspect of developments is that the crisis did *not*

TABLE 9.3 *Per cent distribution of government recurrent expenditure*

	65/6	70/71	73/4	77/8	78/9
1. General public services	33.4	26.6	23.0	14.4	13.6
2. Defence	3.9	6.1	10.9	14.8	23.6
3. Education	14.8	17.5	16.7	14.5	11.3
4. Health	6.8	8.3	9.5	7.3	5.4
5. Other social services	7.3	5.0	5.5	3.2	3.2
6. Water supply	3.0	3.1	3.1	4.9	5.6
7. Agriculture	7.3	10.0	11.7	9.3	6.8
8. Other ec. services	10.3	8.4	8.7	22.5	20.8
9. Financial transfers	13.3	15.0	10.9	9.0	10.0
10. Total BN, defined as 3 + 4 + 5 + 6 + 7	39.3	43.9	46.5	39.2	32.3
11. TOTAL	100	100	100	100	100

NB Includes regions' expenditure.

Sources: *Tanzania, Basic Economic Report, Annex I, Domestic Finance and Resource Use*, World Bank, December 1977, Statistical Appendix, table XIV; and *Economic Memorandum on Tanzania*, World Bank, June 1981, table 2.3

TABLE 9.4 *Recurrent central government expenditure: per cent of total ministerial vote*

	77/8	78/9	79/80	80/81 Ests	81/2 Ests
1. Defence and National Service	21.9	19.3	n.a.	n.a.	18.0
2. Education	12.8	11.5	10.9	10.2	10.4
3. Health	7.1	6.4	6.7	5.2	4.5
4. Social services	1.1	1.0	1.2	0.9	0.8
5. Agriculture	2.9	1.6	4.1	2.2	1.9
6. Water supply and energy	2.0	1.4	1.3	1.2	0.9
BN-sectors = 2 + 3 + 4 + 5 + 6	25.9	21.9	24.2	19.7	18.5
Regional expenditure as per cent total recurrent	27.2	25.2	27.8	24.4	22.5

NB Does not include regional expenditure

Sources: *Financial Statement and Revenue Estimates*, various.

adversely affect domestic food production. Despite much statistical uncertainty, it seems clear that the underlying trend of food production was upward. It seems that there was a switch away from producing cash crops for sale through official marketing channels and towards food production for own consumption. Rural standards of nutrition were not therefore hit by the general economic crisis. This does not mean that the food production/consumption situation was satisfactory overall or for the long term. There were areas of food shortages with rising food prices in the parallel markets in the urban areas and rising food imports. Moreover, the margins were narrow, in the sense that small shortfalls in production could cause major nutritional problems.

POLICY OPTIONS

In the Tanzanian case any adjustment package – especially a BN-oriented one – needed to be mainly expansionary in approach: in other words, the prime aim would need to be to *increase* production so as to create additional resources, and to use these additional resources for exports and (to a lesser extent, as there is limited scope for this) import substitution. This expansionary approach contrasts with orthodox IMF-type approaches which aim to reduce domestic demand, so releasing resources for improving the trade balance. A deflationary approach was not appropriate to Tanzania for a number of reasons: first, imports were already so restricted that there was extremely little scope for additional restrictions, while the existing restrictions were already having major negative effects on production in the economy; secondly, any significant additional exports could only come from the agricultural sector. If levels of food production were to be maintained, a major consideration in a BN-approach, then the additional exports would have to come from additional agricultural production and not from any substantial switch from production for food. Thirdly, there was very limited potential for releasing resources for export by depressing consumption levels, without eating into the standards of living of very poor sections of the community. There were some areas where restrictions on activity would have been appropriate. This was particularly the case with respect to development expenditure and also applied to some elements in government recurrent expenditure (e.g. on administration and defence). But the major impetus in an adjustment strategy needed to be towards expansion of production, with the expansion heavily tilted towards exports.

The prime aim, then was to increase the production of export crops, without substantially affecting the production of food. Hence policies were needed to raise agricultural production in general, and also policies to encourage a proportionately greater effort in export crops.

There were a number of restraints inhibiting total agricultural production. First, there was the availability of agricultural inputs; secondly, of transport for agricultural crops; thirdly, a need for prompt purchase and payment of peasants for produce. Many stories circulated about delayed payment by the marketing authorities. Fourthly, the absence of consumer goods in the rural areas was widely believed to have been a major disincentive to cash crop production.

Changes in these four areas were essential preconditions of improved production. For substantial improvements in these areas, relaxation of foreign exchange restrictions was required as a *prior* condition, in order to provide the inputs directly or to generate production in the industrial sector which would provide the inputs/consumer goods. Hence a substantial inflow of untied foreign exchange was a necessary precondition of improvement.

Finally, there was the question of agricultural prices – which was the issue considered most fundamental by international bodies, such as the IMF and the World Bank. Before considering this, it is important to reiterate that the four changes just listed were essential prerequisites for any change in the price system to be effective. Without the four changes, change in price would have been ineffective: with them, price changes might have been unnecessary.

AGRICULTURAL PRICES

Many observers considered an increase in agricultural prices essential in order to raise production. They justified this recommendation with four types of argument:

1. They pointed to deteriorating terms of trade for the agricultural sector during the 1970s.

TABLE 9.5 *Agricultural price indices (1969–70 = 100)*

Official producer Price indices	1969–70	1975–6	1969–70^a TSh 1978–9	1981–2
Food:				
Maize	100	142	107	97
Paddy	100	96	81	87
Wheat	100	87	77	75
Sorghum	100	124	117	75
Export crops:				
Cotton	100	91	77	76
Cashew nuts	100	55	63	71
Tobacco	100	68	51	55
Tea	100	65	77	50
Pyrethrum	100	70	79	83

^{a}Using National Consumer Price Index. 1981–2 uses June 1981 price index.

Source: *Economic Memorandum on Tanzania*, World Bank, January 1981, table 1.6

As the table shows, the real price of agricultural products fell during the 1970s, with a much sharper fall for export crops than for food crops. Other analyses for smallholder crop producers, using a rural cost of living index, give much the same results.[5] During this period there was a downward movement in the world price of these export crops, but this fall, at least to 1978–9, was not as great as the fall in prices received by Tanzanian farmers.[6]

But while the real returns to smallholders fell, the real incomes of the low paid urban wage-earners fell even more; the real minimum wage in 1979 was around one half the value of the minimum wage in 1969. Consequently, the factoral terms of trade between agricultural work and urban unskilled work moved in favour of agriculture, and income distribution in this period changed in favour of the rural sector. Thus in so far as the relevant comparison and choice was between rural and urban work, there was a shift in favour of farming. On the other hand, to the extent that the relevant comparison was between working more or less intensively within the rural sector, there was some reduced incentive to work intensively. The relevant issue then was how far the latter margin was operational, which is partly dependent on the relative importance of the income effect, which would tend to induce farmers to work harder with reduced prices, as against the substitution effect which might lead farmers to work less hard. In addition there was the question of how much intensity of work can contribute to output levels, given the many other restraints on production. For many crops, special factors, such as disease (coffee), loss in soil fertility (cotton), villagisation and ageing of plants (cashew nuts in some areas), and weather, explained at least some of the poor production performance. Moreover, the factors mentioned earlier (shortages of inputs, transport, etc.) were also contributory factors. For example, in 1980 poor production in tea was partly due to limitations in processing, arising from unavailability of spare parts and frequent power interruptions; in tobacco, there was inadequate supply of curing facilities; in cotton there were transport problems[7]

2. The second fact noted was the decline in production of a number of major cash crops during this period:

TABLE 9.6 *Change in production*

	1970–1 to 1978–9 – 1980–1 Per cent change
Maize	30
Wheat	−51
Rice	30.5
Cotton	−25
Tobacco	42
Pyrethrum	49
Sugar	33
Coffee	− 5
Sisal	−44
Cashews	−58
Tea	87
Cloves	−45
Index of all major crops	−13

Source: *Economic Memorandum in Tanzania*, World Bank, January 1981.

This decline, together with the deterioration in real returns to the farmer was taken as evidence of the significance of price incentives. The fact that food crops did better, in general, than other cash crops was again taken as evidence of the price responsiveness of farmers, since, as shown, the real prices of food crops were sustained much better than those of other crops. However, while cash crop production sold through official channels did rather poorly, agricultural production as a whole increased by 4.9 per cent per annum from 1970 to 1979. It therefore appears that there is no evidence of a withdrawal by labour from agriculture *as a whole*, but strong evidence of a withdrawal from the official cash economy towards food production for own consumption and for unofficial marketing. This would be a rational reaction to the set of price incentives offered the peasant, since while the real returns to production for sale through official channels fell, those to subsistence production remained constant. The evidence supports the view that farmers' cropping patterns and marketing outlets were responsive to the relative prices they were offered, but gives little support to the notion that there was any substantial positive supply elasticity of agricultural production as a whole.

3. The third piece of evidence is of a similar nature. It was argued that the response to particular price changes (e.g. raising the price of cashew nuts) was quick and positive. But this partial supply elasticity tells us nothing about what is likely to happen to agricultural production as a whole, if all prices were raised. It simply indicates that the pattern of production and sales is influenced by the pattern of prices. We have simply no evidence on the *total supply elasticity* of agriculture, which is the relevant elasticity if what we are concerned with is raising total agricultural production. In so far as the concern is not with total production but with increasing the proportion exported, then a rise in the price of exported cash crops would be appropriate. But this would be likely to be at the expense of food production, which conflicts with the objective of maintaining levels of food production.

There were many restrictions on the total level of production, as already noted. These include technology, inputs and so on. Improvements in these factors alone would probably make a major contribution to raising agricultural production. Price was unlikely to be a very significant factor, with a given population, given land supply and given technology.

Nonetheless, even with a very low or zero aggregate supply elasticity, an increase in the real returns to producing for cash, as against own consumption, could lead to a switch of labour towards sale for cash, at the expense of subsistence production. While this might reduce levels of food consumption among peasants, it would increase other types of consumption among peasants. If freely chosen, it can be argued that peasants' real incomes would be raised by such a change, while marketed crops available for export or urban consumption would also increase.

It must be emphasised that any such shift would only occur if the *real* returns to producing for sale increased. The real returns depend on the money returns (or agricultural prices) and on what these money returns can purchase. If there were no increase in the supply of consumer goods, increased nominal returns would involve no increase in real returns. In contrast, if there were a substantial increase in the supply of consumer goods at controlled prices, then there would be a substantial increase in real returns without any change in nominal returns or agricultural prices. It follows that the availability and price of consumer goods was of prime significance in determining real returns; agricultural prices were of secondary importance.

4. A more forceful argument for raising agricultural prices concerned the role of parallel markets. There was sufficient evidence that these were growing in significance. They consisted both of internal and external sales. By bypassing the marketing authorities, these markets permitted the peasant to acquire and spend cash or foreign exchange, in the case of external sales. While internal sales were not of much importance, the external sales generated foreign exchange outside the authority of the government, which could not therefore be allocated in accordance with government priorities.

In sum then, there was a case for a rise in agricultural prices, on two counts: *one*, because there might have been some positive supply response of marketed crops, if not of total production; *two*, to bring some of the parallel trading into the official net. But the price rise would not raise real returns unless accompanied by increased supplies of consumer goods at reasonable prices.

A rise in the price paid to farmers for food would be financed by raising the price of food to consumers. This would involve a reduction in the real incomes of urban consumers, a reduction which would be likely to hit the poorest hardest, since they spent proportionately most on food. These groups could be cushioned by a subsidy, but this would involve a heavy budgetary burden. Moreover, even those on the minimum wage were better off than many rural people. But many of those in the informal sector were thought to have similar incomes to those in the rural sector.[8] A rise in agricultural prices would affect these people very substantially. Most of them did, however, have the option of returning to the rural sector. But the need to avoid too large a cut in real living standards of low-income consumers was a reason for limiting the size of any rise in agricultural prices.

Rises in the prices paid for export crops cannot be passed onto the consumer, but have to be financed either by a direct subsidy from the government, or by a devaluation. The next section considers some of the implications of these two alternatives.

SUBSIDY OR DEVALUATION?

Budgetary burden

A price subsidy involves a direct budgetary cost. Using 1979 values, a 20 per cent rise in the price of export crops would involve a cost of 482 million TSh which is equivalent to 6.2 per cent of recurrent revenue in 1979/80.

Devaluation also involves budgetary costs: first, for direct costs of inputs paid for by the government; secondly, for higher costs of other government expenditure as a result of the inflation in prices throughout the economy, induced by the devaluation. But these higher prices also generate extra revenue in the form of Sales and Excise Tax and taxes on income, while import duties would also rise with the change in the exchange rate. To give an equivalent incentive, the rate of devaluation has to be greater than a subsidy because a devaluation increases costs of imported inputs as well as raising crop prices. Table 9.7 presents estimates of the net budgetary costs of subsidy and devaluation.

TABLE 9.7 *Net budgetary costs, TSh.m, 1979 revenues*

	Subsidy		Devaluation		
Rate	(1) *most exports*[a]	(2) *Cash crops*	Rate	(3) *Inflation of ¼ devaluation*	(4) *Inflation of ½ devaluation*
10%	− 389	− 241	15%	−141	−181
20%	− 778	− 482	30%	−262	−363
50%	−1945	−1205	45%	−655	−90.75

[a]Excludes minerals, petroleum products and re-exports

In general, the budgetary costs of a subsidy tend to be greater than that of devaluation. But it must be emphasised that the results depend on the assumptions.[9] The most relevant comparison is probably between column (1) and column (3), showing that the budgetary costs of a subsidy would be nearly three times those of a devaluation.

In column (1) it is assumed the subsidy would also go to manufactured exports. This seemed desirable in view of the growing significance of manufactured exports as a source of foreign exchange, especially those that consist of processed raw materials (e.g. tobacco, cotton, sisal).

Incidence on different groups

Both measures would raise incomes of producers, but differ in the distribution of burden of so doing. The incidence of a subsidy depends on how it is financed. If it is financed by raising taxation, then it is likely to be progressive. If it is financed by cutting public expenditure, then the incidence depends on which type of expenditure is cut. If financed by additional borrowing, it is difficult to allocate its cost, since it would have an inflationary effect on the economy, which might take the form of a general inflation, or of inflation of black market prices, or might be suppressed.

Devaluation would raise the price of imports. All sectors, including agriculture, were heavy users of imports but the industrial sector was the greatest user. Hence the main burden would fall on consumers of products of the industrial sector. The distribution of the burden was likely to be less egalitarian than a subsidy financed by taxation, but more inegalitarian than one financed by cuts in social expenditure. In either case, the incidence would be altered if wages were raised in response to the measures.

An increase in real returns to agricultural producers, however it is brought about, can only occur with given total incomes if there is a reduction in incomes in the rest of the economy. Either measure, therefore, was likely to reduce real incomes in the urban sector. If incomes as a whole are rising then this reduction might be relative, rather than absolute.

Similarly, an improvement in the trade balance requires proportionately less domestic absorption and more of domestic production going to the outside world. If output is rising this can be achieved without a reduction in absolute income levels domestically. If output is static, then such an improvement is only possible with a reduction in expenditure in parts of the economy.

It appeared that some marketing authorities were paying the growers higher prices than they could recoup from consumers (either domestic or external). In one case (for maize) this was financed by an explicit subsidy. In others, the authorities borrowed from the domestic banks, so that in 1979 44 per cent of commercial bank lending was going to the marketing of agricultural produce; by the end of 1980 credit for the marketing of agricultural crops was estimated to be 75 per cent of total domestic credit, with 503 m. TSh. outstanding from the National Milling Corporation, 325 m. TSh. from the Coffee authority, 254 m. TSh. from the Tanzania Cotton Authority, and 100 m. TSh. from the Tobacco Authority. It seems that there was already a sort of subsidy involved for many crops, in the sense that the prices received by the marketing authorities did not cover the costs of buying from the farmers plus their own operational costs. Delays in purchasing crops from the farmers and in paying them may be partly attributed to the same cause. There was, therefore, a strong case for a change in selling prices of these authorities, so as to eliminate this situation.

Price control system

Devaluation would change the cost of production of almost every commodity sold in Tanzania, and so require revisions in all items subject to price control, therefore involving administrative costs.

The system of price control was not operating satisfactorily, as shown by the very large amount traded in the parallel markets. Estimates vary according to source and commodity, but it was believed that between 40 and 80 per cent of output was going through these markets at prices substantially higher than the controlled prices, with the margin varying according to commodity and region. In the rural areas, prices of two to three times the controlled price were common. In the urban areas, for some commodities prices appeared to be only about one quarter above the controlled prices, but for others the margins were much higher. This situation was highly unsatisfactory because it meant (a) that consumers were not receiving products at controlled prices, so that their real incomes were much less than intended. Moreover, the bias against the rural sector meant the cut in rural incomes from this cause was particularly high. (b) Those who traded on the black market were making large amounts of money, undermining egalitarian policies towards income.

The money made in this way then provided finance for further black market operations. (c) These incomes escaped the tax net. The system, far from contributing to socialist and BN-objectives actually threatened them. The problems arose basically from an attempt to control prices in a situation where there were chronic shortages so that market clearing prices were far in excess of any prices based on cost of production. To contribute to BN-objectives the following changes in the price control system were required:

1. The number of products controlled (515 product types) was far in excess of the number that could be *effectively* controlled, so the system was dysfunctional. From a BN point of view, control should be limited to the basic consumer goods used by rural people and low income wage-earners. The exact commodities to be included would need further investigation, but would probably include most of the six locally produced categories of food and drink (covering twenty-seven product types), most of the nine locally produced textiles (fifty commodities) and a few other items (for example, some drugs), and some essential inputs.
2. To establish *effective* control, it was necessary either to eliminate shortages or to ration effectively. The reduction in the number of commodities controlled would permit either of these policies. Both might be necessary, but high priority would need to be given to increasing supplies of the basic commodities, so as to eliminate shortages and hence make rationing, which is administratively costly and rarely effective and fair, unnecessary.
3. The price of the remaining decontrolled commodities would rise, as compared with the present controlled price, but might fall as compared with the parallel market price. The rise in price would tend to eliminate the middle man who had been making large untaxed profits out of the system and would reduce opportunities for corruption within the system. But substantial profits would then arise for the official producers. An excess profits tax would secure this additional revenue for the state.

A system reformed along these lines would have permitted the government to protect the real incomes of the poor against the ravages of inflation. It would also improve morale generally, by making it much more difficult for some to make large profits out of the country's difficulties.

Import allocation

Some system of exchange control and import licensing was essential, in order to ensure allocation along the lines of government priorities and to ration the available foreign exchange. Use of the price system alone to do this would be extremely inflationary, with unfair incidence and would not lead to allocation according to government priorities. A minor (or even major) devaluation would not eliminate the need for import controls. Inevitably, any system of import allocation would be bound to be a bit arbitrary as between commodities and between firms. Given the extreme shortages, efficiency of use of foreign exchange needed to be an important criterion of exchange allocation.

The import licensing system is an extremely powerful instrument for sectoral planning, and adjustment with BN-orientation. The discussion above suggested the following as priority industries, in a short run adjustment programme: (i) the agricultural sector and associated industries, including transport; (ii) production of simple consumer goods for low income consumers; (iii) goods for socially provided basic needs categories; (iv) manufactured export industries.

Summary of conclusions on devaluation

This question has been discussed at considerable length because it has become such an issue between Tanzania and the international community, in particular, the IMF. Moreover, while the discussion has occurred in the Tanzanian context, it has wider relevance for many other countries in a similar situation, and subject to similar international pressures. The exchange rate is just a price which may be used as an instrument of policy, like other prices. But it is a vital price, which can radically affect internal income distribution and real standards of living, the rate of inflation and even political stability. For these reasons, LDC governments rightly regard the issue with great seriousness.

The conclusions of the above discussion are:

1. That in Tanzania there were many policy changes needed, espe-

cially with respect to increasing agricultural output. The price issue was of relatively minor significance. If prices were radically changed without the other changes suggested, then they would be ineffective in raising output while disruptive in many other ways.
2. There did appear to be a case for some modest upward adjustment in real agricultural prices. But an increase in nominal prices would only bring about an increase in real incentives if accompanied by increased supply of consumer goods to the rural areas. If the price of export crops were raised, then the price of food production would also need to be raised, although by a lesser amount, to avoid reductions in food supplies. The case for some increase in prices rested on the need to bring more of the parallel market production into the official net, and on the hope (rather than any established fact) that there might be some positive supply response.
3. The budgetary costs of a subsidy to finance the price increase would have been very burdensome, which made a modest devaluation plus rise in produce food prices preferable. This change should also have restored the financial position of the marketing authorities, increased the competitiveness of manufactured exports, and encouraged firms to use local resources rather than imports, where possible.
4. Reform of the price control and the exchange allocation systems would also contribute to BN and short-term adjustment. For BN price control needed to be made effective for a few basic commodities while price control of non-basic items appeared to be dysfunctional. The import licensing system could have been used so as to secure import allocation to certain priority sectors.
5. Inflationary consequences of devaluation cannot be avoided. This, as well as other considerations, suggested that only a modest change was advisable in the first instance.

FOREIGN EXCHANGE NEEDS

The import restrictions were vitiating efforts throughout the economy, as argued earlier. In order to get production and exports up, additional foreign exchange was needed for imports in the agricultural sector, to rehabilitate the transport sector, and to permit the industrial sector to produce basic consumer goods and exports. The resulting increase in economic activity would raise revenue and would also raise exports.

Estimates of requirements[10]

The agricultural sector

Estimates by the Marketing Development Bureau[11] were for total import requirements of nearly 1 000 m. TSh for export crops in 1980/1 and 728 m. TSh for food crops – a total of 1 684 m. TSh. These estimates included fertilisers, tractors, machinery spares and renewals, fuel and transport costs.

Other sectors

Import allocations were well below requests in every sector varying from 8.7 per cent in transport to 24 per cent in intermediate products in 1981. Total requests for imports in 1981 amounted to 25.5 b. TSh, excluding all externally financed expenditure, estimated to be 3.9 b. TSh for 1980/1. Non-agricultural requests for import allocations were 24.7 b. TSh. The requests were known to be greatly inflated because firms assumed they would get more if they asked for more. Moreover, in the situation of shortages created by the crisis each firm may have assumed it could operate at full capacity if only it had the imports. In fact, if all firms were free of import constraints supply would exceed demand for some products, and shortages of other kinds (skills, energy and transport for example) would limit operations to something substantially below capacity. If we take half the estimated requirements as a guide, this leaves a total of 12.3 b. TSh for non-agricultural imports, which were not externally financed. Total import requirements then became 17.1 b. TSh.

It is clear that the level of requirements shown as (1) in Table 9.8 was excessive, being four times the level of exports in 1980.

In a realistic adjustment programme, requirements need to be reduced to a level which might reasonably find external finance, while providing sufficient resources to agriculture and industry to revive production and generate foreign exchange. There were two ways in which requirements could be reduced:

1. By cutting development expenditure. While such expenditure was apparently financed externally and therefore costless, the Tanzanian contribution involved foreign exchange. Moreover, once in operation most projects had heavy foreign exchange requirements for raw materials, etc. In addition, the foreign aid devoted to

TABLE 9.8 *Estimated import requirements 1981, b. TSh.*

	(1) Present system: requirements for fuller capacity utilisation	(2) Emergency programme
Agriculture	1.7	1.7
Non-agriculture, not externally financed	12.3	7.4[c]
Externally financed, ex-agriculture[a]	3.1	1.0[c]
TOTAL	17.1	10.1
Imports, 1980 actual	10.3	
Exports, 1980	4.2	
Exports, planned,[b] 1981	6.0	

[a] Deducts half agricultural requirements from estimates for 1981/2 external finance to allow for World Bank loan, which has been included under 'agriculture.'
[b] For 1981, according to National Survival Programme.
[c] The cut in development expenditure would also probably reduce demands for non-externally financed imports. This has not been taken into account above.

development expenditure, might, in one way or another, have been released for balance of payments support. If development expenditure were cut to one-third (i.e. 1.0 b.) this would cut imports by 1.8 b., and might release at least half of this amount to finance other imports.

2. Secondly, by cutting import requirements for raw materials, which accounted for over half the requested allocation in 1981 and 81 per cent of actual allocations; this could have been achieved by shutting down completely, during this emergency, all industries which did not fall into the four priority sectors (see p. 201), plus any industry closely linked to them.

Let us assume these industries accounted for 60 per cent of the total. The estimate of requirements for non-agricultural imports, not financed externally, then would amount to 7.4 b. TSh, roughly the

A Case Study of Tanzania

same as the 1980 imports. But as compared to the 1980 situation, the imports would be concentrated on the priority industries permitting them to provide the products necessary for basic consumption, agriculture and industrial exports. The reduction in development expenditure would have released external resources to finance the balance of trade gap.

These calculations are illustrative only. They are intended to show the direction of changes required for a BN-oriented adjustment programme, and the orders of magnitude likely to be involved. The latter are required to indicate whether the programme is at all realistic, which is of course essential if such a programme is to be presented as a viable alternative to more orthodox programmes.

To determine which projects should be stopped would require detailed case-by-case examination. Considerations determining decisions should include the contribution to import saving/export promotion, contribution to agricultural production (including transport), speed with which the projects would contribute to output, the import requirements for recurrent expenditure of the project when in operation, how far progress had gone in constructing the project, and cancellation charges.

Sources of foreign exchange

Import requirements in the 'Emergency Programme' were for 10.1 b. TSh (see Table 9.9), 1981 figures. Assume exports in 1981 come to 5.0 b. TSh, which is above the 1980 levels, but below those planned leaving a trade gap of 5.1 b. TSh, allowing for the service account. The gap requiring external finance was therefore 5.0 b. TSh for which the sources of finance shown in Table 9.10 might have been available.

The 'sources' of finance table thus suggests a manageable external financial situation on the assumption made – that is, that donors would pick up 50 per cent of their commitments to the cancelled development projects in the form of balance of payments support. This change in the nature of development assistance to Tanzania would not need to mean that the major donors simply issued untied cheques. They could take up particular sectors or subsectors (for example, parts of education, or health, or transport, or even particular industries, or marketing) and add a technical assistance component and a supervisory component in these sectors, while meeting recurrent import costs. They could also introduce an element of

TABLE 9.10 *Sources of finance*

	b. TSh
External assistance for projects (already committed)	1.0
Shift of 50% of money committed to development projects, now cancelled	1.0
World Bank, export rehabilitation	0.4
World Bank, structural adjustment loan	1.0
IMF (45% of quota over 3 years) p.a.	1.2
TOTAL	4.6

'tying' into these recurrent imports (as for instance with textbooks). In addition, Tanzania and the aid community might have to meet cancellation charges. Note that the table assumed a sizeable reduction in donor commitments in total, as a result of these changes. If this did not occur this would obviously ease the situation. Finally, it is assumed that the Fund and the World Bank came to an agreement with Tanzania.

The sort of programme advocated here is rather different from an orthodox stabilisation programme. It differs from a conventional one partly because it puts more emphasis on basic needs and therefore on preserving food production, production of basic consumer goods, and recurrent expenditure on social services; partly because it places less (but by no means no) emphasis on the use of prices to achieve adjustment, intending prices (especially the exchange rate) to be a subsidiary instrument, supporting the rest of the programme, rather than the prime mover. Moreover, it suggests a much smaller initial exchange-rate change because of fears of the political consequences of very large changes and scepticism of how effective they could be. The programme suggested here retains (much modified) price control as an essential element in an equitable system, and exchange controls and import licenses as a vital way of securing production according to priorities. In contrast, conventional programmes rely much more heavily on the price mechanism. Placing the main burden of allocation on the price mechanism, in an economy where shortages are chronic, would be unlikely to secure allocation according to social as well as economic priorities, although prices should be supportive of other policies. Radical price liberalisation of the type recommended by the IMF could lead to rapid inflation and hardship (and even famine) for some groups who are unable to keep their incomes rising as fast as inflation.

These differences (and perhaps others – i.e. lesser emphasis on credit creation as a means of control and indicator of performance) may make it difficult, or even impossible, for the Fund to reach agreement on the kind of programme proposed here. On the other hand, the programme – if ruthlessly carried out – would offer the possibility of medium-term improvements in Tanzania's balance of payments, permitting Tanzania to emerge from the crisis in the longer term with strengthened agricultural and export sectors, and without any major sacrifice of basic needs. If the Fund is serious in its declared intentions of political neutrality, and is able to be neutral about *instruments* of reform, so long as positive results are likely and repayment capacity thereby ensured, then it ought to regard this type of programme as a basis for negotiation.

This discussion has assumed that the Tanzanian Government would accept this type of programme, which they might not; and if they did accept it, that they pursued it ruthlessly and on a sustained basis. Acceptance in principle (apart from the adjustment of the exchange rate) seems quite possible – as indeed much of the programme is in a way an interpretation of the Tanzania's own guidelines contained in the National Programme for Survival. But to carry out the programme with the toughness necessary would require an immense effort of discipline and will. There would certainly be very strong opposing pressure groups to the cuts in development expenditure and industrial consolidation. In some ways the IMF package might turn out to be easier to accept.

10 Conclusions

This chapter will present some conclusions, derived from the analysis in the book, in two areas: first, a brief summary of some positive findings on meeting basic needs; secondly, a consideration of some of the conflicts between BN-objectives and other objectives of development.

SOME POSITIVE FINDINGS

The very large difference in BN-performance among countries which are quite similar suggests that most countries can improve their BN-performance substantially. Some improvements in the basic indicators are likely to occur almost automatically as economic growth proceeds – this is shown by the progress that has been made over time during the past few decades by virtually every country in the world, as well as by the strong association between average income per head across countries and BN-achievements. But countries can also improve their performance without waiting for growth to do it for them.

Three types of economy were identified as likely to be especially successful in relation to BN: socialist countries, with egalitarian income distribution and planned production and consumption; those capitalist economies which experienced rapid and labour-absorbing economic growth; and mixed economies with effective government interventions to promote BN. Most developing countries could improve their BN-achievements quite markedly by changing their government welfare-state type interventions. Economic conditions and political constraints will determine what is possible in any particular case. The detailed case study of Nigeria provides an example of the sort of combination of policy changes required in a mixed economy where neither radical redistribution nor Taiwan-type eonomic growth can be expected.

Improvements in BN performance, do not require extreme achievements with respect to income distribution, nor with respect to economic growth: they are potentially within the reach of most types of economy.

Improved BN-performance involves changes at the level of the macroeconomy: these changes must occur simultaneously and consistently with respect to each of the three aspects of the planning framework – production, organisation and incomes. Different aspects may form the 'lead' sector in any particular case; but in a permissive way the other aspects must adapt, or the changes will prove ineffective.

A key link in planning for BN is the meta-production function, relating BN-goods to BN-achievement. This function enters each of the aspects of the framework, and an improvement in this relationship will therefore automatically increase BN-performance. One reason why education turns out to be a critical variable is that it affects the meta-production function.

Attempts to identify social and economic variables that are positively related to BN-performance have generated rather few definite results. This may not be surprising in view of the complexity of the relationships involved. The strongest positive association among social variables was between measures of education (e.g. primary school enrolment ratios) and BN-achievement, as measured by life expectancy. Apart from education, some studies found a positive association between indicators of health service provision and BN-performance; no strong association was found for variables often emphasised in the BN-literature such as water supplies and calories per head. Among economic variables, overwhelmingly the most important was income per head. Some studies found some positive relationship between measures of income distribution and BN-performance, but this was not found consistently across studies. Contrary to what might have been expected, public expenditure as a share of GDP (and expenditure on social services as a share of GDP) was not found to have a positive association, nor was defence found to have a negative association, with BN-performance. Industrialisation tended to be positively associated and mineral exports negatively associated with performance.

The absence of a firm association in some areas where it might have been expected, is due to the nature of the variables and relationships involved. In the first place, the variables (e.g. social expenditure) are aggregates making no allowance for distribution or composition. For example, 'health expenditure' could be expected to have different results according to how the expenditure was allocated between modern hospitals and rural clinics, curative and preventive medicine. In addition, complementarities between the variables may prevent any one variable appearing effective when examined on its own. Inevitably, relevant issues get concealed in looking at aggregate variables. Hence comparative micro-studies are likely to shed more light on some of the relationships than cross-country aggregate studies.

Nonetheless, while a broad look at country experience strongly indicates a potential for markedly improving performance on BN in many countries, the weakness of the relationships identified among economic and social variables suggests some caution about claiming to know precisely how to achieve this potential. Given the difficulties, the positive findings then appear particularly strong: these are education, among social variables; and income per head, among economic factors.

CONFLICTS

Conflicts between objectives have been asserted or implied – often in order to justify avoiding emphasis on BN. Johan Galtung (1978) has described the conflict between BN, advocated by advanced countries, and the New International Economic Order (advanced by the Third World) as 'Grand Designs on a Collision Course'.

This conflict is premissed on assumed conflicts between BN and other objectives which form part of the NIEO – that is, a conflict between economic growth and BN; a conflict between industrialisation and BN; and a conflict between the desire to avoid dependency and BN.

The reality of these conflicts is a very important issue because to achieve BN requires, above all, political commitment by Third World

Conclusions 211

governments and so long as these conflicts exist, *or are believed to exist*, they will provide major obstacles to the achievement of BN.

The analysis and evidence in this book strongly suggests that these conflicts are not real.

A conflict between BN and economic growth would occur if BN-achievement required a shift in resources from investment in growth-enhancing activities. But the evidence shows that BN may be achieved by redistributing resources within the social sectors and by a reorientation of growth, so that the deprived participate. Countries which do better on BN do not, typically, have lower investment ratios, or higher expenditure on social services, or lower growth rates. Typically, they have higher incomes per head suggesting that economic growth will permit better achievement on BN. Moreover, better achievement on BN is likely to enhance the growth potential by increasing the quality of people, a country's major productive asset. Hicks (1979) has done a systematic and convincing empirical investigation into the question and found no empirical evidence for a conflict between economic growth and BN.

The hypothesised conflict between industrialisation and BN is also non-existent. In general the evidence suggests that there is some *positive* relationship between measures of industrialisation and BN-achievement. As with economic growth, it is a question of the nature of the industrialisation. Patterns of industrialisation using advanced technology, producing sophisticated products, and employing rather few people would be likely to be associated with poor BN-performance. But labour-intensive industrialisation and rural industrialisation would tend to be positively associated with BN. Industrialisation which conflicts with agricultural production, where food production lags behind the growth in incomes (as in the example of Nigeria) will tend to be associated with poor performance. But in those countries which combine industrial and agricultural growth this will not be the case.

The dependency issue is complex, partly because of the various meanings attached to *dependency*. In part BN is believed to perpetuate dependency because of the supposed conflicts just discussed – i.e. because it is assumed to retard growth and industrialisation. It is difficult to find any other reason why a conflict should occur: a healthy, educated people would seem to be a necessary precondition of true independence. It is difficult to believe that a people, as against its rulers, can be independent without health and education. But while BN might be thought to be necessary for the achievement of independence, it is not sufficient. What is sufficient depends on the precise interpretation of 'independence'. Casual consideration of the 'successful' and 'unsuccessful' countries on BN (Chapter 4) does not suggest any strong conclusions – though it is clear that countries in the unsuccessful group are by no stretch of the imagination more independent than the successful ones.

The threat to BN posed by the current debt and balance of payments crisis of many LDCs, (see Chapter 9) also points to the fact that financial dependence threatens BN-achievements.

The emphasis on a conflict between BN and the NIEO despite the absence of any real basis for it, suggests there may be some underlying motivation for stressing the existence of a conflict. On the one hand, the developed countries have tended to use BN to avoid meeting the demands of the NIEO; on the other, advocates of the NIEO, the leaders of the Third World, may wish to use a supposed conflict as a way of avoiding the redistribution of public expenditure and of incomes that would be needed for BN. For both, the 'conflict' is a useful political device.

Another conflict that has been suggested is between human rights and BN (except in so far as fulfilment of human rights is defined as part of BN, when there can be no conflict, though there could remain a conflict between the material aspects of BN, and human rights). The possibility of a conflict here has been suggested[1], by pointing out that an effective way of meeting BN in some societies is to go to prison. In practice, failure to ensure human liberties is to be found in many societies, both among those which have 'succeeded' in BN and those that have failed. Among the successful types, neither the socialist nor the capitalist are strongly achievers on human rights. It seems from casual analysis that the welfare-state type successes most often respect human rights. Among the countries classified as failures, there is near universal failure on human rights. It does not seem that there is any necessary conflict between achieving the material aspects of BN and fulfilling human rights. But the tough political systems associated with successes of the socialist and capitalist type have not so far had a good record in terms of liberal virtues. This may not be accidental: a more liberal political system may be incapable of producing and sustaining the reorientation in the economy necessary for these types of success.

CONCLUSION

In almost every area this book has touched it has become apparent that more knowledge is required. This includes the definition of the objective, its measurement, and the empirical relationships between BN-inputs and the BN-objective. The BN-approach emphasises the need to move beyond economists' normal identification of welfare with *utility* to the real welfare effects that consumption confers. This involves investigation of consumption behaviour within the household, an area which has been hardly studied. But while there is a need for theoretical imagination and empirical investigation, enough is known about the direction of change required. It is not lack of knowledge but lack of commitment that keeps so many deprived.

Appendix A: Table of Income, Life Expectancy and Adult Literacy

TABLE A.1

Country	Income (SNP) per capita $ 1979	Life expectancy at birth (years) 1979	Adult literacy rate (per cent) 1976
Low-income countries			
1. Bhutan	80	44	
2. Bangladesh	90	49	26*
3. Chad	110	41	15*
4. Ethiopia	130	40	15*
5. Nepal	130	44	19
6. Somalia		44	60
7. Mali	140	43	10
8. Burma	160	54	67
9. Afghanistan	170	41	12
10. Vietnam		63	87
11. Burundi	180	42	25
12. Upper Volta	180	43	
13. India	190	52	36
14. Malawi	200	47	25*
15. Rwanda	200	47	
16. Sri Lanka	230	66	85
17. Benin	250	47	
18. Mozambique	250	47	
19. Sierra Leone	250	47	
20. China	260	64	66*
21. Haiti	260	53	
22. Pakistan	260	52	24*
23. Tanzania	260	52	66*
24. Zaire	260	47	15
25. Niger	270	43	8
26. Guinea	280	44	20*
27. Central African Republic	290	44	
28. Madagascar	290	47	
29. Uganda	290	54	50*
30. Mauritania	320	43	17*
31. Lesotho	340	51	52*
32. Togo	350	47	18
33. Indonesia	370	53	62*
34. Sudan	370	47	20

Appendix A

	Income (GNP) per capita $ 1979	Life expectancy at birth (years) 1979	Adult literacy rate (per cent) 1976
Middle-income countries			
35. Kenya	380	55	45*
36. Ghana	400	49	
37. Yemen Arab Republic	420	42	13*
38. Senegal	430	43	10*
39. Angola	440	42	
40. Zimbabwe	470	55	
41. Egypt	480	57	44
42. Yemen PDR	480	45	27*
43. Liberia	500	54	30
44. Zambia	500	49	39*
45. Honduras	530	58	60*
46. Bolivia	550	50	63*
47. Cameroon	560	47	
48. Thailand	590	62	84
49. Philippines	600	62	88*
50. Congo, People's Republic	630	47	
51. Nicaragua	660	56	90*
52. Papua New Guinea	660	51	
53. El Salvador	670	63	62*
54. Nigeria	670	49	
55. Peru	730	58	80*
56. Morocco	740	56	28*
57. Mongolia	780	63	
58. Albania	840	70	
59. Dominican Republic	990	61	67
60. Colombia	1010	63	
61. Guatemala	1020	59	
62. Syrian Arab Republic	1030	65	58*
63. Ivory Coast	1040	47	20
64. Ecuador	1050	61	77*
65. Paraguay	1070	64	84*
66. Tunisia	1120	58	62
67. Korea, Dem. Republic	1130	63	

Appendix A

	Income (GNP) per capita $ 1979	Life expectancy at birth (years) 1979	Adult literacy rate (per cent) 1976
Middle-income countries			
68. Jordan	1180	61	70
69. Lebanon		66	
70. Jamaica	1260	71	
71. Turkey	1330	62	60
72. Malaysia	1370	68	60*
73. Panama	1400	70	
74. Cuba	1410	72	96*
75. Korea, Republic of	1480	63	93
76. Algeria	1590	56	35*
77. Mexico	1640	66	82
78. Chile	1690	67	
79. South Africa	1720	61	
80. Brazil	1780	63	76*
81. Costa Rica	1820	70	90*
82. Rumania	1900	71	98
83. Uruguay	2100	71	94
84. Iran		54	50*
85. Portugal	2180	71	70
86. Argentina	2230	70	94
87. Yugoslavia	2430	70	85
88. Venezuela	3120	67	82
89. Trinidad & Tobago	3390	70	95*
90. Hong Kong	3760	76	90
91. Singapore	3830	71	
92. Greece	3960	74	
93. Israel	4150	72	
94. Spain	4380	73	

	Income (GNP) per capita $ 1979	Life expectancy at birth (years) 1979	Adult literacy rate (per cent) 1976
Industrial Market Economies			
95. Ireland	4210	73	98*
96. Italy	5250	73	98
97. New Zealand	5930	73	99*
98. United Kingdom	6320	73	99
99. Finland	8160	73	100
100. Austria	8630	72	99
101. Japan	8810	76	99
102. Australia	9120	74	100
103. Canada	9640	74	99
104. France	9950	74	99
105. Netherlands	10 230	75	99
106. United States	10 630	74	99*
107. Norway	10 700	75	99*
108. Belgium	10 920	72	99
109. Germany, Fed. Republic	11 730	73	99
110. Denmark	11 900	75	99
111. Sweden	11 930	76	99*
112. Switzerland	13 290	75	99
Capital-surplus Oil Exporters			
113. Iraq	2410	56	
114. Saudi Arabia	7280	54	
115. Libya	8170	56	50*
116. Kuwait	17 100	70	60
Non-market Industrial Economies			
117. Bulgaria	3690	73	
118. Poland	3830	72	98
119. Hungary	3850	71	98
120. U.S.S.R.	4110	73	100
121. Czechoslovakia	5290	71	
122. German Dem. Republic	6430	72	

* For year other than 1976.
Source: *World Development Report 1981* (World Bank, August 1981) table 1 (annex).

Appendix B: List of people who helped in Nigeria*

Anne Bamishaye, Institute of Child Health, University of Lagos
Professor L. Bown, Department of Adult Education, University of Lagos
Dr A. Callaway, UNESCO, Lagos
Dr E. Fapohaunda, Department of Economics, University of Lagos
Professor A. Opuber, Department of Mass Communication, University of Lagos
Dr Ndagi, Director of Institute of Education, A.B.U.
Dr Odufalu, Department of Economics, Lagos
Dr B. d'Silva, Department of Agricultural Economics and Rural Sociology, Institute of Agricultural Research, A.B.U.
Professor A.O. Omololu, Department of Nutrition, University of Ibadan
Professor Teriba, Department of Economics, Ibadan
Professor T. Williams, Department of Agriculture, Ibadan
Katherine McKee, Ford Foundation, Lagos
Dr Ramsome-Kuti, Department of Medicine, Lagos
Dr Ejiga, Department of Agricultural Economics & Rural Sociology, Institute of Agricultural Research, ABU.
Dr Okello, Department of Political Science, ABU
Professor Hallaway, Department of Biochemistry, ABU
Professor Okediji, Department of Sociology, Lagos
Members of UNFPA team

*Apart from government officials.

Notes and References

1 A BASIC NEEDS APPROACH TO DEVELOPMENT

1. See ILO (1976), ILO (1977), Streeten *et al.* (1981), Lederer (1980), Leipziger (1981).
2. This term is used in ILO (1976).
3. Jesse Collings declared the objective of land reform in Britain in the nineteenth century to be three acres and a cow for each household. Henri Quatre (in sixteenth-century France) promised each household a chicken every Sunday.
4. The term 'BN-goods', should be taken to mean 'BN goods and services'.
5. See discussion in Lederer (1980).
6. See Hicks and Streeten (1979).
7. There is a parallel here with the 'headcount' approach to defining poverty and Sen's more sensitive index, which allows for the extent of variation in incomes of the poor below the poverty line (see Sen, 1981a).
8. Sen (1981b) illustrates this choice with respect to Sri Lanka.
9. See especially Hicks (1970) and later chapters of this book.
10. Drums and toddy were the items which made life worth living for a very poor man in one novel of Indian village life (see Shivaram (1978)).
11. See, for example, the weighting systems discussed in Chenery *et al.* (1974).
12. This has been well analysed by Streeten in Streeten *et al.* (1981).
13. See, for example, the writings of Frank, Furtado and Prebisch.
14. Although not sharply growing. See Morawetz (1977) pp. 34–5.
15. Turnham (1971) provides a good analysis and summary of the evidence in the 1960s.
16. See, for example, ILO (1970).
17. Kuznets (1955).

18. Adelman and Morris (1973) p.189.
19. Morawetz (1977) p.43 and references in his footnote 17.
20. One case where it was sufficient it appears was Taiwan. (See Fei, Ranis and Kuo, 1979.)
21. Griffin and Khan (1978) and ILO (1977), for example, describe a number of Asian cases where poverty increased alongside increasing per capita incomes.
22. See ILO (1972) and Chenery *et al.* (1974).
23. Chenery *et al.* (1974).
24. See Stewart and Streeten (1976).
25. See Sen (1981a).

2 A MACROECONOMIC FRAMEWORK

1. It is clearly difficult, if not impossible, to establish a functional relationship between the intermediate outputs and, say, 'love of art'.
2. For example, subsidies to private producers.
3. All categories of income are after deducting tax. In this case, income from self-employment is imputed to wages and property income. A less arbitrary and artificial procedure might be to include it as a separate category.
4. We have neglected the community production sector for simplification.
5. On the assumption of a closed economy and ignoring stock accumulation or decumulation. With trade, net imports must be added to production, in each sector.
6. See Chenery *et al.*, 1974; Fei, Ranis and Kuo, 1979.
7. In this analysis we are using C_b to represent consumption of the BN-commodity. In fact there are a number of BN-goods, $C_b{}'$, $C_b{}''$, $C_b{}'''$ etc. But for simplicity we assume a single one here.
8. See, for example, Meerman, (1979).

3 PLANS AND POLICIES

1. See, for example, ILO (1977).
2. See, for example, *World Development Report, 1980*, Part II, 'Poverty and Human Development', (World Bank, 1980).
3. See Griffin and James (1981).
4. For example in Sheehan and Hopkins (1979).
5. See Stewart (ed.) (1983) for a discussion of implications for income distribution and efficiency of a variety of organisational alternatives.
6. See, for example, Becker (1981).

4 COUNTRY EXPERIENCE IN MEETING BASIC NEEDS

1. I have benefited greatly from research assistance from H.V. Singh in writing this and the following chapter.
2. For example, for Nigeria the *World Development Report* 1981 gives a figure of 49 for life expectancy in 1979, while best-guess local estimates are for 42–45. See Chapter 6.
3. Most studies find a high correlation between life expectancy and literacy. For example, Berg (1981) found a simple correlation co-efficient of 0.91.
4. As has been suggested by Eberstadt (1978).
5. See Kravis *et al.* (1978) and Isenman (1980a).
6. Using quadratic relationship, equation l_j in Table 4.2.
7. This account relies on statistics in the World Bank's *World Development Report, 1981*; a report of a World Bank team which visited Cuba in 1978 and Brundenius (1981a).
8. One estimate was that food subsidies in 1980 amounted to 25 pesos per head per month: this, if accurate, is enormously high, since monthly salaries were between 65 (retired worker) and 248 pesos (university teacher). See Brundenius (1981a), pp. 157, 158.
9. See detailed discussion in Brundenius, chapter 5.
10. See Brundenius, chapters 1 and 2.
11. This account relies on the World Bank's *World Development Report*, 1980, Fei, Ranis and Kuo (1979) and Kuo, Ranis and Fei, (1981).
12. Having refused to admit the existence of mainland China for many years and provided figures only for Taiwan, the World Bank shifted in 1981 and since then has accepted mainland China in its statistics, but has omitted all reference to Taiwan. One consequence of this ludicrous attitude (both pre and post 1981) is that we use the 1980 edition *World Development Report* for data for Taiwan. Hence the figures are somewhat out of date.
13. Figures from Fei, Ranis and Kuo (1979), pp. 66, 92.
14. See discussion in Fei, Ranis and Kuo (1979).
15. Kuo, Ranis and Fei (1981) table 2.7.
16. According to Fei, Ranis and Kuo (1979) the land reform was among the most substantial (as measured by a change in Gini co-efficient for land concentration) among a group of countries which instituted land reforms between 1948 and 1960 (p. 252).
17. See the discussion in Ranis (1983).
18. This account relies heavily on Isenman (1980b) and Richards and Gooneratine (1980).
19. Isenman (1980b).
20. Data from Lee (1977) and Chenery (1980).
21. Chenery (1980).
22. *Review of the Economy, 1980*, Central Bank of Ceylon, table 93.
23. *Central Bank of Ceylon*, Annual Report, 1981.
24. Bowring, *Financial Times*, 27 August 1980.
25. See the World Development Report's estimate of 69 for 1977; others estimated the figure as being nearer 66 then (the level it is reported for 1980).

Notes and References 223

26. This account relies heavily on *Zambia: Basic Needs in an Economy under Pressure*, ILO, (JASPA), 1981.
27. Quoted in introduction to ILO Report.
28. ILO Report on Zambia (1981), para 0.6.
29. Ibid, table 0.1.
30. Ibid, para 13.
31. Ibid, p. xlii.
32. Bloom, *Financial Times*, 15 December 1980.
33. A. Berg (1981), table B.1.
34. World Bank, *Accelerated Development in sub-Saharan Africa*, 1981.
35. Ibid.
36. Ahluwalia, Carter and Chenery (1979).
37. Leipziger (1981).
38. In 1982 Keith Griffin and Shyam Nigam led an ILO/JASPA team to Ethiopia to consider economic development and poverty elimination. Discussions with members of this team have been very useful in preparing this section.

5 ECONOMIC AND SOCIAL VARIABLES AND BASIC NEEDS PERFORMANCE

1. Hicks (1980, 1982).
2. Sheehan and Hopkins (1979).
3. The sample excludes the four oil surplus countries.
4. Leipziger and Lewis (1980) also find that the Gini co-efficient is related to various measures of BN for countries with incomes above $500 per capita, but not for low-income countries.

    A similar view is suggested in Ahluwalia, Carter and Chenery in Chenery (1979, P. 492):

    A poor country such as Indonesia that can move quite rapidly parallel to the Kuznets curve may make more progress in reducing poverty than a slow growing country with better distribution such as India or Bangladesh ... On the other hand, in the typical middle-income countries, which tend to have more rapid growth and less equal distribution, improved distribution is often more effective in reducing poverty than is accelerated growth.

5. The figures are taken from Ahluwalia, Carter and Chenery: their poverty line is derived from Indian data, being roughly that income level necessary to ensure 2250 calories per person.
6. This is recognised by Ahluwalia, Carter and Chenery in Chenery (1979, p.458):

    Not only is the notion of some biologically determined absolute poverty level imprecise, it is in any case wrong to think that poverty should be defined solely in terms of biological requirements. Ultimately concepts such as poverty lines are operationally meaningful only when they acquire some social reality, that is, when there exists a sufficient social consensus that a particular level represents an objective which claims a high social priority ... it follows that poverty lines used in national policy debates will vary across countries reflecting differences in level of economic, social and political development.

7. The fact that the two sets of results (for income distribution and absolute poverty) are similar may merely reflect common sources of data.
8. See Berg (1981), Appendix B.
9. The method was devised by Reutlinger and Selowsky (1976).
10. Leipziger and Lewis (1980).

6 BASIC NEEDS IN NIGERIA

1. The chapters on Nigeria are based on a report written for the World Bank in 1980. While working on this report I had the privilege of participating in many of the discussions of Dudley Seers' ILO Mission to Nigeria on basic needs. I benefited enormously from the work and ideas of all members of his group (see the ILO Report *First things First: Meeting the Needs of the People of Nigeria* 1980). References to the ILO Report appear as ILO (1980). Apart from extremely useful discussions, material and comments I received from people I met in Nigeria, listed at the end of the book (Appendix B), and those who participated in the World Bank Mission to Nigeria in February 1980, led by Irfan ul Haque, I should like to thank H. Callaway, D. Davies, V. Diejomoah, G. Ranis and G. Williams for very valuable suggestions and comments.
2. *World Development Report*, 1981.
3. A statistical assessment relating life expectancy to per capita income among developing countries as a whole in 1979, showed that Nigeria's life expectancy was *ten years* below that expected for countries at that per capita income. See Chapter 4.
4. The official' population figure is 81m. for 1978. But this is widely believed to be an overestimate. In these chapters alternative estimates are used (see note 15) unless explicitly stated.
5. For a comprehensive account of the Nigerian economy in the 1950s and 1960s see Helleiner (1966).
6. See Chapter 8 for analysis and discussion of these effects.
7. This is the figure in *World Development Report 1981* (World Bank 1981). Any figure is rather arbitrary because it depends on uncertain GDP estimates, uncertain population estimates and which exchange rate is used.
8. See E.B. Simmons (1976).
9. UNFPA (1979)
10. See ILO (1981) Technical Paper 1, table 4.
11. H.M. Gilles (1965).
12. N. Bankole (1977).
13. UNFPA (1979) table 10. There seems to be no particular reason for this rise which may be purely statistical or random.

14. *Health Sector Policy Paper*, World Bank, 1980, Annex 1.
15. Per capita figures are dependent on the population figures adopted. The official population figures are widely believed to be overestimates. Here (and elsewhere) 'best-guess' population estimates are used:

millions

1963	1965	1969	1975	1977	1980
48.3	51.0	56.7	66.5	70.1	75.9

16. See World Bank (1980), *Health Sector Policy Paper*, table 6. p. 38.
17. Arowolo (1979).
18. 'Guidelines for the Fourth National Development Plan, 1981–85', p. 75.
19. ILO Technical Paper.
20. Annual Report of Medical Statistics Division, Federal Ministry of Health, 1975.
21. Another nationwide survey in 1966 found average daily consumption of calories varied from 1,545 in the Midwest to 2,470 (East Central) while protein consumption varied from 41.7 grams (West) to 66.7 (East Central). Omololu (1974).
22. World Bank (1979). Nigeria, *Agricultural Sector Review*, Vol. II, Paper 4, Report No. 2181-UNI, p. 126: the average calory estimates per person were 2,450 (USDA, 69/70), 2,182 (FAO, 63/4) 2,199 (Olayide 68/9), 2, 460 (IBRD Food Study, 1978).
23. Omololu, a pediatrician, Professor of Nutrition and Director of the Food Science and Applied Nutrition Unit, University of Ibadan, Nigeria.
24. Simmons (1976).
25. Morley, Bicknell and Woodland (1968).
26. Collis, Dema and Omololu (1962). Dr M. James of the Institute of Child Health at Ibadan found similar substantial differences in height and weight between children in the traditional sector of Ibadan and children with educated parents (secondary completion for both mother and father). Similar results were found for rural children in eastern Nigeria (International Geographical Union, World Land Use Survey, Occasional Paper No. 6, 'Uboma: A Socio-Economic and Nutritional Survey of a Rural Community in Eastern Nigeria', 1966).
27. Data from the Institute of Child Health, Lagos supplied to ILO.
28. Tomkins, Drasar, Bradley and Williamson (1978).
29. Paper prepared for joint Population Council/UNFPA Workshop, Oct. 1978.
30. ILO Technical Paper 2A.
31. US Department of Health, Education and Welfare, March 1967.
32. Omolulu (1974).
33. Omolulu (1974).
34. Ransome-Kuti, Obajumo and Olaniyan (1972).
35. See Lesi (1978); Ransome-Kuti *et al.* (1972), and Okungbowa and Akesode (1978).
36. Ransome-Kuti *et al.* (1972).
37. Okungbowa and Akesode (1978).
38. Information supplied to ILO by Institute of Child Health.
39. Okungbowa and Akesode (1978).
40. See Umoh and Bassir (1976).

41. This section relies heavily on the background paper for the ILO Mission prepared by F.R. Banugire and ILO Technical Paper 3, 'Water'.
42. This is the average target for an urban population, which allows for some degree of unequal distribution. A supplementary target is a minimum of 21 litres per person per day for *every* family.
43. See ILO (1981), Technical Paper 3, table 26.
44. A 1938 Board of Education Report stated that, 'This country is in the invidious position of providing fewer opportunities in regard to education than any other British possession in Africa.' In 1944 it was estimated that the number of children in government or government assisted schools was 40 per 10,000 of the population in Nigeria, compared with 134 in the Gold Coast and 568 in Nyasaland. (ILO, 1981, Technical Paper 6, para. 21).
45. Second National Development Plan.
46. In 1965, only one-fifth of the children in primary schools were girls, according to UNESCO estimates. In 1970 the ratio had risen to 37 per cent.
47. See 'Education: Sector Working Paper', World Bank, Dec. 1974.
48. The Blueprint gives the following cost breakdown:-

	N Capital costs per student	Recurrent costs per student
Primary (basic facilities)	100	86
Secondary, junior	700	205
Secondary, senior	1,000	430 – tuition 880 – boarding
Teachers College ex-boarding	1,000	325 – tuition 720 – boarding

Source: 'Blueprint' Report of the Implementation Committee for the National Policy on Education, 1978–9.

49. In Nigeria as a whole enrolments in 1976–7 were nearly 700 000 (or 31 per cent greater than expected). (Blueprint, p. 54).
50. Blueprint, p. 53.
51. The Blueprint estimates that enrolment in Form I of secondary schools will need to more than double between 1978–9 and 1988–9, given a 40 per cent transition rate.
52. Estimate by L. Bown, Head of Department of Adult Education, University of Lagos.
53. Cited in table 9.22 of R.W. Morgan (1975).
54. M.M. Konan (1975).
55. There were over 10 000 unqualified primary school teachers in some states in 1976–7 (Anambia, Bendel, Benue, Cross River, Kaduna, Kano and Oyo) and under 5000 in others (Banchi, Borno, Kwara, Lagos,

Niger). With UPE secondary school differences are likely to become the most significant source of regional inequality. In 1976–7 transition rates from primary to secondary schools varied from 36 per cent (Anambra) to 83 per cent (Niger).
56. Theses by students of ABU's Institute of Education show almost 100 per cent support for UPE in all states surveyed. But in Benue support was slightly lower among Muslims (75%) than others (100%) and in Anambra support was lower among farmers (75%) than others (89–100%).
57. Dr Ndagi, Director of Institute of Education, ABU, Zaria.
58. Dr Ndagi.
59. D'Silva's study of the Funtua Project (1979).
60. This is a programme devised by David Morley (Institute of Child Health Care, London) to educate children in simple health skills – e.g. the administration of nutrition tests, easy first aid, information about immunisation etc. In Lagos there was Workship for teachers in July 1979, in honour of the Year of the Child.
61. See summary of studies in the next chapter pp. 164–5).

7 A MACRO APPROACH TO BASIC NEEDS IN NIGERIA

1. It could also mislead about trends if domestic industrial processing's share is changing over time. During this period there were two offsetting trends: on the one hand, there was a fall in producer prices for cash as against food crops encouraging a shift towards the production of food. Some of this has been taken into account (implicitly) in using the net import trend. Secondly, there was growth in the share of textiles as a proportion of manufacturing, while manufacturing as a whole rose much faster than agricultural output. Hence agriculture may have provided an increasing proportion of its output to supply cotton, etc.
2. Similar trends have occurred since 1975 – however because of changes in classifications, the 1975 figures are used here.
3. Which is a rather conservative estimate.
4. The figure given for food per capita is in fact an estimate of the value of the output of agriculture, fishing and livestock plus net imports per capita – it should thus be expected to exaggerate because it includes the value of non-food crops, e.g. cotton. An alternative approach is to look at household consumption surveys; the national survey of 1974–5 gives a figure of 42.5 per cent for the proportion of total income all households spent on food. Thus both approaches give very similar results.
5. Ozgediz (1980) for a general discussion and more details.
6. At present over a quarter of the medical doctors in Nigeria are expatriates – see Ozgediz (1980) for a more general discussion and more examples.
7. According to the Blueprint: 'The problem facing the whole Federation now is what to do with 2.1 million primary school leavers in June 1982. Unless a drastic restructuring of the primary school curriculum is achieved which would make primary school leavers not dissatisfied with

the rural districts where they were brought up, the whole country is in for serious trouble, because even with 40 per cent of them proceeding to junior secondary schools, 1.3 million of them would still be waiting to be catered for.'
8. Basu (1969).
9. Clark and Akinbode (1968) and Voh (1979).
10. Van den Burne and Roling (1973) find that over twice as many cocoa farmers with high contact with extension workers have been to school as those with low contact.
11. Taiwo Williams (1969): 32 per cent of the farmers got their information from extension workers with radio (at 29 per cent) being the second main source.
12. Konan (1975).
13. Norman, Pryor, Gibbs (1979).
14. Berry (1975).
15. Grant and Anthonio (1973).
16. See Simmons (1975); Remy in Williams (ed.) (1976); and C. Dimonenico and Lacey Majuetan (1976), which describes the limitations imposed on Muslim Hausa women and the more active role, especially in marketing, of Yoruba women.
17. Konan (1975).
18. Adeyeye (1978).
19. Ibid., p. 172.
20. Grant and Anthonio (1973).
21. It has been claimed that this is true of some of the major World Bank interventions in agriculture – see B. D'Silva and M. Rafique Raza (1979).
22. King (1980).
23. See, for example, Matlon's study (1977) and (1981). Because households of all income levels participate in the cash economy to some degree there is no automatic relationship between additional production and additional consumption even where the actual production for own-consumption forms a very large element of total production. Farmers make production decisions (as between cash and subsistence crops) and consumption decisions (as between food and other items) in the light of economic and other considerations in much the same way as in a non-subsistence context.
24. Ittah (1979) quotes studies showing Gini ranging between 0.5 and 0.6. Diejomaoh and Anusionwu (1980) 'The Structure of Income Inequality in Nigeria: A Macro Analysis' in Bienen and Diejomaoh (1981) (eds) suggest that the Gini co-efficient was around 0.5 in 1960 rising to about 0.6 in 1970 and to 0.7 in mid-1979.
25. Hays (1978).
26. Rouis (1980).
27. These results are very different from those of ILO (1981a); a much higher urban–rural differential of income per capita of over four, is estimated. The main reason for the difference is that petroleum is included in urban income, and rural income is assumed to come exclusively from agriculture while all other income is urban.

28. Teriba and Phillips (1971).
29. See Williams (1982) for a survey of those studies. Much of what follows is taken from Williams.
30. Female income added 58 per cent to male income for households in the 1st decile and 8 per cent to those in the 10th decile.
31. Williams, table 8.
32. Williams (1982) table 10.
33. E.g. Matlon (1980).
34. Fajana, in Bienen and Diejomaoh (1981).
35. See evidence in Bienen and Diejomaoh (1981).
36. L. Barreiros, 'Wage Policy Issues in Nigeria', Background Paper for ILO BN Mission, mimeo (1979).
37. Household Income and Expenditure Survey.
38. However, the household survey occurred just after a huge wage increase; this probably distorted relativities – and also consumption patterns.
39. Member of World Bank Mission, 1980.
40. ILO Mission, 1979.
41. Simmons (1976).
42. This is a rather over simplified view of the migration process, ignoring cultural/educational factors in causing migration and also the Harris–Todaro critical variables – that is, the differential between earnings in the rural sector and earnings in the urban modern sector plus expectations of potential migrants about the probability of getting a job in the urban modern sector. In the Harris–Todaro model, higher rural earnings would reduce the flow of migrants, because it reduces the rural/urban modern sector earnings differential. However, a major weakness of the Harris–Todaro model, in its initial form, was that it ignored the existence of urban earning opportunities in the informal sector. But while cultural/educational and Harris–Todaro factors may influence migration, the immediate choice for most migrants is between rural earnings opportunities and those in the urban informal sector, and *ceteris paribus*, it is likely that these will bear some functional positive relationship to each other, so that large movements of either will eventually be followed by movements in a similar direction in the other.
43. Essang and Mabawonku (1975).
44. For example, Sada in Bienen and Diejomaoh (1981).
45. See D'Silva and Rafique Raza (1979); Forest (1980); and Williams (1982).
46. Teriba and Phillips (1971).
47. Omorogiuwa, in Bienen and Diejomaoh (eds) (1981).
48. Omorogiuwa reports evasion of personal income taxation of 50 per cent in Nigeria as a whole and 67 per cent in Western State – though the nature of the data must make these claims difficult to substantiate.
49. G.S. Sahota, 'The Distribution of the Benefits of Public Expenditure in Nigeria', report prepared for the World Bank, June 1980.
50. Sahota (1980).
51. Sahota (1980).
52. Matlon (1977, 1980).
53. Sada, in Bienen and Diejomaoh (1981).
54. See Morley (1974).

55. Orubuloye and Caldwell (1975).
56. ILO (1983) technical paper C.
57. Okungbowa and Akesode (1978).
58. Imrana Yazidu, Phd. (1978) ABU.
59. Bamishaye (1979).
60. Working paper prepared for Joint Population Council/UNFPA Workshop, October 1979, New York.
61. Ohadike, 'A Demographic Note on Marriage, Family and Family Growth in Lagos, Nigeria' found that age of marriage and fertility were associated with education level in a 1964 survey; Okediji in a survey of females in Ibadan (1965–6) found that improved education, higher prestige jobs, higher incomes are all associated with reduced fertility; education was a significant negative determinant of fertility according to a survey of Yoruba women in the 1970s by Arowolo. See also Caldwell and Caldwell (1978).
62. Ilori in a survey of Ife and rural areas in Oyo in 1974 (Ilori, 1978).
63. Olusanya (1969 and undated) in studies of Ibadan, Ife and Oyo finds a positive relationship between education and fertility which he attributes to improved health and reduced taboos associated with increased education.
64. The matrix does not show the effects which may result from subsequent changes in productivity; nor the effects on fertility.
65. Orubuloye and Caldwell (1975) and Caldwell (1979).

8 A BASIC NEEDS STRATEGY FOR NIGERIA

1. Several studies (see Health section, Chapter 6) show that the average weight of children with high income parents is substantially greater than that of children of low income parents, as is their height. Levels of education at all levels are correlated with incomes (see, for example, Ransome-Kuti *et al.* (1972), while use and benefit from the various social services are strongly related to both income levels and education.
2. See p. 158.
3. People may choose à la Harris–Todaro to accept a lower (or even zero) income in the urban informal sector while seeking modern sector jobs, so that urban informal earnings fall below rural opportunities, but the direction and broad magnitude of change in the two areas are likely to move in line.
4. These have been discussed at length elsewhere. See, for example, ILO (1977); Chenery *et al.* (1974); Fei, Ranis, Kuo (1979).
5. The role of agricultural performance in relation to *urban* poverty seems to have been under-emphasised in general and needs investigation in other countries.
6. One study of W. Nigeria showed that over 70 per cent of those between twenty and forty had migrated (S.M. Essang & A.F. Mabawonku, 1975).
7. See ILO (1977).
8. See Bienen and Diejomaoh (1981).

9. Problems of estimating targets were more fully discussed in Chapter 3.
10. Countries with high life expectancy generally have supplies of food per capita in excess of 110 per cent (on average) of FAO 'requirements'. The more unequal the food distribution the greater this excess needs to be to eliminate malnutrition. According to the World Bank indicators Nigeria's ratio was 88 per cent in 1974. An increase of a quarter would thus raise this to precisely 110 per cent.
11. See World Bank (1974) *Education Sector Working Paper*.
12. See table 6 of World Bank (1980) *Health Sector Policy Paper*.

9 BASIC NEEDS AND THE INTERNATIONAL CRISIS: A CASE STUDY OF TANZANIA

1. This chapter draws heavily on work done for a JASPA BN Mission to Tanzania in 1981, under the leadership of Shyam Nigam and Paul Streeten. I am grateful to them and JASPA for permission to use the material, some of which has appeared in *Basic Needs in Danger: a Basic Needs Development Strategy for Tanzania*, JASPA (1982).
2. For more discussion of the nature of IMF conditionality see Stewart and Sen Gupta (1982), and Killick *et al.* (1982).
3. Bank of Tanzania estimates.
4. Green *et al.* (1980).
5. See Ellis (1982).
6. See World Bank (1981), p. 15.
7. Reported by Bank of Tanzania.
8. See JASPA/ILO Report.
9. In order to make these calculations it was necessary to make assumptions on (i) the rate of subsidy which would be equivalent to any particular rate of devaluation; (ii) the coverage of the subsidy; (iii) the proportion of government expenditure that goes directly on imports (iv) the subsequent rate of inflation; (v) the consequent effects on revenue from Sales Tax and Excise Taxes.
10. The estimates are based on 1981 figures.
11. See Schluter and Sackett (1981).

10 CONCLUSIONS

1. By Paul Streeten in discussion.

Bibliography

Aboyade, O.(ed.) (1978) *The National Accounts of Nigeria, 1973–75*, Lagos.
Adelman, I. and C.T. Morris (1973) *Economic Growth and Social Equity in Developing Countries*, Stanford University Press.
Adeokun, L. and A. Odebiyi (1977) 'Physical Planning and Cultural Factors Determining Optimum use of Modern Facilities in Nigeria', *Journal of Medical and Pharmaceutical Marketing*, 5.
Adeyeye, S.O. (1978) *The Cooperative Movement in Nigeria, Yesterday, Today and Tomorrow*, Göttingen-Vandenboeck and Ruprecht, Marburg, Federal Republic of Germany.
Ahluwalia, M.S., N. Carter and H.B. Chenery (1970) 'Growth and Poverty in Developing Countries', *Journal of Development Economics*, 6.
Akiwowo, A. and A.C. Basu (1968) 'Tobacco Growers in the Northern Oyo Division and Adoption of New Farming Ideas and Practices', Nigerian Institute of Social and Economic Research, Ibadan.
Arowolo, O.O. (1979) 'Fertility and Mortality Trends: Implications for Education, Health and Housing Expenditure in Nigeria', Paper presented at National Workshop on Interactions between Economic and Demographic Processes in Nigeria, University of Lagos.
Bamishaye, A. (1979) 'Health Service Use in Lagos: Socio-economic, Cultural and Organisational Factors affecting Use of Child Health Services in Somolu, Lagos with Some Strategies to Improve Coverage', PH.D. thesis, Ann Arbor.
Bankole, N. (1977) in O. Adejuyigbe (ed.) *The Location of Rural Basic Health Facilities in Ife–Ijesa Area of South Western Nigeria*, University of Ife.
Basu, A.C. (1969) 'The Relationship of Farmers' Characteristics to the Adoption of Recommended Farm Practices in Four Villages of the Western State of Nigeria', *Bulletin of Rural Economics and Sociology*, 4.
Becker, G.S. (1981) *A Treatise on the Family*, Harvard University Press.

Bibliography 233

Berg, A. (1981) *Malnourished People, a Policy View*, World Bank.
Berry, S.S. (1975) *Cocoa, Custom and Socio-Economic Change in Rural Western Nigeria*, Clarendon Press.
Bienen, H. and V.P. Diejomaoh (eds) (1981) *The Political Economy of Income Distribution in Nigeria*, Holmes & Meier.
Bloom B. (1980) *Financial Times*, 15 December.
Bowring P. (1980) *Financial Times*, 27 August.
Brundenius, C. (1981a) *Economic Growth, Basic Needs and Income Distribution in Revolutionary Cuba*, University of Lund, Sweden.
Brundenius, C. (1981b) 'Growth and Equity: The Cuban Experience 1959–1980', *World Development*, 9.
Caldwell, J.C. and P. Caldwell (1978) 'The Achieved Small Family: Early Fertility Transition in an African City', *Studies in Family Planning, Population Council 9*.
Chenery, H.B., M.S. Ahluwalia, C.L.G. Bell, J.H. Duloy and R. Jolly (1974) *Redistribution with Growth: An Approach to Policy*, Oxford University Press.
Chenery, H.B. (1979) *Structural Change and Development Policy*, The World Bank and Oxford University Press.
Chenery, H.B. (1980) 'Poverty and Progress–Choices for the Developing World', in *Poverty and Basic Needs*, World Bank.
Caldwell, J.C. (1979) 'Education as a Factor in Mortality Decline. An Examination of Nigerian Data', *Population Studies*, 33.
Clark, R.C. and L.A. Akinbode (1968) 'Factors Associated with Adoption of Three Farm Practices in the Western State of Nigeria', *Research Bulletin*, 1, Faculty of Agriculture, University of Ife.
Collis, W., I. Dema and A. Omololu (1962) 'On the Ecology of Child Health and Nutrition in Nigerian Villages: Environment, Population and Resources', *Tropical and Geographic Medicine*, 14.
Dimonenico, C.M. and L. Lacey Majuetan (1976) 'Female Industrial Recruits: Women Workers of the Nigerian Tobacco Company Factory at Ibadan', paper delivered at National Conference on Nigerian Women and Development in Relation to Changing Family Structure. University of Ibadan, April 1976.
D'Silva, B. and M. Rafique Raza (1979) 'Integrated Rural Development in Nigeria. A Case Study of the Funtua Project', mimeo, Department of Agricultural Economics and Rural Sociology, Institute of Agricultural Research, A.B.U.
Eberstadt, N. (1978) 'Has China Failed?', *New York Review of Books*, XXVI.
Ellis, F. (1982) 'Agricultural Price Policy in Tanzania', *World Development*, 10.
Essang, S.M. and A.F. Mabawonku (1975) 'Impact of Urban Migration on Rural Development: Theoretical Considerations and Empirical Evidence from Southern Nigeria', *Developing Economics*, 13.
Fei, J., G. Ranis and S. Kuo (1979) *Growth and Equity, The Taiwan Case*, Oxford University Press.
Forrest, T. (1980) 'Agricultural Policies in Nigeria, 1900–1978', in Heyer, J., P. Roberts and G. Williams (eds), *Rural Development in Tropical Africa*, Macmillan.

Galtung, J. (1978) 'Grand Design on a Collision Course', *Development/ Development/Desarrollo*, 20.

Gilles, H.M. (1965) *Akuto: An Environmental Study of a Nigerian Village Community*, Ibadan University Press, Nigeria.

Grant, B. and Q.B.O. Anthonio (1973) 'Women Cooperatives in the Western State of Nigeria', *Bulletin of Rural Economics and Sociology*, 8.

Green, R.H., D.G. Rwegasira and B. Van Arkadie (1980) *Economic Shocks and National Policy Making: Tanzania in the 1970s*, Institute of Social Studies, The Hague, Research Report Series No. 8.

Griffin, K. and J. James (1981) *The Transition to Egalitarian Development*, Macmillan.

Griffin, K. and A.R. Khan (1978) 'Poverty in the Third World: Ugly Facts and Fancy Models', *World Development*, 6.

Harris, J.R. and M.P. Todaro (1970) 'Migration, Unemployment and Development', *American Economic Review*, 60.

Hays, H.M. (1977) 'The Mobility and Storage of Food Grains in Northern Nigeria', *Samaru Miscellaneous Paper*, no. 50, ABU.

Helleiner, G.K. (1966) *Peasant Agriculture, Government and Economic Growth in Nigeria*, Richard D. Irwin.

Hicks, N. and P. Streeten (1979) 'Indicators of Development: the Search for a Basic Needs Yardstick', *World Development*, 7.

Hicks, N. (1979) 'Growth vs Basic Needs: Is there a Trade-off?', *World Development*, 7.

Hicks, N. (1980) *Economic Growth and Human Resources*, World Bank Staff Working Paper No. 408, Johns Hopkins University Press.

Hicks, N. (1982) 'Sector Priorities in Meeting Basic Needs: Some Statistical Evidence', *World Development*, 10.

ILO (1970) *Towards Full Employment: A Programme for Colombia*, ILO, Geneva.

ILO (1972) *Employment, Incomes and Equality: A Strategy for Increasing Productive Employment in Kenya*, ILO Geneva.

ILO (1976) *Employment, Growth and Basic Needs, A One World Problem*, ILO, Geneva.

ILO (1977) *Poverty and Landlessness in Rural Asia*, ILO, Geneva.

ILO/JASPA (1981a) *First things first: Meeting the Basic Needs of the People of Nigeria*, Addis Ababa.

ILO/JASPA (1981b) *Zambia: Basic Needs in an Economy under Pressure*, Addis Ababa.

ILO/JASPA (1982) *Tanzania, Basic Needs in Danger*, Addis Ababa.

Ilori, F.A. (1978) 'Factors determining Fertility Differentials in Western Nigeria: A Case Study of Ife, Ilesha, and Selected Areas in Oyo Province', University of Ife.

Isenman, P. (1980a) 'Inter-Country Comparison of "Real" (PPP) Incomes: Revised Estimates and Unresolved Questions', *World Development* 8.

Isenman, P. (1980b) 'Basic Needs: The Case of Sri Lanka', *World Development*, 8.

Ittah, Y. (1979) 'Prices and Income Distribution Data Review', mimeo. World Bank, September.

Killick, T. (ed.) (1982) *Adjustment and Financing in the Developing World: The Role of the IMF*, Overseas Development Institute, London.
King, R. (1980) 'Cooperative Policy and Village Development in Northern Nigeria', in Heyer, J., D. Roberts and G. Williams (eds), *Rural Development in Tropical Agriculture*, Macmillan.
Konan, M.M. (1975) 'Occupations and Family Patterns among the Hausa in Northern Nigeria', *Samaru Miscellaneous Paper*, 52.
Kravis, I.B., A. Heston and R. Summers (1978) 'Real GDP *per capita* for more than One Hundred Countries', *Economic Journal*, 88.
Kuo, S., G. Ranis and J. Fei (1981) *The Taiwan Success Story*, Westview Press.
Kuznets, S. (1955), 'Economic Growth and Income Inequality', *American Economic Review*, 45.
Lederer, K. (ed.) (1980) *Human Needs: A Contribution to the Current Debate*, Oelgeschlager, Gunn & Hain.
Lee, E.L.H. (1977) 'Rural Poverty in Sri Lanka, 1963–1973' in ILO, *Poverty and Landlessness in Rural Asia*, Geneva.
Leipziger, D.M. and M. Lewis (1980) 'Social Indicators, Growth and Distribution', *World Development*, 8.
Leipziger, D.M. (1981) *Basic Needs and Development*, Oelgeschlager, Gunn & Hain.
Lesi, F.W. (1978) 'Infant Mortality, Diet and Disease in Nigeria', *Nigeria Medical Journal*, 8.
Maslow, A.H. *(1966) The Psychology of Science*, Harper & Row.
Maslow, A.H. (1970) *Motivation and Personality*, (Rev. ed.), Harper & Row.
Matlon, P.J. (1977) 'The Size Distribution, Stucture and Determinants of Personal Incomes in the North of Nigeria', Ph. D. thesis, Cornell University.
Matlon, P.J. (1980) 'The Structure of Production and Rural Incomes in Northern Nigeria: Results of a Three Village Case Study', in Bienen, H. and Diejomaoh, V.P. (eds), *The Political Economy of Income Distribution in Nigeria*, Holmes & Meier.
Meerman, J. (1979) 'Public Services for Basic Needs in Malaysia', *World Development*, 7.
Morawetz, D. (1977) *'Twenty-five Years of Economic Development, 1950 to 1975*, World Bank, Washington, DC.
Morgan, R.W. (1975) 'Fertility Levels and Fertility Change' in Caldwell, J. C. (ed.) *Population Growth and Socio-Economic Change in West Africa*, Columbia University Press.
Morley, D. (1974) *Pediatric Priorities in the Developing World*, Butterworth, London.
Morley, D., J. Bicknell and M. Woodland (1968), 'Factors Influencing the Growth and Nutritional Status of Infants and Young Children in a Nigerian Village', *Transactions of the Royal Society of Tropical Medicine and Hygiene*, 62.
Norman, D.W., D.H. Pryor and C.J.N. Gibbs (1979) 'Technical Change and the Small Farmer in Hausaland, Northern Nigeria', *African Rural Economy Paper*, no. 21, Michigan.

Okungbowa, P. and F. Akesode (1978) 'Protein Calorie Malnutrition in Lagos', mimeo.
Olusanya, P.O. (1969) 'Modernisation and the Level of Fertility in Western Nigeria', *Proceedings of the International Population Conference*, London.
Olusanya, P.O. (undated) 'Rural Attitudes to Family Size and its Limitations in Western Nigeria', mimeo, Nigerian Institute of Social and Economic Research, Lagos.
Omolulu,. A. (1978) in B. Winikoff (ed.), *Nutrition and National Policy*, MIT Press.
Omolulu, A.O. (1974) *Food, Famine and Health*, Ibadan University Press.
Orubuloye, I.O. and J.C. Caldwell (1975) 'The Impact of Public Health Services on Mortality: A Study of Mortality Differentials in a Rural Area of Nigeria', *Population Studies*, 29.
Ozgediz, S. (1980) 'Manpower Constraints to Development in Nigeria', mimeo, World Bank, April.
Pearce, A.J. (1979) *Choice, Class and Conflict. A Study of Southern Nigerian Factory Workers*, Harvester.
Ranis, G. (1983) 'Alternative Patterns of Distribution and Growth in the Mixed Economy: The Philippines and Taiwan', in F. Stewart (ed.) *Work, Income and Inequality*, Macmillan.
Ransome-Kuti, O., W.O. Obajumo and M. Olaniyan (1972) 'Some Socio-Economic Conditions Predisposing to Malnutrition in Lagos', *Nigerian Medical Journal*, 2.
Reutlinger, S. and M. Selowsky (1976) *Malnutrition and Poverty, Magnitude and Policy Options*, World Bank Staff Occasional Paper No. 23, Johns Hopkins University Press.
Richards, P. and W. Gooneratine (1980) *Basic Needs, Poverty and Government Policies in Sri Lanka*, ILO, Geneva.
Rouis M. (1980), 'Income Distribution and Poverty profiles', mimeo, World Bank, June.
Sahota, G.S. (1980) 'The Distribution of the Benefits of Public Expenditure in Nigeria', mimeo, World Bank, June.
Schluter, M. and M. Sackett (1981) 'Estimates of 1981/82 Import Requirements for the Production, Processing and Marketing of Major Crops in Mainland Tanzania', Marketing Development Bureau, Tanzania.
Selowsky, M. (1981) 'Income Distribution, Basic Needs and Trade-offs with Growth: The case of Semi-industrialised Latin American Countries', *World Development*, 9.
Sen, A.K. (1981a) *Poverty and Famines: An Essay on Entitlement and Deprivation*, Clarendon Press.
Sen, A.K. (1981b) 'Public Action and the Quality of Life in Developing Countries', *Oxford Bulletin of Economics and Statistics*, 43.
Sheehan, G. and M. Hopkins (1979) *Basic Needs Performance, An Analysis of Some International Data*, ILO, Geneva.
Shivaram, K.K. (1978) *Choma's Drum*, Hind Pocket Books.
Simmons, E.B. (1975) 'The Small-scale Rural Food Processing Industry in Northern Nigeria', *Food Research Institute Studies*, XIV.
Simmons, E.B. (1976) 'Rural Household Expenditure in Three Villages of Zaria Province. May 1970–July 1971', *Samaru Miscellaneous Papers*, 56.

Stewart. F. (ed.) (1983) *Work, Income and Inequality*, Macmillan.
Stewart, F. and A.K. Sengupta (1982) *International Financial Co-operation: a Framework for Change*, Frances Pinter.
Stewart, F. and P. Streeten (1976) 'New Strategies for Development: Poverty, Income Distribution and Growth', *Oxford Economic Papers*, 28.
Streeten, P., J. Burki, M. ul Haq, N. Hicks and F. Stewart (1981) *First Things First: Meeting Basic Human Needs in Developing Countries*, World Bank and Oxford University Press.
Teriba, O. and A. O. Phillips (1971) 'Income Distribution and National Integration', *Nigerian Journal of Social and Economic Studies*.
Tomkins, A.M., B.S. Drasar, A.K. Bradley and W.A. Williamson (1978) 'Water Supply and Nutritional Status in Rural Northern Nigeria', *Transactions of the Royal Society of Tropical Medicine and Hygiene*, 72.
Turnham, D. (1971) *The Employment Problem in Less Developed Countries: A Review of the Evidence*, OECD, Paris.
Umoh, I. and O. Bassir (1976) 'Nutrient Changes in Some Nigerian Traditional Food during Cooking, (1) Vitamin Changes', *West African Journal on Biology and Applied Chemistry*, 19.
UNFPA (1979) 'Nigeria: Background Report Needs Assessment for Population Assistance', Working paper prepared for Population Council, UNFPA Workshop, Oct 1979, New York.
Van den Bone, B. and N. Roling (1973) 'Extension Workers and Farmer Characteristics', *Bulletin of Rural Economics and Sociology*, 8.
Voh, J. P. (1979) 'An Exploratory Study of Factors Associated with Recommended Farm Practices among Giwa Farmers', *Samaru Miscellaneous Papers*, 73.
Williams, S. K. T. (1969) 'Source of Information on Improved Farming Practices in Some Selected Areas of Western Nigeria'. *Bulletin of Rural Economics and Sociology*, 4.
Williams, G. P. (ed.) (1976) *Nigeria: Economy and Society*, Rex Collins.
Williams, G. P. (1982) *Inequalities in Rural Nigeria*, Occasional Paper No. 16, School of Development Studies, University of East Anglia.
World Bank (1978) 'Report on Cuba', Washington, DC.
World Bank (1980) *World Development Report, 1980*, Oxford University Press.
World Bank (1981) *World Development Report, 1981*, Oxford University Press.

Index

Aboyade, O.   150, 152
Adelman, I.   10, 221
Adeokun, L.   110, 118
Adeyeye, S.O.   228
advertising and propaganda   44, 45, 49, 181
Afghanistan   67, 69, 215
Africa, sub-Saharan   81, 82
agriculture   80, 81, 83, 85, 86, 91, 94, 98, 189–207. *See also under* Nigeria; extension workers; food production
Ahluwalia, M.S.   223
aid, international   36, 100. *See also* IMF; World Bank
Akesode, B.   123, 225, 230
Akinbode, L.A.   228
Albania   67, 71, 216
Algeria   67, 69, 81, 217
anaemia   121
Anambra   125, 226, 227
Angola   65, 67, 81, 216
Anthonio, Q.B.O.   234
Anusionwu, E.C.   228
Argentina   8, 69, 217
Arowolo, O.O.   225, 230

balance of payments   79, 183–7, 198, 203–5, 212
Bamishaye, A.   163, 219, 230
Bangladesh   67, 68, 77, 81, 82, 112, 215
Bankole, N.   224
banks, government borrowing from   187, 199
Banugire, F.R.   226
Barreiros, L.   229
basic needs (BN): definition   1, 2, 54, 109; macro-framework for   14–35, 88, 209; applied to Nigeria   106, 109, 131–82; performance   54, 56–86, 208–13; policy for   36, 40–53, 72, 170–82, 191–2. *See also* targets
Bassir, O.   225
Basu, A.C.   228
Bauchi, Nigeria   159, 226
Becker, G.S.   221
Bendel   138, 226
Benin   77, 215
Benue   125, 226, 227
Berg, A.   99, 102, 103, 222, 223, 224
Berry, S.S.   141, 228

Bhutan   67, 68, 81, 215
Bicknell, J.   225
Bienen, H.   228, 229, 230
birth and death rates   39. *See also* mortality
black market   199, 200, 202
Bloom, B.   223
Bolivia   67, 69, 70, 81, 216
Borno   125, 226
bottle feeding   123
Bown, L.   219, 226
Bowring, P.   222
Bradley, A.K.   225
Brazil   8, 32, 47, 63, 65, 74, 78, 217
Brundenius, C.   222
Burma   65, 67, 69, 215
Burundi   67, 69, 215

Caldwell, J.C. and P.   110, 111, 163, 164, 167, 168, 230
Callaway, A.   162, 219, 224
calory supply: as BN indicator   100–104; FAO requirement   118; in different countries   57, 74, 76, 77, 82, 84, 86, 90, 94, 96, 118–20, 151, 225
Cameroon   65, 67, 216
capital as production resource   15, 23
capital–output ratio   36–7
capitalism and BN   12–13, 52, 71–3, 75, 77, 81, 84, 175, 208
Carter, N.   223
Central African Republic   67, 81, 215
Central Bank of Ceylon   222
Chad   67, 69, 215
Chenery, H.B.   36, 220, 221, 222, 223, 230
child care   49, 120–22
child mortality   55, 79, 113–15, 164, 165
China   63, 67, 70, 71, 73, 75, 76, 215, 222
Clark, R.C.   228
clinics. *See* health clinics; maternity care
collectives   52
Collings, Jesse   220
Collis, W.   225
Colombia   8, 216
colonial era, effect of   75, 77, 81, 107, 127, 226
communes   49
communities in organisation of production   22, 23, 25
Congo   65, 67, 81, 216

Index

consumer goods in Tanzania 185, 189, 192, 196, 201, 202, 206
consumption: of non-basic goods 4, 7, 15, 16, 27, 29–33; patterns of 21, 27–34, 41, 43–5, 48–50; planning of in socialist countries 71; relation to BN achievement 4, 5, 11, 15, 29–34, 131. *See also* meta-production function
co-operatives 22, 52, 141–2
Costa Rica 67, 69, 71, 72, 217
'crafts' 107
credit institutions and policies in Nigeria 141, 175
Cross River State, Nigeria 121, 125, 164, 226
Cuba 54, 67, 69, 71, 73–5, 79–80, 114, 217, 222
cultural differences 34, 107–9, 128. *See also* Hausa; language; religion; Yoruba
Cyprus 65

Davies, D. 224
defence expenditure, effect on BN performance 6, 21, 33, 91, 95, 98, 103, 104, 190, 210
Dema, I. 225
dependency 8–9, 210–12
devaluation as solution for Tanzania 197–202
development, planning for 1, 2, 7–13, 36, 54, 203–7
diarrhoea 114, 115, 123
Diejomaoh, V. 224, 228, 229, 230
Dimonenico, C.M. 228
diseases: and child mortality 55; in Nigeria 106, 110, 113, 114, 121, 124; of the rich 61. *See also* diarrhoea; dysentery; gastro-enteritis; infectious diseases; leprosy; malaria; measles; meningitis; parasitic diseases; pneumonia; smallpox; water-related diseases
dispensaries 79, 118
distribution of goods and services 5–6, 11, 16, 33–4, 41, 55, 86, 89, 95, 99, 109, 141–2, 158–60, 171, 176–9. *See also* equality; income, distribution of; resources
doctors per population 57, 74, 76, 79, 82, 85, 86, 90, 94, 96, 100–103, 117
Drasar, B.S. 225
drugs, medical, access to 52, 200
D'Silva, B. 219, 227, 228, 229
dysentery 113

Ebendo, Nigeria 111
Eberstadt, N. 222
Ecuador 69, 216
education: as constituent of basic needs 1, 3–5, 15–16, 23, 55, 60, 96, 102, 103, 209, 210
as requirement in differing societies 49, 71, 72
effects: on consumption patterns 41; on health 38, 122, 129; on incomes 33, 149; on life-expectancy 100; on organisation
expenditure on 91, 95
female 53, 73, 82, 85, 90, 94, 96, 101–3, 122–3, 127–9, 161–8, 180–2, 226
primary 57, 76–8, 82, 94, 127–30, 138–40, 160, 226
secondary 57, 76, 82, 90, 94, 226
See also life expectancy; literacy; numeracy; opportunity costs; school; skill; university
Egypt 8, 112, 216
Ejiga, Dr. 219
El Salvador 67, 68, 216
electoral regularity as BN indicator 100
Ellis, F. 231
employment: objectives 1, 10, 83; growth of in Taiwan 76; unemployment 9, 79. *See also* labour surplus; self-employment
Engels, F. 12
entitlement approach (Sen) 11–12
Enugu, Nigeria 152–3
environmental improvement 21, 23, 33, 39
equality in distribution of income and land 76, 77, 81, 85, 103, 104, 146, 148, 175–6
Essang, S.M. 229, 230
Ethiopia 54, 67, 69, 81, 82, 85–6, 215, 223
exchange rates: effects on statistics 63, 64; policy 72, 76; effects in Nigeria 108, 174
exports 19, 82, 91, 95, 98; Nigerian 107, 108, 172; Tanzanian 185–8, 191–3, 195, 197, 198, 202–5, 207
extension workers in agriculture 138, 160, 161, 180

Fajana, O. 229
family: income distribution 25–35, 41, 44, 48–9, 74, 75
production and consumption of BN goods 22–35, 41, 47, 49–52; in Nigeria 107, 119. *See also* households
Fapohaunda, E. 219
Fei, J. 141, 221, 222, 230
fertility 39, 164, 230
feudalism 85–6
fly-eradication 23
food: allotment among families and households 39, 53, 119, 122
cooking and storage 53, 88, 122–3, 141
distribution 88, 122
prices 47–8, 72, 134, 145
production 15, 16, 23–5, 72, 84, 86
production and consumption in Nigeria 106, 109, 118–24, 130, 132–4, 137–45, 150–4, 162–3, 177, 231
requirements for health 1, 38–9, 88, 150–4, 211
supply, production and prices in Tanzania 186, 191–7, 200, 202–3, 206

food (*cont.*)
  trade in 19
  See also under agriculture; calories;
    nutrition; protein; rationing;
    subsidies; subsistence
Food and Agriculture Organisation 106, 118,
  225, 231
Forrest, T. 229
Frank, A.G. 220
Furtado, C. 220
fuels, exports of 91, 95, 98. *See also* oil;
  petroleum
full-life objective 3–6, 15–18, 23, 25, 26, 28,
  37–42, 51, 53, 88, 132
Funtua Project 227

Gabon 65
Galtung, J. 210
gastro-enteritis 114, 115, 123
Germany 218
Ghana 8, 65, 84, 114, 216
Gibbs, C.J.N. 228
Gilles, H.M. 224
Gold Coast 226
Gongola 125
Gooneratine, W. 80, 222
government: as element of BN
    production 25–7, 51, 72;
    interventions in welfare economies 71, 72,
      77, 79, 208–9; in Nigeria 108, 171,
      178. *See also* public goods; public
      sector; public services; subsidies;
      taxation; transfers
Grant, B. 228
Greece 65, 217
Green, R.H. 231
Griffin, K. 221, 223
gross domestic product (GDP): as variable in
    BN performance 91, 94, 95
gross national product (GNP): growth of 36–8,
    90, 103;
    relation with defence 91, 95, 98; relation
      with BN performance 95, 101–5
growth, economic: as object of
    development 8–11; relationship with
    BN performance 6, 10, 11, 32, 34, 37, 45,
    46, 62–3, 71–2, 74–85, 97, 100, 103, 104,
    155, 158, 170, 179, 182, 208–11; in
    Nigeria 106–8, 158, 179, 182. *See also*
    incomes; labour; 'trickle-down'
Hallaway, Professor 219
Haque, Irfan ul 224
Harris–Todaro model 229, 230
Harrod–Domar planning model 36
Hausa 139, 141
Hays, H.M. 228
health: as a basic need 1, 3–5, 15, 16, 23, 33,
    55, 60, 161, 209
    clinics, use of 53, 160, 181
    expenditure on 89, 91, 95, 116, 209
    in Nigeria 106, 109–18, 122, 123, 130,
      161–4, 177, 180, 181, 183

services in varying countries 23, 24, 39, 72,
    74, 75, 77, 78, 83, 86
  in Tanzania 187, 190
  See also under disease; dispensaries;
    doctors; drugs; education; food;
    hygiene; immunisation; medicine;
    maternity care; nurses; nutrition;
    sanitation
Helleiner, G.K. 224
Hicks, N. 99, 101–4, 211, 220, 223
'hijacking' of public goods 47, 49, 72
Hong Kong 62, 65, 68, 71, 217
Hopkins, M. 99, 100, 103, 221, 223
Houphouet-Boigny, F. 84
households: as producer and consumer of BN
    goods and services 17, 24, 35, 52–3, 73,
    82, 85, 139, 142, 180–2, 228, 229; incomes
    of 11, 20, 25–8; Nigerian 119–23, 139,
    142–3, 159, 170, 180–2. *See also*
    education, female; family; hygiene;
    women
housing 78, 109, 160
human rights 212
hygiene, practices and standards 53, 73, 78,
    123, 181

Ibadan 121, 165, 168, 225, 230
IBRD 225
Ife 113, 121, 128, 230
Ilori, F.A. 230
Ilorin 151
immunisation 118, 164
Imo 125
import-substitution 71, 77, 83, 84, 107, 108,
    191
imports: and production framework 19; of
    managers and technology 82, 84, 107;
    Nigerian 133, 173; Tanzanian 184–206
incentives 45, 46, 189
incomes: relationship with BN 5, 9–10, 12, 14,
    56, 58–68, 71, 81, 84, 97, 112, 208–11,
    215–18
  distribution 7, 9–11, 20, 21, 32–4, 41, 45–9,
    52, 71, 72, 74, 85, 86, 91, 95–9, 103,
    104, 107, 131, 142–4, 146–50, 171, 209
  'full income' 20–3, 25–32, 35
  in Nigeria 106–8, 112, 141–60, 170–5, 182
  of the poor, raising of 10, 11, 43, 44, 72,
    220
  statistics 63
  in Tanzania 193–4, 196, 198–200
  See also equality; family; household;
    money-incomes
independence 6, 100
India 8, 67, 68, 70, 71, 78, 215
Indonesia 32, 69, 215
industrial production: as % of GDP 91, 98; in
    Nigeria 108, 172; in Tanzania 185, 187,
    189, 192, 198, 202, 203, 205
industrialisation 8, 9, 81, 83, 84, 104–5, 210,
    211
infant mortality 38–9, 85, 100; in

Nigeria 106, 108, 110–14, 122, 161, 164
infectious diseases 100, 122
inflation in Tanzania 191, 200–2, 207
International Labour Organisation 10, 79, 83, 110, 125, 151, 157, 220, 221, 223–6, 228–31
International Monetary Fund 72, 79, 183–4, 191, 192, 201, 206–7, 231
investment: as element in BN performance 11, 15, 16, 18, 19, 37, 45, 46, 80, 97, 101, 211; as % of GDP 91, 94; allocation of in Nigeria 135–7, 179
Iran 67, 69, 81, 217
Iraq 61, 67, 81, 218
Isenman, P. 222
'Iso-care' 118
Ittah, Y. 134, 145, 156, 228
Ivory Coast 65, 67, 69, 81, 84–5, 216

Jain, S. 92
Jamaica 63, 67, 71, 72, 114, 117
Jamal 151, 228
James, J. 221
James, M. 225
Japan 75, 76, 218
JASPA 223, 231

Kaduna 121, 125, 148, 152–3, 226
Kano 128, 148, 151, 226
Katsina 121, 122, 161, 163
Kaunda, President 82
Kenya 67, 81, 112, 114, 130, 215
Khan, A.R. 221
Kibbutzim 49
Killick, T. 231
King, R. 228
Konan, M.M. 226, 228
'Koranic' schools 140
Korea (South) 62, 65, 69–70, 74, 216, 217
Kravis, I.B. 222
Kuo, S. 221, 222, 230
Kuwait 61, 69, 218
Kwara 118, 125, 226
Kuznets, S. 10, 220, 223

labour: as resource 15, 23; costs 64; mobility of 157; surplus 9, 71–2, 76, 79
Lacey Majuetan, L. 228
Lagos 65, 109, 111–15, 117, 118, 122–5, 128, 129, 151, 157, 161, 164, 165, 168, 173, 225, 226, 227
land: availability and distribution 15, 43, 75–6, 86, 222; in Nigeria 107, 146, 148, 160, 172, 175–6
Lederer, K., 220
Lee, E.L.H. 222
Leipziger, D.M. 97, 220, 223, 224
leprosy 113
Lesi, F.W. 225
Lesotho 65, 69, 215
Lewis, M. 223, 224
Liberia 65, 69, 216
Libya 61, 67, 69, 81, 216

life-expectancy: as measure of BN performance 38, 39, 54–5, 60, 61, 70, 88, 89, 96, 100–2, 104
in different countries 57, 73–5, 77, 79, 82, 84–6, 112, 184
measurement of and statistics for 39, 55–6, 63, 222
relation to income and literacy 58–69, 100, 112, 215–18
in Nigeria 106, 108, 110, 112, 113, 161, 222, 224
literacy: as measure of BN performance 15, 38, 55, 68–70, 100–2
in different countries 57, 74, 75, 77, 82, 84, 86, 90, 94, 101
in Nigeria 106, 108, 128, 138
relation to income and life-expectancy 56, 58–60, 215–18
statistics of 55, 56
living space 76, 78, 100, 109, 160

Mabawonku, A.F. 229, 230
McKee, K. 219
Madagascar 69, 70, 215
maize 151, 193, 194, 199
malaria 113, 115
Malawi 69, 70, 82, 112, 114, 215
Malaysia 8, 67, 68, 114, 217
Mali 69, 70, 112, 114, 215
malnutrition 83, 114, 118–24, 162–4
managers, imported 82, 84
manufactured exports 76, 91, 95, 98, 103, 104, 198, 202, 205
manufacturing in Nigeria 107, 108, 172, 174
market; in production and consumption of BN 22, 23, 28, 33, 34, 71
Maslow, A.H. 4
maternal deaths 113
maternity care 118, 161
Matlon, P.J. 143, 148, 228, 229
Mauritania 65, 67, 69, 215
measles 113–15, 118, 122, 123
medicine, curative and preventive 89, 116–17, 130, 135
Meerman, J. 221
meningitis 15
metals, exports of 91, 95, 98
meta-production function: definition and role 5, 11, 15, 17–21, 23, 26, 28, 37, 38, 88, 132, 209; and life-expectancy 39–40; and participation 50–1; in households 52; in Nigeria 160–9
Mexico 8, 69, 217
migration 229. See also rural–urban relationship
milk consumption 122
minerals, exports of 91, 95, 98, 100, 101, 103, 104. See also oil
money-incomes 33–4, 99
Mongolia 71, 216
Morawetz, D. 8, 220, 221
Morgan, R.W. 226

Morley, D. 225, 227, 229
Morocco 69, 70, 216
Morris, C.T. 10, 221
morbidity. *See* disease
mortality: in Nigeria 110, 113, 164–8. *See also* child mortality; infant mortality; maternal deaths; violence
motor cars and motor cycles 79, 108
Mott, F.L. 111
Mozambique 65, 215

Ndagi, Dr. 219, 227
Nepal 69, 70, 215
New International Economic Order 210, 212
Nicaragua 65, 69, 216
Nigam, S. 223, 231
Niger 67, 69, 114, 215, 227
Nigeria: access to goods and services 160
  advertising, effect on household behaviour 181
  agriculture: education for 138–9, 180, 181; extension workers 138, 160, 161, 180; imports, incomes and production 107, 108, 119, 132–4, 143, 145, 146, 148, 155, 172–6; investment in 135–7, 176, 179; priorities for 174–5, 180–2; subsidies 160; women in 139–41
  basic needs policy for 170–82
  capital expenditure in 159–60
  child care and mortality 113–15, 120–2
  colonial era 107, 127, 226
  credit policies and institutions 141, 175
  cultural differences 107–9, 128
  diseases 106, 110, 113, 114
  distribution of goods and services 109, 141–2, 176–9
  economic growth 106–8, 158, 179, 182
  education 106, 127–40, 149, 160–3, 177–82, 226, 227–8
  exchange rates 108, 174
  exports 107, 108, 172
  family 107, 119
  food 106, 118–24, 130, 132–4, 137–45, 150–4, 162–3, 177
  government interventions 108, 171, 178
  health 106, 109–18, 122, 123, 130, 161–4, 177, 180, 181, 183
  household 119–23, 139, 142–4, 159, 170, 180–2
  housing 109, 160
  hygiene 123, 181
  import-substitution 107, 108
  imports 133, 173
  incomes 106–8, 112, 141–60, 170–5
  industrial production 108, 172
  infant mortality 106, 108, 110–14, 122, 161, 164
  investment allocation 135–7, 179
  'Iso-care' 118
  land, availability and distribution 107, 146, 148, 160, 172, 175–6

life-expectancy 67, 106, 108, 110, 112, 113, 161, 222, 224
literacy 106, 108, 128, 138
manufacturing 107, 108, 172, 174
meningitis 15
meta-production function 160–9
mortality 110, 113, 164–8
motor-car assembly 108
nutrition 106, 108, 114, 118–24, 130, 143, 161–4, 225
oil boom, effect of 106–8, 155, 158, 171–5, 182
organisation of BN production 131, 139–42, 170
political system 178
population 107, 108, 155
poverty line 146, 156
prices 145, 175
private sector 139, 178
production of BN goods 132–9, 170, 176–80
public-sector priorities 158–60, 176–80
recurrent expenditure 159–60
resource allocation 177–80
rural–urban relationship 112, 114, 117, 130, 144–50, 154–7, 159, 171–3, 175
sanitation 123, 125, 140, 180
school attendance 129, 181
seasonal variations in food supply 119
skill, effect on earnings 137, 149, 157
statistics 108–9, 161, 165
subsidies 160, 174
taboos 122
taxation 158–60, 171, 176
urbanisation 138, 160
universities 149
wages 149–50, 152–3, 157
water supply 106, 123–6, 130, 132–7, 140, 162–3, 177, 180
women, role of 139–42, 148, 165
Nigerian Tobacco Company 138
Nkrumah, President 84
Norman, D.W. 228
Northern Nigeria 139, 143, 145, 160, 161
numeracy 55
nurses per population 57, 74, 90, 94, 96, 100, 102
nutrition 1, 32, 84, 106, 108, 118–24, 130, 143, 161–3
Nyasaland 226

Obajumo, W.O. 225
Odufalu, D. 219
Ogun 125, 148
Ohadike, P.O. 230
oil: effect of boom 79, 183, 185, 187; exports 61, 81, 98; effect in Nigeria 106–8, 155, 158, 171–5, 182. *See also* petroleum
Okediji, Professor F.O. 219, 230
Okello, Dr. 219
Okungbowa, P. 123, 225, 230

Index

Olaniyan, M. 236
Olayide 225
Olusanya, P.O. 230
Omolulu, A. 119, 162, 219, 225
Omorogiuwa, P.A. 229
Ondo 125, 148
opportunity costs of school and clinic attendance 34, 171
Opuber, A. 219
organisational elements in BN production 14, 19–25, 50–2, 73, 78, 82, 83, 86; in Nigeria 131, 139–42, 170
Oruboloyo, I.O. 111, 163, 164, 230
Oyo 118, 125, 128, 148, 226, 230
Ozgediz, S. 137, 227

Pakistan 69, 70, 215
Panama 67, 217
Papua New Guinea 65, 67, 216
Paraguay 65, 69, 216
parasitic diseases 113, 123
participation 1, 3, 50, 51, 100, 109
Paukert, F. 92
Pearce, A.J. 157
Peru 8, 69, 78, 216
petroleum 145, 156–7
Philippines 8, 65, 67, 71, 78, 114, 216
Phillips, A.O. 146, 147, 229
Plateau, Nigeria 125
pneumonia 114, 115
policy for BN 36, 40–53, 72, 170–82, 191–2
political economy: types of in relation to BN performance 1, 2, 7, 11, 33, 34, 40–4, 46, 49, 51, 54, 70–86, 178, 207–9, 211. *See also* capitalism; feudalism; socialism; welfare states
population 90, 94, 97, 100–3; of Nigeria 107, 108, 155, 224, 225
Port Harcourt 118, 119, 151
Portugal 65, 217
Portuguese Timor 65
poverty line 7, 9–11, 37, 44–5, 72, 85, 91, 95, 99, 146, 156, 175, 220
Prebisch, R. 220
preferences and tastes, effect on consumption 34, 43–5
prices: effect on consumption patterns 34, 41, 43, 45, 47, 48; exchange rates 76; of food 74, 145, 175; of non-tradable goods 63–4
private borrowing, consumption and expenditure 23, 56, 82, 139, 178, 183
production of BN goods: analysis, organisation and planning of 14–25, 27–9, 35, 37, 41, 71, 72, 191, 192, 209; in Nigeria 132–9, 170, 176–80. *See also* meta-production function
productivity 9–10, 42, 137
property income 25, 28, 221
protection 64, 84
protein consumption 76, 100, 118–20, 225
protest demonstrations 100

Pryor, D.H. 228
public-sector provision for basic needs 20–3, 27, 28, 32–4, 41, 47–9, 56, 72, 82, 85, 91–5, 98–9, 103, 158–60, 209–10
purchasing-power parity estimates of income 63–6

Rafique Raza, M. 228, 229
Ranis, G. 14, 221, 222, 224, 230
Ransome-Kuti, O. 123, 219, 225, 230
rationing 47–8, 72, 74, 77, 200
recurrent expenditure 50, 159–60, 187, 189, 191, 206
religious differences 107, 128
Remy, D. 228
reproduction rate 39
resources 15, 18, 19, 23, 36–42, 131, 135, 177–80, 191, 211
Reutlinger, S. 224
rice 71, 77–9, 194
Richards, P. 80, 222
Rivers State, Nigeria 118, 125
road maintenance in Tanzania 189
Roling, N. 228
Romania 69, 217
Rouis, M. 151, 228
rural area, BN standards in 90, 94, 96, 112, 114, 117, 191
rural–urban relationship 83, 84, 89, 117, 130, 144–50, 154–7, 159, 171–3, 175, 191, 193, 198, 199, 228, 229
Rwanda 65, 114, 215

Sackett, M. 231
Sada, P.O. 229
Sahota, G.S. 229
sanitation 23, 39, 75, 123, 135, 140, 180
Saudi Arabia 61, 67, 81, 218
savings 26, 29, 36–7
Schluter, M. 231
school attendance 34, 53, 129, 181
school equipment, meals and staffing 49, 52, 83, 181
seasonal variations in food supply 119
Seers, Dudley 224
self-employment 149, 150, 152–3, 157, 172, 221
Selowsky, M. 99, 224
Sen, A.K. 11, 99, 220, 221
Senegal 65, 67, 69, 114, 216
Sengupta, A.K. 231
Sheehan, G. 99, 100, 103, 221, 223
Shiveram, K.K. 220
Sierra Leone 65, 82, 215
Simmons, E.B. 120, 224, 225, 228, 229
Singh, H.V. 222
Sipasi, O.N. 150, 152
skill 39, 137, 149, 157
smallpox 39
social services. *See* public-sector provision
socialism and BN performance 51, 71–3, 75, 77, 80, 81, 208

Sokoto 148, 152–3
Somalia 69, 215
South Africa 65, 67, 81, 217
South Korea 62, 65, 69–70, 74
Spain 65, 76, 217
spare parts 189, 194
Sri Lanka 33, 45, 46, 63, 65, 67, 69, 71–3, 77–80, 112, 114, 215, 220
statistics, deficiencies in 55, 89, 108–9, 161, 165
Streeten, Paul 220, 221, 231
subsidies 43, 45, 46, 48, 49, 71, 72, 74, 77–80, 160, 174, 184, 197–9, 202, 221, 222
subsistence food production 11, 24, 143, 195, 196
Sudan 65, 67, 69, 215
sugar 194
sustainability of performance 72–3, 80. *See also* recurrent expenditure
Swaziland 65
Syrian Arab Republic 67, 68, 216

taboos 122
Taiwan 8, 32, 62, 63, 65, 67, 68, 71–3, 75–6, 79–80, 221, 222
Tanzania
  agriculture 189–207
  balance of trade 184–207
  BN performance 69
  banking 187, 199
  consumer goods 185, 189, 192, 196, 201, 202, 206
  defence 190, 191, 210
  devaluation or subsidies? 197–202
  development and IMF 191, 201, 203–7
  education 87, 90
  food 186, 191–7, 200–3, 206
  health 130
  incomes 193–4, 196, 198–200
  inflation 191, 200–7
  life-expectancy 112
  outputs 82, 83, 185–7, 189, 192, 194, 198, 199, 202, 203, 205
  prices 200
  recurrent expenditure 187, 189, 191, 206
  rural and urban areas 191, 193, 198, 199
  taxation 187–9, 197–8
  transport 185, 189, 192, 194, 201–3
targets in BN planning 2, 4, 6, 7, 36–40, 176–7
tastes and preferences 34, 43–5
taxation 43, 46, 48, 158–60, 171, 176, 187–9, 197–8, 200, 221, 229
tea 77, 86, 193, 194
technology, imported 82, 84, 107, 195
Teriba, O. 146, 147, 219, 229
Thailand 65, 67, 69, 114, 216
time: element of BN planning 6, 37, 42; household allocation of 53
Tinbergen 36
tobacco 152, 185–6, 193, 194, 198, 199
Togo 67, 69, 215
Tomkins, A.M. 225
tradable and non-tradable goods 63–4, 173–4

trade, effect on BN performance 19, 83, 85, 100, 103
traders, 149
trading by women 141
transfers, government 33, 43, 46, 47, 71. *See also* subsidies
transport 83, 185, 189, 192, 194, 201–3
'trickle-down' effect of growth 10, 45, 62, 158, 170
Turnham, D. 220

Umoh, I. 225
unemployment. *See* labour, surplus
UK 74, 218
UNFPA 109–10, 114, 115, 219, 224, 225, 230
USA 76, 218, 225
USDA 225
USSR 75, 218
university graduates 149
Upper Volta 67, 215
urban areas and BN performance 83, 97, 98, 101–3, 138, 153, 160
'use-value' 12
Usoro 146

Van den Borne, B. 228
Venezuela 67, 70, 81, 217
Vietnam 67, 68, 215
violence, political, death from 100
Voh, J.P. 228

wages 11, 25–6, 28, 149–50, 152–3, 157, 221
water: access to and use of 1, 3, 57, 76, 78, 82, 85, 90, 94, 96, 100, 101, 103, 180, 187, 190; in Nigeria 106, 123–6, 130, 132–7, 140, 162–3, 177
water-related diseases 113, 162
weaning practices 122
welfare states 71–3, 79, 209
Western Nigeria 111, 120, 141, 165
Williams, G.P. 224, 228
Williams, S.K.T. 219, 228
Williamson, W.A. 225
women, role in household and society 53, 139–42, 148, 229. *See also* education, female; family
Woodland, M. 225
World Bank 8, 9, 10, 57, 79, 92, 112, 186, 188, 190, 193, 194, 204, 206, 218, 221–5, 229, 231
World Health Organisation 118

yam 122, 151
Yazidu, Imrana 230
Yemen 67, 69, 216
Yoruba women 165, 230
Yugoslavia 217

Zaire 69, 215
Zambia 65, 67, 69, 81–4, 216
Zaria 119, 152, 227
Zimbabwe 216